THE ARCADIAN CIPHER

☆

Having developed a keen interest in art and art history from his father, PETER BLAKE went on to become a fine art restorer, establishing his own company. His interest in the artists behind the paintings soon developed into a broader fascination with the history of their patrons, the sponsors of some of western culture's greatest treasures. More recently, he has become interested in the origins of and history of religion. Peter Blake lives in London.

With an honours degree in geology, PAUL S. BLEZARD became a stockbroker in the City of London. Ten years ago he left finance for a more diverse career path. Now a novelist and screenplay writer he divides his time between London, Warsaw and the South of France. This is his first work of non-fiction.

PETER BLAKE & PAUL S. BLEZARD

THE
ARCADIAN
CIPHER

THE QUEST TO CRACK
THE CODE OF CHRISTIANITY'S
GREATEST SECRET

PAN BOOKS

First published 2000 by Sidgwick & Jackson

This edition published 2001 by Pan Books
an imprint of Pan Macmillan Ltd
Pan Macmillan, 20 New Wharf Road, London N1 9RR
Basingstoke and Oxford
Associated companies throughout the world
www.panmacmillan.com

ISBN 0 330 39119 4

A CIP catalogue record for this book is available from
the British Library.

Typeset by SetSystems Ltd, Saffron Walden, Essex
Printed and bound in Great Britain by
Mackays of Chatham plc, Chatham, Kent

PETER BLAKE

To my family

PAUL S. BLEZARD

For Alexandra, a wonderful mother,
and for Nicholas, our son.

Acknowledgements

☆

We would especially like to thank the staff of a number of libraries, without whom many of the books and documents which have been so important to us would have remained elusive. Among these are the British Library, The Bodleian Library, the Bibliothèque National in Paris, The Bridgeman Art Library and the Kensington and Chelsea Library, Kings Road, London plus others too numerous to mention.

Thanks must also go to those of our friends who managed to stay the course and whose assistance and support was invaluable, together with our families who always understood.

We would also like to express our gratitude to Jonathan Harris and Annabel Leung at our agents, Associated Publicity Holdings Ltd whose unswerving belief in us kept us going.

Finally our thanks go to our editor, Gordon Wise at Sidgwick and Jackson, whose informed comments and suggestions were inspirational.

Good frend, for Jesus sake, forbeare
To digge the dust encloased here!
Bleste be ye man yt spares thes stones
and curst be he yt moves my bones

Inscription on the tomb of William Shakespeare,
Holy Trinity Church, Stratford-upon-Avon

CONTENTS

☆

CONTENTS

FOREWORD

☆

My involvement with *The Arcadian Cipher* began in the spring of 1998 when I first met Peter Blake at the invitation of my literary agent Jonathan Harris. During the course of that meeting, Peter described the work that he had carried out in the course of researching what appeared to be a code concealed within a number of paintings and how, by following that code, he had made a most extraordinary discovery in the south of France.

Given the nature of his revelation, my first reaction was one of scepticism, as although now a novelist, my early academic training was in the sciences; and whilst Peter's material was fascinating in its content, it appeared to me to have little methodology or structure. However, by the end of the meeting, having seen Peter's notes, listened to his account and viewed some of the images, my interest was piqued and I agreed to collaborate with him, to augment the research that he had already conducted and to write the manuscript of the story.

This book is the result of that collaboration. It is the story of Peter's search through the history-clouded evidence that led him to his discovery and his work in unravelling the disparate facts that allowed him to draw his conclusions. However, in much the same way that whilst Sir Alexander Fleming is remembered as the discoverer of penicillin, it was the diligent work of Sir Ernst Chain that enabled it to be brought to a wider public. The same principle of teamwork is applicable here.

I consider myself fortunate to have been involved in this project, to have contributed to both the research and the investigation, to have had my own ideas and discoveries incorporated into the wider arguments and to have given voice to Peter's fascinating work.

Paul S. Blezard
Chelsea
January 2000

INTRODUCTION

☆

I owe my interest in art history and picture conservation to my father, Henley Blake, who, after returning from the last war in Europe, won a place at the Courtauld Institute in London to study Art and Conservation. After his studies he became a fine-art restorer at the National Gallery.

One of my earliest memories is of being taken as a young boy to the Tower of London to see the murals he had uncovered in the Beefeaters' rest room and hearing him explain to me why Henry VIII had plastered over them and the reasons for the decline in Catholic taste in England. I remember that the Beefeaters were not amused by my father's discovery as they now had to find a new room in which to play darts! Occasionally I was allowed to accompany my father on long trips to the stately homes and palaces of England, where, in his capacity as a restorer, he was commissioned to write reports on the condition of paintings in their collections. These excursions became informal lectures with my father as tutor and myself as his diligent student, following a wide range of subjects from paintings, clocks, furniture, china and porcelain to architecture and the gardens. It was on such a trip that I was shown into a great dining hall to see a secret room hidden behind the wall panelling. To my amazement there was a tiny staircase littered with straw leading to a small, windowless room and there in the corner was a rough bed of straw, a pair of clogs and a single candle. I felt I was the first person ever to have seen this undisturbed room and as a child I wondered what poor souls must have spent their time in this airless room, perhaps at the beck and call of the master's voice.

Some time later I visited the Royal Naval College at Greenwich to see the Thornhill ceiling, which my father was restoring. Climbing the ladders to the scaffold stretched out across this vast painting, I saw him on his back, cleaning the old varnish from it. He looked so tired that I was reminded of how Michelangelo must have suffered during his work at the Sistine Chapel. Such experiences and many others kindled my inquisitiveness about art and the minds of those who commissioned and painted it.

At the age of nineteen I found a position at the fine-art dealers Frost and Read of Bond Street as a fine-art restorer and it was not long before I set up my own company in Lots Road, Chelsea as a fine-art restorer and canvas reliner. It was through starting on my own that I pioneered the new process of wax-vacuum relining, had the first machine in private use and numbered among my clients such galleries as Ackerman, Richard Green, M. Spink and Coetzer and many private collections. This process today has been adopted throughout the world as a superior alternative to the glue lining of the past.

One of my most exciting times was a result of my purchase of Luca Giordano's *Venus with the Water Sprites*. I had invited Lord Clark to come to my studio to give his opinion on this great painting and was amazed when, without any hesitation, he informed me that the work had disappeared during the Blitz in London and had at one time hung in the Globe Theatre. I moved to the USA for some years, still restoring and dealing.

On my return to England my interest had broadened and I devoted my time to researching the history and religions of the ancient civilizations, working to uncover the many aspects of these past great cultures which mainstream historians ignore.

This book is the result of nineteen years of endeavour. It is the story of my discovery of a code, a cipher, clues to the existence of which I found in a number of paintings, including Poussin's *The Shepherds of Arcadia* (*Les Bergers d'Arcadie*). But why Arcadian? And what code?

The accepted definition of Arcadia is a land of rural idyll, unspoiled countryside inhabited by rustics. It is often thought that the advent of the plough hastened the demise of Arcadia, the ploughshare tearing up Arcas, the virgin Mother Earth. However, it was only much later that I realized the true significance of the Arcadian scene portrayed in Poussin and the other artists' paintings.

My work in fine-art restoration had brought me into contact with a wide range of paintings and subject matter. It was while researching a painting for a client that I first came across Luca Signorelli's *The Education of Pan*. In studying this work I became aware that the composition was underpinned by a hidden geometry. It was many years later, having been given a copy of a book by Henry Lincoln called *The Holy Place*, that I realized that there was a correlation between the Signorelli work and that by Poussin which Lincoln had been working on. And it was while looking closely at *The Shepherds of Arcadia* that I realized that it also told a hidden story using the same principles that I had discovered in the Signorelli. My imagination was fired by the possibility that two Renaissance artists had concealed information within their paintings and I began to look for other works that might also have hidden meaning. What I detected set me on a path of discovery, for in the additional paintings that I had found, the same formula was at work. It appeared to me that this was nothing less than a code and that I was the first person to be aware of its existence in recent times.

During my research I had become aware of a mystery surrounding a village in south-west France called Rennes-le-Château. The many books co-authored by Michael Baigent, Richard Leigh and Henry Lincoln which focused on this are remarkable, for they set great store by an interpretation of Poussin's painting and documents found in the village church. But I felt that there was more. Their work, together with that of Lynn Picknett and Clive Prince, was fascinating and inspired me in my quest. However, I felt that my own line of enquiry was going in a different direction, that the code was concerned with something far greater than a local mystery. The paintings had led me to discover not only that the code was hidden in art, but also, given that each of the paintings was Arcadian in theme, that art was the key.

This seemed to fit with a clue in Baigent, Leigh and Lincoln's *The Holy Blood and the Holy Grail*. They explain that the priest of Rennes-le-Château, Abbé Bérenger Saunière, during a stay in Paris, made a number of visits to the Louvre, where he is thought to have bought reproductions of three paintings. One was a portrait of Pope Celestine V by an unknown artist, one a work by David Teniers the Younger entitled *St Anthony and St Jerome in the Desert* and the third Nicolas Poussin's *The Shepherds of Arcadia*. In the latter work, a picture of a tomb in a pastoral setting, there is a strange Latin inscription, 'Et in Arcadia Ego', which has been variously translated as 'And in Arcadia I am' or 'Even in Arcadia I am'. Much has been made of this enigmatic phrase and many researchers have put forward theories to explain what they think Poussin was trying to say. Indeed a viewer of Henry Lincoln's television documentary on the subject, realizing that there was curiously no verb in the phrase, proposed that it is a Latin anagram which, when the letters are rearranged, results in 'I Tego Arcana Dei' or 'Begone, I conceal the secret of God'.

Richard Andrews and Paul Schellenberger published in 1996 a book called *The Tomb of God*. They were primarily concerned with the Rennes-le-Château mystery and in their attempts to solve it they boldly claimed that they had found the tomb of Jesus Christ. The basis for their claim was largely drawn from their analysis of the parchments found by Saunière, which they then endeavoured to link to the Poussin painting and to the other two works in which the priest had shown interest. Despite their best endeavours, however, their theory proved inconclusive. At the time that their book was released, amid much publicity, my quest had already quietly reached its own conclusion and their work served only to confirm in my own mind that their area of research was only part of the much larger enigma which is described here.

THE DISCOVERY

☆

'All I can think about as I draw near is that this is the place. Suddenly I am there. A large, flat boulder lies across my path, I negotiate around it and there in front of me is a large upright stone, five to six metres high and four, four and a half metres across. I look to my right and there is the same small, flat rock that the figure in red is resting his foot on in the Poussin painting *The Shepherds of Arcadia*. I am so excited . . . He is buried here . . . I know it. I stand back to appreciate the scale and there, amazingly, are oaks growing out of the back and the sides, just like in the painting. This is just too incredible. I think of the painting and reflect that in the background there appears, behind the tomb, to be a drop-off, a void. I walk towards the headstone, around the small rock and suddenly I am hit by a strong wind, coming up from the valley. I look down and there below me is a sheer drop of some fifteen to twenty metres . . .

'I step back immediately and recover some of my composure. I sit down on the small rock, the same small rock from Poussin's painting . . . Well, there's no doubt in my mind now that this is the place – the clues Poussin left in his painting were all visual . . . the tomb, for instance, in the painting is the work of masons, but it's written on the tomb "Et in Arcadia Ego . . ." ("And in Arcadia I am . . .") But what does Arcadia mean? The dictionary says that it is the land of shepherds and shepherd-esses, a rustic place, so if the tomb is Arcadian then it should be made by nature, or by Pan the rustic God on the left of the tomb in the painting . . .

'I get up off my flat rock and look over the escarpment. Down at the bottom I can make out a hole in a very large slab of rock leaning against the mountain. The slab is covered in moss and has small box trees growing over it in profusion. I look for a way to climb down and to my right the ground slopes away. I might be able to hang on to one box tree at a time and lower myself down. This I manage to accomplish and eventually I find myself standing on the slab. I try to look into the hole but it's too small, so I pull some of the old moss away. This has not been disturbed for a long time, but to my surprise I manage to enlarge the hole to about three-quarters of a metre by a metre.

'I look in and see that the bottom, about a metre and a half down, is covered in large and small stones. I ease my way down the cliff and find that I am at one end of a triangular chamber about five metres long and at its highest about one and a half metres. The width of the floor is also about one and a half metres and at the end furthest away from me is a small triangular opening. I am on my hands and knees on the floor and I feel stones beneath the earth. I scrape some of the soil away with my bare hands. The stones feel regular and smooth. The tops of them are all flat, but digging one up, the bottom is jagged and irregular. The stone next to it is the same. This floor has been prepared, someone has worked here to make the floor flat and even, turning the stones so that all the flat sides face upwards. This is incredible. The tomb is Arcadian but it has been worked on to make it perfect for a burial. I crawl through and emerge the other side to find I am standing in the exact middle of the escarpment. I turn to my right and to my amazement there is another stone slab, this time slightly smaller . . . I lean my back against the rock face and contemplate what I have just found. Not one tomb but two!'

It is my belief that this discovery of mine solves a mystery that has surrounded a small village in south-west France for almost a hundred years. But more than that, it would appear to me to raise fundamental questions about the veracity of some of the central tenets of Christianity.

However, the path that led me to this extraordinary disclosure was far from being a direct one. For the first stumbling steps that led ultimately to a beautiful hillside in rural France were taken hundreds of miles away in London with my uncovering of a code, a secret cipher that had been concealed not just in one painting but in several.

It is with this discovery, and with an investigation into the background of the men who painted these works and those who commissioned them, that the story begins.

CHAPTER ONE

THE PAINTINGS AND
THEIR PATRONS

☆

In Rome in the mid-seventeenth century Cardinal Guilio Rospigliosi, who was later to become Pope Clement IX, commissioned a number of paintings from Nicolas Poussin, the artist whose highly distinctive, individual work had already attracted favourable attention among the European intelligentsia of the time. The two men had met through the enormously influential literary and artistic circle of Cardinal Maffeo Barberini, who was himself elected to the papal throne as Urban VIII in 1623 and who is perhaps best known for his sponsorship of and friendship with Galileo. This meeting of men and minds is indicative of the openness of the Italian High Renaissance, a period which witnessed an explosion of progress in nearly all areas of human artistic endeavour. But it is also more than that, for the legacy of literature, diaries, court records and other documents which are still extant attests to the control held by the relatively small group of people who were the driving force behind this extraordinary cultural expansion. These were the power brokers and spin doctors of their time. The Roman Church, so called as it was based in Rome, was the most powerful institution in the world. Its personnel were key figures, not only in religion but also in the politics and economy of the period, and they formed the core of the intelligentsia which influenced both the arts and the sciences.

Giulio Rospigliosi was a man known for his kindness, courtesy and extreme personal modesty. He was a distinguished man of letters and while he was recognized as a poet of some quality, it was as the author of such moralizing plays as *Sant' Alessio* and *Chi Soffre, Speri* (*Who Suffers, Hopes*), which were staged in the theatre of the Barberini palace, that he gained fame.[1] This theatre seated three thousand people and was actually inaugurated with a production of another Rospigliosi play, a dramatization of the life of St Alexius which, set to the music of Stefano Landi, featured flying angels and the apparition of Religion on a chariot of clouds floating across the stage to the thunderous applause of the audience.[2] Indeed it is as a result of his work in writing the libretto for *Chi Soffre, Speri*, which was set to the music of Virgilio Mazzocchi and Marco Marazzoli and of which Milton had attended the opening night,[3] that he is credited with creating the world's first comic opera, which was premiered in Rome in 1639. He was also a keen art lover, not content with merely collecting works but becoming actively involved in the development of those artists he admired, first as the patron of Claude Lorrain and subsequently of Carlo Maratta. A close adviser to Barberini when he became Pope Urban VIII, he was extremely well connected, numbering among his friends a man well known at the time, the influential Jesuit, scientist and historian Athanasius Kircher.

An extremely significant character in the highest levels of Italian political and religious society, Kircher nevertheless had origins both inauspicious and far distant from Rome. Born in May 1602 near Fulda in Germany, he was the youngest of nine children, whose father was a doctor of divinity who taught the Benedictine monks at the nearby town of Heiligenstadt and who, rarely for the time, owing to the cost and rarity of books, had amassed a large personal library (although this was to be lost during the Thirty Years War). This learned parent seems to have given Athanasius a head start in education, for while still a young boy he had proven himself precocious enough to be given Hebrew lessons by a rabbi in addition to his normal lessons, conducted in Latin and Greek, at the Jesuit school of Fulda. Athanasius completed his noviciate in 1620, but his education was continually interrupted by the fighting of the Thirty Years War, which began in 1618, and he was forced to move frequently to avoid the rise in anti-Jesuit feeling that was being promulgated as a result of Protestant and Calvinist expansionism. Eventually, however, he was ordained a Jesuit priest in Mainz in 1628, having by then shown himself to be something of a prodigy whose interests went far beyond the boundaries of theology. Indeed, moving to France to escape the Protestant armies of Germany, he made his way to Avignon, where he taught mathematics, philosophy and Oriental languages. It was here that he entered into the world of cosmopolitan learning and met Nicolaus Claude Fabri de Peiresc, a wealthy patron of scholars, who had already heard of Kircher's linguistic skills and had noted his developing interest in Egyptian hieroglyphs. Peiresc even owned a number of Egyptian manuscripts. With texts that Kircher was able to borrow from the Jesuit library in Sepia, where he had once taught, and Peiresc's copy of the Bembine tablet of Isis, the pair embarked on research that they hoped would solve the mystery of the hieroglyphs. But the work had barely started when in 1633 Kircher was summoned to Vienna to receive the honour of succeeding Johannes Kepler, who had died in 1631, as Court Mathematician to the Habsburgs. This did not fit in with his personal plans, as he was keen to continue his research in Avignon, but he dutifully set off for Austria while Peiresc fired off letters of protest to, among others, Cardinal Barberini.

The next stage in Kircher's career is indicative of the individual dynamism of the man and the extraordinary coincidences that marked his life. To travel to Austria he would normally have taken the shortest route, which would have led him through Germany. However, as that was dangerous for Jesuits, he decided to travel by way of northern Italy.[4] The first part of the journey was by river to Marseilles, but both he and the Jesuit brothers with whom he was travelling were so ill that the captain of the vessel had to put into an island to allow them to recover, but having done so, he promptly sailed off with all their possessions. On finally reaching Marseilles, they transferred to a more substantial ship to sail to Genoa. But no sooner had they started the voyage than a storm blew up and they had to seek shelter in a cove for three days until it passed over. As they continued their journey, another storm overtook them and this time they had to hug the coastline for protection, narrowly avoiding shipwreck through the skill of the captain. Finally Genoa was reached and there Kircher stayed for two weeks, seemingly in no hurry to continue his voyage, for on a whim he boarded another vessel heading south towards the seaport of Leghorn (Livorno). It seems that Kircher and boats were not a happy combination, for once again a storm came up and they were blown completely off course to Corsica and back before they were eventually able to dock far beyond their intended destination, at Civitavecchia, the main port serving Rome. Kircher could not forgo this opportunity to see the Eternal City and so he started out on the forty-mile journey on foot and on finally arriving he found to his utter surprise that he was expected. As a result of the letters Peiresc had sent, his orders had been changed and he was to stay at the Roman College, at the time the centre of the entire Jesuit movement, in order to take on a special commission, which he had been granted in his absence, to study hieroglyphs.

It was while he was in Rome that Kircher's career really took off. A true polymath, he was at the time the leading expert on Egyptian and Coptic history and was well versed in Sumerian, Chaldaic and Babylonian scripts. Nor were his skills limited to linguistics, for his ability in Greek, Latin and Hebrew opened up to him the greatest collection of written works and through this his personal research extended into the fields of astronomy, geography, mathematics, medicine, music, architecture and art. He is widely regarded as the last of the Renaissance men, not least because he became the most important focus for cultural and scientific knowledge garnered both within Europe and from the many far-flung outposts of Jesuit influence. So highly thought of was he that during his lifetime a museum was founded for him and called the Museo Kircheriano. He was, as the *Encyclopædia Britannica* describes him, 'a one man intellectual clearing house'.[5]

Kircher's knowledge of the transformation of Egyptian Gnosticism into the teaching of Christ was encyclopaedic. He had specialized in finding the origins of all the subjects to which he applied his impressive intellect and his approach to theology was no different. He was of the opinion that Egyptian idolatry and polytheism had been not only the source of the religions of the Greeks and the Romans but also the basis for the beliefs of the later Hebrews. But he did not stop there, for as a result of the information that he was receiving from his Jesuit colleagues around the then known world, he also conjectured about an Egyptian origin for the religions of India, America, China and Japan. This period of research resulted in one of the most extraordinary books to have been written during the Renaissance, the *Oedipus Aegyptiacus*. At least half of this book was devoted to expounding the theosophies of Orpheus, Zoroaster, Pythagoras, Proclus and Plato, all of which Kircher derived from the Egyptian wisdom which had been passed down through the Hermetic writings (of which more later). Many of the theories that he expounded in this and his many other works were thought to have been founded on sound scientific bases – he once lowered himself into the crater of Vesuvius to observe what happens after an eruption, apparently completely unconcerned about the dangers – although the validity of these has since been questioned. Nevertheless, his realization that in virtually every religious tradition there is both an exoteric, publicly disseminated knowledge and an esoteric, hidden knowledge, and that the esoteric part is not only generally closer to the truth but is also closer to the other esoteric doctrines, remains an enduring legacy.

A major part of the *Oedipus Aegyptiacus* is devoted to the links that Kircher found between the theologies of Zoroaster, Pythagoras, Plato and Orpheus, but more important are the connections he saw between these belief systems and the Hebrew Kabbalah. He also drew the conclusion that this wisdom was directly related to the knowledge of the Egyptians and that it had been handed down through the Hermetic writings. Intriguingly, much of what Kircher includes in this spectacular book he also actively criticizes. Nowhere is this more true than in the passages on the possibility of magic, which he introduces by saying, 'he who knows the great chain joining the upper world with the lower, knows all the mysteries of nature and becomes a worker of miracles'.[6] Although not sparing in his censure, he includes such fine detail on these subjects that there are large sections of the *Oedipus Aegyptiacus* which are no less than textbooks in Kabbalist knowledge, Egyptian astrological magic and Hermeticism. This strange contradiction has led some to conclude that despite his protestations to the contrary, Kircher was actually an avid exponent of these doctrines and that, given his exalted position, he felt moved to dismiss them for his own protection while at the same time expounding them. Indeed a clue to his thoughts on these subjects may lie in his choice of image for the colophon at the end of his magnum opus: a picture of Harpocrates, the Graeco-Egyptian God of Silence, holding his finger to his lips as if to say, 'If you know the secret message, keep it to yourself'.[7]

It is easy to understand how, with his immense learning, Kircher became both an extremely powerful and somewhat mysterious figure. Indeed while he had been publicly dismissive of the alchemists who were attempting to transmute base metals into gold, he admitted to discovering one basic alchemical secret: that the 'language of art is not only to be taken literally ... but also metaphorically as a description of psychic or spiritual things',[8] a direct reference to the dual uses of art, as both decoration and a vector for the dissemination of secret knowledge.

This was, of course, a time of intellectual revolution. When Kircher was writing what was to become the most highly sought-after oeuvre of the Renaissance, both Descartes and Newton were busy developing the theories that were to change for ever their particular fields of endeavour. Kircher's contribution to the shift in thinking brought about at this time was to draw together the various strands of Egyptian wisdom, Greek knowledge and Kabbalist and Christian philosophy and to propose the first unified theory of the transmission of knowledge through the ages.

It was into this world of erudition that the painter Nicolas Poussin eventually found himself not only admitted but entirely at home. However, the path there was far from direct. Born in the hamlet of Les Andelys in Normandy in 1594, he was the son of poor parents who scraped a living running a smallholding; his father had once been a soldier but seems to have succumbed to hard times. He attended the village school, and wrote in later years of the good education he had received there. Poussin seems to have shown no aptitude for the arts until his eighteenth year. In 1612 the painter Quentin Varin came to the village to produce several works depicting the church at Les Grands Andelys and in so doing sowed the seeds of artistic interest in the young Poussin. Realizing that he would have to find a master under whom he could learn the rudiments of his calling, he left the village, seemingly against the wishes of his parents, for Rouen, later moving to Paris. However, his poverty and lack of knowledge made his quest difficult. In order to remain in the city and at least start his career he spent some time in the studios of several minor painters, working on portraits and the like. It was through this work that he was asked by a young (and unidentified) nobleman from Poitou to stay in his chateau[9] and paint for him. For a short while this seems to have been a convenient and beneficial arrangement, although one account suggests that the nobleman's mother began to treat Poussin as a mere servant and that as a result he fled the house, utterly humiliated. Initially setting out to return to Paris, he found the journey on foot and without money too difficult, the 'greatest hardship that he endured'.[10] He fell ill and was forced to return to his parents' village to recuperate and not until a year later was he able to set off again for Paris, this time with ample funds and the blessing of his parents.

During his first period in the capital Poussin had made the acquaintance of Marie de' Medici, Louis the XIII's queen, who had introduced him to the work of Raphael and other artists of the Italian High Renaissance. This had fired his enthusiasm to go to Rome, the centre of artistic and literary attention and a magnet for anyone with artistic aspirations and talent. It took him three attempts. The first ended in disaster in Florence. The second resulted in his being arrested over a debt with a merchant in Lyon, then something of a halfway house for those on the road to Italy, and being forced to return to Paris, where he lived in the Jesuit Collège de Navarre. There his luck began to change. He was commissioned by the Jesuits to paint a series of six large decorative pictures for the celebrations to commemorate the canonization of Saints Ignatius and Francis Xavier, due to take place in mid 1622. These paintings caught the eye of Giovanni-Battista Marino, generally known as the Cavalier Marin, who was the court poet to Marie de' Medici. By this time elderly and ill, Marino took a liking to the young Poussin and recommended him to Cardinal Francesco Barberini, nephew of Maffeo Barberini, Pope Urban VIII. Marino also intended to effect personal introductions to many of his art connoisseur friends who had made Rome their home and he and Poussin set off together for that city. However, failing health dictated that Marino went to Naples and Poussin was left to travel by himself, to arrive unfêted.

From 1624 to 1630 Poussin experienced deep privation, for during this time Marino died and Cardinal Barberini was dispatched to France, leaving the painter with no patrons and very few contacts of any worth to him. He was cared for by the Dughets, kindly neighbours who all but adopted him as their son. Indeed Poussin would not only marry the daughter of Jacques Dughet but would also teach painting to one son[11] and employ the other as his personal secretary. With this stable background he soon built up a reputation for his work, developing his art and his experience, especially when, between 1638 and 1639, having found a firm patron in Cassiano dal Pozzo, the secretary to Barberini, he painted a number of well-received works – not least of which was the altarpiece of St Peter's, commissioned by Barberini himself on his return to Rome from his diplomatic travels. As a result of this success Poussin came under intense pressure to return to Paris and become a member of the Royal Academy of Painting and Sculpture, which was being formed by Cardinal Richelieu. Poussin was not interested in this offer: he had made his home and his friends in Rome, and he had no wish to return to the stifled and restricting atmosphere of the French court. However, he eventually had to bow to the united demands of Richelieu and Louis XIII, and in October 1640 he set out for Paris.

Poussin's time in France was not a happy one. Although hailed and received with great honours, he was commissioned to do work he neither liked nor wanted. Requests to him to apply his talents to altarpieces and tapestry designs did nothing to improve his humour, and even his work on the majestic ceiling painting of the Grand Gallery at the Louvre Palace left him bored and uninspired. He bitterly missed the retinue of artists and patrons with whom he had surrounded himself in Rome, and in late 1642 he returned to his beloved Italy.

It is on Poussin's return to Rome that a marked change becomes apparent, not only in his work but also in his life. He maintained a strict daily regime, with time set aside for painting, exercise and conversation. The patronage and friendship of dal Pozzo had a powerful stabilizing influence, as did his marriage.[12] It was also during this period that he was commissioned by none other than Cardinal Rospigliosi to paint a series of four works, and in accepting the commission he seems to have found a new confidence in his painting style and a calmness in his life in general.

Two of these paintings are now lost and we only know of them and their subject matter through engravings; they are *The Rest on the Flight into Egypt*, which featured an elephant in the background of the work, and *Time saving Truth from Envy and Discord*. Of those remaining and extant today, the third in the series, *Happiness subdued by Death* has been the focus of the most attention although not necessarily by art historians. Better known under the title *The Shepherds of Arcadia*, this work has been particularly dissected in all manner of ways in an attempt to discover what clues it holds to the mystery of Rennes-le-Château. But it is the last in the series of works that Poussin painted for Cardinal Rospigliosi, *A Dance to the Music of Time*, that I have come to recognize as most revealing in the context of this quest, both for how it relates to ideas expressed in the earlier work and for what I believe is its profound impact on how we can interpret various paintings by other artists.

It was a number of things that drew me to these paintings by Poussin and led me to believe that these and his own personal circumstances were important in solving this mystery. I believe that the painter was inducted into a great secret in order that he could transmit this through his art to those who understood the code. The basis for this belief is twofold. It is known that Rospigliosi himself chose the themes of the works that he had commissioned, but what is less well known is the fact that Poussin received instruction in the painting of perspective from none other than Kircher, the one man in Rome above all others whose key interests were ciphers and secret knowledge. Would he not have put this secret knowledge into practice in the works that he himself tutored? Fascinatingly, Rospigliosi chose to hang the completed *The Shepherds of Arcadia* not on public view in his offices, which would seem the natural choice for a superb painting by the most celebrated artist in Rome, but in his private apartments, where it would be seen only by himself and his guests. Could it be that he wanted the painting to remind him of the hidden secret but to do so in a way that only those who were aware of it would see it in the painting?

There may be a further clue to the complicity of Poussin in this mystery. Six years after painting *The Shepherds of Arcadia* he was visited by Abbé Louis Fouquet, the brother of Nicolas Fouquet, Superintendent of Finances to Louis XIV of France. After the meeting the Abbé wrote to his brother:

He and I discussed certain things, which I shall with ease be able to explain to you in detail – things which will give you, through Monsieur Poussin, advantages which even Kings would have great pains to draw from him, and which, according to him, it is possible that nobody else will discover in the centuries to come. And what is more, these are things so difficult to discover that nothing now on this earth can prove of better fortune nor be their equal.[13]

If Poussin had been made privy to this information, his learning of it could well explain why both his style of painting and his own personal circumstances changed considerably. Certainly, with even a cursory glance at *The Shepherds of Arcadia* it becomes apparent that its subject, three shepherds and a shepherdess in front of an antique tomb bearing the peculiar inscription 'Et in Arcadia Ego', carries enigmas within, which are deepened if one has an understanding of some of the imagery the artist has employed. Further, it is clear that there is some sort of geometry at work here, especially when one considers the deliberate positions of the shepherds' staffs.

But *The Shepherds of Arcadia* and *A Dance to the Music of Time* are not the only Poussin paintings which suggest very significant meanings lying beneath their more obvious subject matter. *The Deluge* (or *Winter*), one of a series of paintings called *The Four Seasons* which also depict *Spring*, *Summer* and *Autumn*, was commissioned by Cardinal Richelieu's nephew, the Duc de Richelieu, in 1664. It was the Cardinal who had so much contact with Poussin during his unhappy return to Paris in 1640 and the two continued to meet in Rome until Richelieu's death.

Cardinal Armand Jean du Plessis de Richelieu is today remembered best as a consummate political manipulator and the figure for whom the term 'the power behind the throne' could have been coined. He was an intelligent and devious man, whose origins, while not utterly humble, were certainly inauspicious. The 'Éminence Rouge', as he became known, was born in 1585 to the family of du Plessis de Richelieu in Poitou (coincidentally the same region to which the unnamed nobleman had taken the young Poussin). The family had fairly insignificant feudal origins but had made the most of them through a series of intermarriages with the legal and administrative classes and had thereby been granted the Seigneury of Poitou, which had led to Armand Jean's father, François, becoming the grand provost to Henry II. François died when Armand Jean was just five years old. By then the family was in a parlous financial state, many of their estates having been ruined by mismanagement during the Wars of Religion of 1562–98. This seems to have had a great effect on the young boy, the constant threat of impending poverty instilling in him a will to learn, a capacity for hard work and a talent for charming those in authority.

Armand Jean's mother discovered that one of the few remaining family assets was the bishopric of Luçon, near the port of La Rochelle, granted to them by Henry III under the Concordat of 1516. At the time the cathedral chapter was in disarray and it became necessary for a member of the family to become bishop there if they were to maintain it as one of their estates. Although he was the youngest of three sons, the role fell to Armand Jean, then a student. His eldest brother, Henri, was already heir to the Seigneury of Richelieu, while his other brother, Alphonse, had already taken his orders as a Carthusian monk. The prospect of a religious career actually appealed to Armand Jean. Although he was a sickly boy, his aptitude for education had developed into a strong ability to debate and an even greater interest in being able to control the lives of those around him. However, because he was not yet above the canonical age for consecration, dispensation had to be granted by the

Pope in order for him to take up his position. This required him to travel to Rome, where he worked his charms on Paul V and was in April 1607 both ordained as a priest and consecrated to the Holy See of Luçon. On taking up his position he found that there was much to do. The diocese had been ruined in the Wars of Religion, the chapter was hostile and the clergy was demoralized in the extreme; but, undaunted, Richelieu set to work and soon the industry and authority that started to emanate from the Episcopal Palace won his opponents round. Divisive and manipulative though he may later have become, this period of his life is marked by his incredible work rate and the highly developed sense of conscience that he exhibited. He became the first bishop in France to introduce the reforms that had been determined at the Council of Trent and as a theologian he was not only the first to write in French but also the first to establish the convention of vernacular exposition.

Richelieu's greatest concern at this time was that France was in danger of falling back into the disorder of the Wars of Religion. This is the first point at which we see him broadening out from strengthening the position of his family to adopting a wider national perspective. The assassination of Henry IV in 1610 had resulted in the rise of his wife the queen mother, Marie de' Medici, as regent for her son, Louis XIII, but under her the government was corrupt and self-serving. In 1616, after spending some years developing a reputation as a clever negotiator between the various factions of the royalty, the nobility and the Third Estate (professionals, the middle class, artists and peasants), he was appointed Secretary of State. But a palace revolt in 1617 overthrew the regency and Richelieu was banished, first to Luçon and then to the papal city of Avignon.

It was not until 1624 that he found himself returning to a position of real power with his appointment as Secretary of

State for Commerce and the Marine and Chief of the Royal Council, the office that was later to be given the title First Minister of France. The crisis that resulted in the renaming of this post was the invocation of a protection treaty between France and the Protestant Swiss canton of Grisons against Spanish ambitions in the Valtellina valley. This treaty threatened to destabilize French domestic relations, for the Protestants had sided with Grisons and the Catholics with the Spanish Habsburgs. Richelieu's response was both swift and ruthless. He expelled the papal troops from France, indicating support for the Grison Protestants and for ever opposing Catholic interests. Indeed in 1635, at the outbreak of what was to become the Thirty Years War, he also aligned the nation with the Protestant powers.

Richelieu's relationship with Marie de' Medici was a strained one, reflecting the distance that existed between her and her son, who was by then a close confidant of the Cardinal. In a relationship which at times declined into outright hostility, Richelieu at the best of times provoked Marie de' Medici into a state of near hysteria, leading her to claim that the First Minister was the man responsible for her lack of influence. She tried to influence her son to dismiss Richelieu, effectively forcing Louis XIII to choose between having what he perceived as his own independence or the domination of an overbearing mother. Determining that there was no one but Richelieu who could relieve him of the complicated responsibilities of decision making, Louis gave his full support to the Cardinal, causing his mother and brother to seek refuge in the Spanish-owned Netherlands. After this crucial time for Richelieu, he had in almost every sphere the unswerving support of the King, who became increasingly reliant on the advice and political stratagems of his First Minister. Indeed Richelieu terrorized Louis to such an extent that he ultimately became the power behind the throne of France.

In Richelieu's employ there was a now little-known man named Gaffarel. A highly learned and extraordinarily erudite scholar who had a wide knowledge of Egyptian, Sumerian and Babylonian languages and history, Gaffarel was fully conversant with the principles of Gnosticism and was extremely interested in the occult,[14] on which he wrote many works, including *Abdita Divinae Kabbale Mysteriae* and *Unheard of Curiosities concerning Talismanic Magic*.[15] Gaffarel was heavily relied upon by his master for instruction, acting not only as librarian and teacher but also as something of a sage.[16] Intriguingly, Richelieu is documented as carrying with him a staff or wand which he evidently used to cast spells and to influence the outcome of meetings and audiences with those whom he wished to control. This may seem odd until we remember that, even to this day, the Roman Catholic Church is in the business of exorcism and relies heavily on the belief that poltergeists and ghosts are the manifestation of souls which the Church has been unable to help.

Richelieu came to depend more and more on Gaffarel, who was also working on a book which he considered to be his magnum opus, *The Holes of Man and the Holes of the Earth*. This, thought to have been a collection of occultist and Kabbalist knowledge, was never published and Gaffarel mysteriously vanished in 1661.

Thus we come to have a deeper understanding of the Duc de Richelieu, the Cardinal's nephew and Poussin's patron for *The Deluge*. With access to the voluminous library of arcane knowledge that his uncle had amassed and, having had the guiding hand of the mysterious Gaffarel to instruct him, the Duc de Richelieu bears all the hallmarks of the significant personalities connected with the formulation and promulgation of the Arcadian cipher. Strangely, none of the works in the series of which *The Deluge* forms a part is ever mentioned in the letters of the artist himself, nor are they described in Bellori's early biography of Poussin.[17] The themes of each of the four are drawn from Old Testament imagery. *Spring* or *The Earthly Paradise* depicts Adam and Eve in the Garden of Eden; *Summer* or *Ruth and Boaz* shows the meeting of the Moabite Ruth with the Israelite Boaz, leading to the union that gave birth to the line of David (and ultimately Christ); *Autumn* or *The Spies with the Grapes from the Promised Land* shows the scene of Moses' spies returning from the land of Canaan, 'the land of milk and honey'; and the final work, *Winter* or *The Deluge*, is based on the Flood of the Old Testament. When the series was completed and shown in Paris it met with mixed reviews, some of which were highly critical. Indeed it did not long stay in the possession of Richelieu, as the series of paintings was lost by him as a wager on a real tennis match with Louis XIV. The King had coveted these works and used the tennis match merely as a method of obtaining them. He is known to have reimbursed Poussin by paying him 50,000 livres, a considerable amount at the time.

While the central theme of the Flood had been a popular one in Baroque and Renaissance art, Poussin's rendering has some strikingly original factors which set it aside from those of Uccello, Raphael and Michelangelo. *The Deluge* is generally regarded as being a much finer work than the other three, and is also significant for Poussin's choice of subject matter, considering that it forms part of a seasonal quartet. A depiction of winter would normally be expected to include motifs of wood-cutters carrying faggots of firewood and pigs rooting through the frozen earth, and would also show figures skating on frozen lakes and rivers. It is therefore curious that the artist has chosen very different subject matter. As a treatment of the Flood the painting is also singular, its scene of a group of helpless and seemingly insignificant people coming ashore inspiring awe in many of its admirers. However, the picture's details have great relevance in terms of the cipher.

There is another painting, by Luca Signorelli (1441–1523), which is also of great import. It was commissioned by Lorenzo de' Medici, grandson of that benevolent despot Cosimo, uncrowned 'King of Florence'. Perhaps unsurprisingly, the family background of the Medici who commissioned the painting bears some interesting similarities to those other artistic patrons we have already encountered. And again it is such a background that makes this work an important key in the unlocking of the cipher.

The Medici were the most powerful family in Italy, ruling Florence and Tuscany from 1434 until 1737 with only two brief interruptions and providing the Church of Rome with four of its Popes: Leo X, Clement VII, Pious IV and Leon XI. They also married into Europe's royal families, most notably in France, where two queens, Catherine de' Medici and Marie de' Medici, represented the family interests. There were effectively three lines of the family that acquired or tried to acquire power: the Minor Branch headed by Chiarissimo II, which failed to gain Florence in the fourteenth century; the Grand Duchy, which renounced any republican notions and which set itself up as a dynasty of Grand Dukes of Tuscany in the sixteenth century; and perhaps the most influential arm of the family, and the one which is of particular interest to us, the Principate.

The family's origins are something of a mystery. It is known that the Medici were originally of Tuscan peasant stock and came to greatness from the village of Cafaggiolo, set in the valley of the River Sieve, north of Florence. By the thirteenth century they had become wealthy notables in Florence, although not so elevated that they were in the first flight of Florentine society. It would appear that the depression which had a hold on Europe throughout the 1340s resulted in the bankruptcy of many of the larger and wealthier families, leaving the Medici to take a position in the city's élite. But all was not smooth running, for a stream of political miscalculations posed difficulties for the family until the late fourteenth century.

The founding father of the Principate branch, Cosimo the Elder (1389–1464), had inherited the persistent traits which mark the entire dynasty. Adept at courting favour with both the professional and peasant classes, he maintained a huge fortune which allowed him to follow the same passion for building magnificent edifices – and collecting books and works of art to fill them – that had marked the family's activities since the fourteenth century. Cosimo the Elder's grandfather was the distant cousin of the last of the members of the Minor Branch and it was his son, Giovanni di Bicci, who inherited the family business of cloth and silk trading upon which much of the family fortune had been built. Cosimo augmented this wealth handsomely when in 1462, having already been charged with the responsibility of managing the papal finances, he was granted a monopoly on the alum mines at Tolfa, alum being an integral part of Florence's burgeoning textile industry. This, among other fortunate dealings, made him the richest man of his time, his bank providing funds for profitable loans through branch offices in most of the trading centres and financial markets of Europe. The power that such near-unimaginable wealth bestowed on him made him a target for the jealousies of other powerful families, not least the Albizzi, who attempted a coup to overturn his influence. In 1431, when Cosimo was taking a holiday in Caffaggiolo, he was summoned to the city to answer the charge 'of having sought to elevate himself higher than others', which attracted the maximum penalty of capital punishment. He was imprisoned in a small dungeon in part of the Palazzo Vecchio but it was not long before the Albizzi realized that removing the influence of Cosimo was not going to be plain sailing. The same wealth and power that had made him friends in high places worked wonders on those who were employed to keep him contained. The gaoler was bribed to act as Cosimo's food taster in case of poisoning and government officials succumbed to the offers of riches in order to reduce his sentence from death to banishment. On his release Cosimo effectively retired from public life to take up residence in Padua and Venice. But a year later a turn of fortune, in part engineered by the manipulation of election results, returned the government of Florence to the Medici family. Cosimo resumed his seat of power while the Albizzi fled into permanent exile. This period, beginning in 1434, saw the establishment of the Medici Principate and the foundation of a firm future for the most successful branch of the family

Significantly, Cosimo was not solely employed in furthering the family fortunes through a quest for wealth and power. He was at first interested in, and later became obsessed with, collecting ancient manuscripts, both from within the Christian kingdoms and, having been granted the permission of Sultan Mehmed III, from the East and Byzantium. In order to maximize his chances of success he approached the sourcing and acquisition of the books, codices and manuscripts that he wanted in a highly methodical fashion, employing a small army of agents to find and buy them and a team of highly respected copyists and translators to work on them. This work resulted in what became known (somewhat unfairly) as the Laurentian library, after Cosimo's grandson, and was without equal in the Western world, not only for its contents but also because it was open to the public.

One of the books Cosimo de' Medici spent much time, and

a large fortune, acquiring was the *Corpus Hermeticum* or *The Book of Hermes*, named after the Greek god Hermes the Messenger, who had the ability to speak and be heard by both the 'world above and the world below'. This book is thought to have been written between the first and third centuries CE and deals with the connections between all religious thought. It explains the links between the Orphics, Platonists, Pythagoreans, Chaldeans, Jews and Christians. Cosimo realized the importance of this highly Kabbalist work to an understanding of the truths of the Golden Ages of the Romans, Greeks, Egyptians and even further back in time, and it was the one text that he wanted to gain above all others.

An indication of the importance he placed on this unique work may be gained from the responsibility he gave in connection with it to the humanist Marsilio Ficino. This scholar had been in the employ of Cosimo primarily as a translator of Plato – a subject that so enthralled Cosimo that he is sometimes credited with being the driving force behind the entire Neo-Platonist movement. Indeed Cosimo had been so impressed by the intelligence shown by the young Ficino that he had persuaded him to forgo his training as a doctor in Bologna and instead to concentrate his energies on studying philosophy in Florence. He installed him in his own house in the city and gave him a small estate at Carreggi so that he would not be distracted from his intellectual task by the mundanity of earning a living or worrying about the material aspects of life.[18] Ficino had an extraordinary intellect, and although he was physically weak, lame and hunchbacked, it was as if these deficiences were compensated for by a brilliant mind. Cosimo now commissioned him to reconcile paganism, in the guise of Platonic thought, with Christianity – a theme that had been proposed by Cosimo, who had become an ardent admirer of Plato, and which Ficino took to readily.[19] Indeed the young scholar had become so adept at fusing the two schools of thought that his work was followed by many of the great thinkers of the time, keen to reconcile adherence to the orthodoxies of Christianity with their passion for the heritage offered by antiquity. Ficino and Cosimo shared a desire to prove once and for all that the two disciplines were not mutually exclusive, and it was this that fuelled Cosimo's craving to find those antique documents still extant which would support Ficino's argument.

Thus, when in 1463 one of Cosimo's agents, a Greek monk named Leonardo del Pistoja, returned from Macedonia with a Greek manuscript that contained a near-complete copy of the *Corpus Hermeticum*, it was passed immediately to Ficino in order that he might translate it straight away. Ficino had hitherto seen the translation of the entire works of Plato, the manuscripts of which had been assembled in readiness, as his priority, not least because Cosimo was over seventy years old and in failing health. But notwithstanding the fact that such a translation, and the act of patronage, would have lasting value to the learned world and would cause him to be remembered, Cosimo deemed the *The Book of Hermes*, its rarity and the hidden secrets it contained, of even more importance.[20] Ficino, perfectly aware of the importance of these works, set to immediately and was able to translate them in full for Cosimo to be able to read them before his death on 4 August 1464.

On the death of Cosimo, who only after his demise was granted the title Pater Patriae (Father of His Country), power passed into the hands of his son Piero. Known as Piero the Gouty for his affliction with the condition that troubled so many of the Medici, he was nonetheless a brave and successful ruler, despite being so crippled that he was frequently able to move only his tongue. His rule over Florence lasted only five years and he was succeeded on his death in 1469 by his sons Lorenzo and Giuliano. The assassination of Giuliano in the

Pazzi Conspiracy of 1478 left Lorenzo to rule on his own. He was to contribute more than any other individual to the flowering of Florence.

The man who was to become known as Lorenzo the Magnificent seemingly inherited the brilliance of his grandfather and on acceding to power he publicly announced his intention to follow closely both Cosimo's and his father's footsteps. He succeeded in perfecting the political and diplomatic accord that Cosimo had set in motion, creating a firm balance of power between the various dukedoms and protectorates of Florence, Naples, Milan, Venice, the Papal States and with the states that surrounded Florence. Political diplomacy and affairs of state aside, as with his grandfather, Lorenzo's passion lay in the arts and philosophy and his tutor had been none other than Marsilio Ficino. He also counted among his closest friends the humanist Giovanni Pico della Mirandola and the poet Politian (Poliziano, born Angelo Ambrogini), who had actually saved his life on the day that his brother had perished at the hands of the Pazzi. He continued the quest for ancient texts, spending the equivalent today of two million pounds a year on books alone and sending new agents far into the East to acquire ancient manuscripts which would then be copied and distributed among the many colleges he both founded and financially supported for the dissemination of knowledge. At the tender age of twenty-three he founded the University of Pisa for 'the study of the Latin language and those branches of science of which it was the principle vehicle',[21] second only to the University of Florence, the only place in Italy where Greek, the language of the greats, was taught.

It was through Lorenzo's tutorship by and subsequent friendship with Ficino that the Golden Age of Florence really developed. Nowhere was this more so than in the Platonic Academy, a loose grouping of Lorenzo's good friends presided over by Ficino, which discussed all things Platonic, staged re-enactments of the *Symposium* and kept a lamp burning before a bust of the great man. It was within this forum that della Mirandola, fourteen years younger than Lorenzo and already a renowned precocious talent, took on the search for a reconciliation between Platonism and Christianity and stretched its boundaries further than any of his contemporaries. He read Hermes Trismegistus, the great Greek mystical inventor of writing associated with the Egyptian God Thoth, and then brought the mysteries of the Kabbalah into the debate. This seems to have fired the imagination of the group, for a number of them subsequently learned Hebrew – an extremely rare occurrence among Gentiles – and sought out such Jewish teachers as Eliah del Medigo.

Part of the dominance that Florence was to gain in poetry, art and sculpture can be directly linked to the patronage that Lorenzo bestowed on many of the finest artists of the time. A highly respected poet himself and one whose talent seems to have been genuine rather than the result of sycophantic adulation, Lorenzo wrote in the local Tuscan dialect rather than the more common Latin. Towards the end of his life he opened a school of sculpture in his garden in San Marco and, having already been the patron-protector of such talents as Botticelli, Verrocchio and Verrocchio's best-known pupil, Leonardo da Vinci, he spotted another talent, a fifteen-year-old who seemed to exhibit an unnatural flair and feel for the stone he was working. The boy was Michelangelo and as a result of Lorenzo's discovery he was brought up in the Medici palace as if he were Lorenzo's own son.

Lorenzo the Magnificent died on 9 April 1492. His demise marked the end of one spectacular era but it also heralded the onset of another; just a few months later Christopher Columbus would set sail for the Indies and discover the Americas.

Lorenzo's death at the age of forty-three moved the entire Florentine population, all of which, it is said, attended the simple burial ceremony that he had requested. His last words were fittingly to his closest friends, Politian and Pico della Mirandola, telling them, 'I wish that death had spared me till I had completed your libraries.'

In the year before he died, however, he had commissioned a painting from one of his favoured artists, Luca Signorelli, to whom he was both friend and patron. Signorelli was already recognized as one of Florence's emergent geniuses and the painting, *The Education of Pan*, when finished, was installed in the Chapel of the Madonna di Brizo in Orvieto Cathedral. During the Second World War it was thought to have been lost for ever as the result of an air raid on Berlin, but it is now considered to be among the war plunder hidden from public view in the enormous basements of the Hermitage in St Petersburg. It is this painting that I was drawn to, for it bears the hallmarks of having been painted by someone who used the same principles as Poussin, a geometry which underlies the scene being painted and which hints at messages concealed in the image itself. It would seem that someone with Kabbalist knowledge, an understanding of how to code information, had a hand in this painting.

Lorenzo's heritage of learning at the hand of Ficino and Pico della Mirandola, the vast libraries of ancient tracts at his disposal and the proximity of the family of which he was a key member to the centre of the Roman Church's power, would indeed have made him well placed to be inducted into any secret truth that the Church feared. It would also have brought more power to himself and more influence to his line. Is it mere coincidence that his son Giovanni became the first of the Medici to be elevated to the papal throne as Pope Leo X? It is my belief that Italy's most prominent family was inducted into a great secret and that the art commissioned by them contains a trail of clues that leads eventually to the revelation of a great truth.

There is another link with Lorenzo de' Medici which would seem to have a bearing on this mystery. Leonardo da Vinci was not only about the same age as Lorenzo but shared with him a passion for philosophy, music, riddles, beauty, knowledge and intellectual games of all types. As Lorenzo was the patron to Leonardo's master, Verrocchio, he cannot fail to have known of the existence of Leonardo and indeed there are records which show that Leonardo 'in the days of his youth was admitted to the company of "Il Magnifico", who paid him an allowance and had him work on the garden in the Piazza San Marco'.[22] Given Lorenzo's ability to spot and promote talent, it is curious in the extreme that while almost certainly aware of Leonardo and his skills as an artist and sculptor, he never once offered him a major commission. There is not even one painting of Leonardo's that can be directly associated with Lorenzo. The reason for this absence of patronage from Lorenzo has been lost to history. Perhaps there was an unresolved dispute early in their relationship; indeed there was the charge of sodomy on which Leonardo was arrested at the age of twenty-four and tried with three others, with which Lorenzo would hardly have wanted to be associated. But the case was eventually dismissed and the charges dropped for good, the accusations having been anonymous and no witnesses making themselves available to provide signed statements or evidence. Whatever the case, Lorenzo never showed the young man from Vinci the level of support that was granted to others within the same close circle. As a result the frustrated Leonardo left Florence in 1483 to try his fortune in Milan, two hundred miles away, and there he blossomed, feeling that he could at last spread his wings without the criticism of the snobbish fast set of Florence. Milan must have suited him well, for it was not long before he won favour at the court of the Sforza family, the Milanese Medici, and won commissions from his new patron, Ludovico Sforza.

However, in one of the paintings completed early in his Milanese period there is an oddity that leads me to believe that Leonardo too may have come into contact with the same great secret shared by his contemporaries and the near-contemporaries we have encountered. That painting is *The Virgin of the Rocks*, a work which, although Leonardo painted only thirteen major works in oil, he executed twice. It is the earlier work, now hanging in the Louvre, that is most revealing. The later version, now in the National Gallery in London, has been also worked on by Ambrogio da Predis and, while showing the same peculiarity, has various other aspects that have been altered.

As we have seen, these paintings are all by highly respected artists, who were patronized or commissioned by extremely wealthy and powerful individuals each of whom had a connection with the papacy and behind them a librarian or mentor with an interest in the Kabbalah and ancient or esoteric texts. We shall see that each of these works bears a hidden symbolism which is Kabbalist in theme. In untangling this we are led to a fascinating discovery.

CHAPTER TWO

THE ESOTERIC ARCHAEOLOGY
OF FINE ART

☆

Before setting out to try to understand fully what depths of common meaning might lie in these works of art, it was of course necessary to establish proof positive that Poussin, Signorelli and the other painters concerned had indeed been aware of a knowledge that would have given rise to such a cipher as I was discerning.

We know that Poussin started work on *The Shepherds of Arcadia* in 1650, having been commissioned by Cardinal Rospigliosi, later to become Pope Clement IX. Far from being a dry and blinkered theologian, Rospigliosi was a highly artistic man with a broad range of interests which encompassed an understanding of the arcane and esoteric through his librarian Athanasius Kircher. Indeed pursuit of modes of thought far beyond the boundaries of accepted Christian theology led to his becoming known as the 'free-thinking Pope'. If Kircher had discovered deeper secrets than the Christian tradition maintained, it is not only possible but extremely likely that he would have shared and discussed with his open-minded employer matters which would have been considered by others as heresy. On this basis it is also plausible to suppose that Rospigliosi, as a dramatist and intellectual, would have wished to encapsulate this knowledge in a form which, while preserving the secret and keeping it hidden from the general public, would be visible to him as a reminder of the fallacy upon which the Church, of which he was an officer, was based. Certainly, as his career was leading powerfully towards accession to the papacy, he would not have wanted to jeopardize himself in any way. A broad-minded, free-thinking Pope could be acceptable to the Holy See; a heretical Pope, for obvious reasons, would not.

There is evidence that Poussin was disillusioned by religion in general and the teachings of the Roman Church in particular. Despite his close proximity to the personalities and the seat of the Church, he was renowned for his intellectual independence, especially where formal religion was concerned. But it is also clear that he even had distinctly non-Catholic leanings. He is known to have been a Stoic and a Gnostic and to have had strong Pythagorean tendencies, leading some authors to label him a Rosicrucian. References to contemporary religious affairs in his letters are scant, but according to Anthony Blunt, 'all display a surprising degree of flippancy'.[1] Indeed, on hearing of the death of Pope Urban VIII, Poussin wrote: 'God grant that we may be better governed in the future than in the past.' That he counted Kircher, the repository of an enormous amount of heretical and arcane information, among his circle of friends is also telling. Kircher's instruction of Poussin in the art of perspective, which itself was an overturning of established mores, even extended to his showing Poussin how to construct a shadow-box and to place small wax figures inside it, lighting it with candles in order to conjure up the atmosphere of a planned painting and demonstrating how the shadows of the figures would fall on the scene. Could it be that Poussin, a trusted free-thinker, was being coached so that he might be told a great secret, the better to paint *The Shepherds of Arcadia* with a concealed code?

On first viewing the work it becomes apparent that its quality differs from that of Poussin's previous commissions. Whereas before he had employed a robust and broad style resembling that of the artist Philip Peter Roos, better known as Rosa da Tivoli (1656–1706), his art now takes on a more refined and balanced quality, showing a subtlety more akin to that of Claude Lorrain (1600–82).

The picturesque scene of three shepherds and a shepherdess standing by a hilltop tomb and pointing at the mysterious inscription 'Et in Arcadia Ego' is, without doubt, of great beauty. Interestingly, though, the figures are wearing distinctive, highly coloured clothing of rich fabric, not the rough, dull clothes of rural peasants, innocents in an Arcadian idyll. The footwear of three of the figures is extremely fine in both detail and workmanship, their delicately strapped sandals not the normal footwear of those who make their living following and protecting animals on the rough, rocky hillsides the landscape indicates. And why is one of them wearing no footwear at all but is unshod on the harsh earthen surface? Given the minds of the men behind the work, there is reason to suppose that this connotes something more than merely a highly stylized vision of rustics. These elements alone are so distinctive that they cannot be an arbitrary choice by the artist.

As for the use of colours, I believe that this is an encoding of Kircher's, and through him Rospigliosi's, knowledge of the Egyptian heritage and of the ascription of colours to various of the gods that was practised by the pharaohs and their priests. For applying the same rules to this work shows that the choice of colours is far from random.

The female figure on the right of the work wears a rich blue skirt with an impressive golden shawl around her shoulders and golden sandals on her feet. To the Egyptians blue was related to the god Amen-ra, who was concerned with the resurrection of the god Horus. Gold was frequently used to signify a relationship with the godhead, and the golden steps that led up to the temple; gold was also associated with the harvest, not just of crops but of the gathering in of spirits in order to return them to their Father creator, leaving the mortal, physical remains to their owner the Earth (or, in the Greek tradition, Pan). When we study the other figures it becomes even clearer that Poussin wanted to convey that this country idyll is in fact an allegory with religious overtones. But it is this figure who indicates that we have the licence to do so.

To the right of the shepherdess is a shepherd wearing a laurel wreath who has his foot on a raised stone and is pointing at the tomb's inscription. He is dressed in a luxuriant vivid-red robe and wears equally impractical brilliant-white sandals. In the Egyptian tradition red was a highly important colour which signified the very senior god Shu, the representation of the power of the godhead incarnate here on Earth in the form of man. It has also been found to illustrate the presence of the Lord of Truth or the eye of Ra – in Christian terms a simulacrum of the Christ figure.

On the other side of the tomb is a curious character. Clean-shaven like the shepherd, he wears the same leafy headgear and is clothed not in brilliant colour but in a simple white shroud. In this instance the white is significant as it represents Death, white being the colour of both bloodless flesh and the swaddling bandages which were used to wrap the bodies of the dead pharaohs in the process of mummification. Also significant here is the fact that this figure is the only unshod member of the group, his feet thus directly connecting with the ground. In the Greek tradition this confirms him as Pan or, in Cathar terminology, Rex Mundi, the god of the physical world, the king of the Earth, who was sealed or chained into his earthly domain, unable to rise to the heavens until the end of the world. While

Pan is the god of all things physical, the possessor of the flesh, the God of the Christian belief is the god of the soul and the spirit. Could the two wreathed figures each be half of the same whole, a godhead comprising the earthly Pan/Rex Mundi and the spiritual Shu/Ra or the representation of the risen Christ, flanking each side of the tomb?

The final figure is of no less importance in terms of meaning and the cipher. His clothing, a simple robe draped around him, is of the same blue as that of the shepherdess; he also is wearing sandals. The implication is that he is of spiritual rather than earthly significance. The blue, as we have seen, indicates a connection with the resurrection. Yet if this painting is meant to represent a holy family of sorts we have already determined the Jesus character. It is my conclusion that this figure, heavily muscled and the only man in the piece to be wearing a beard, signifying wisdom, is the representation of John the Baptist, the wild man, dressed in furs. Jesus himself said he paved the way for his own coming. Could it be that Poussin is trying to indicate a continuing relationship between Jesus the preacher and John, whose sacrifice made that ministry possible?

So we have a painting which, far from merely representing a rural scene, is laden with historically religious overtones which resound, albeit in a cryptic fashion, with the Jesus story. Further, is it not odd, for a painting which is supposed to be of shepherds, that there are no sheep evident anywhere? Are we meant to assume that the flock is of a spiritual nature?

In *The Deluge* the same colour coding for the various characters can be easily discerned. In the foreground is a small, rudderless boat, washed into a rocky cove at the mercy of the wind and tide and carrying what one assumes to be survivors of the Flood – in the background is an ark. Beside it is a figure adorned in red, who is being dragged to the shore by an ass, a powerful image directly evoking Jesus through his association with this animal and confirmed by the colour of the robe. Here we also find the same female figure as in *The Shepherds of Arcadia*, still dressed in blue and gold, but in this painting depicted holding up a small child who is also dressed in red. We already have an adult Jesus, with the ass, so this is unlikely to be the Madonna and child. Could this be the son of the Jesus figure being held by his mother? That there is a relationship between the woman and the man would seem to be borne out by the contact that there is between the Jesus figure in *The Shepherds of Arcadia* and the woman there, who also has her hand resting on his back.

If using the Egyptian code is right, the colours alone link *The Deluge* with Jesus and his family. The painting as a whole, far from being based on the Bible story of the Flood, thus becomes a representation of the coming ashore of a holy family, although not an orthodox one. There are other curious images contained within this work which have baffled previous interpreters. A figure swimming in the water holds a large book. Dressed in a robe with a cowl covering his head, he appears to have no face but two shining dots for eyes. Why is he carrying a book, especially in such desperate circumstances as a shipwreck? One would suppose that only the most important artefacts would require risking life and limb to save. My sense is that the book represents the book of souls, the record of those pledged to the faith of Jesus, who will stand behind him on the Day of Judgement. On the left-hand side, climbing up a rock out of the water, is a snake which seems to have come ashore with the Jesus figure and his family. In mystic symbolism the snake is often used to represent wisdom. Mercury the messenger, the bringer of knowledge, is often depicted as having a snake coiled around his staff (a sign which today can still be found in the emblem of the Royal College of Surgeons). It would seem that the implication here is that as Jesus sought sanctuary, so did the knowledge that he possessed, coming ashore with him. On the far horizon we see a pyramid, an obvious allusion to Egypt. Does this not suggest that to decipher the secret one has to look to the knowledge of the Egyptians? Indeed there is, as we shall see, a distinct link between the Gnosticism of Jesus and the teachings and ascetic lifestyle of the Essenes of Nag Hammadi in Egypt.

It is worth bearing in mind that this is the last significant painting that Poussin finished before his death. As I have already mentioned, his style is acknowledged to have changed dramatically after the influence of Kircher and Rospigliosi, as if the scales had been removed from his eyes. The richness of detail that he now allows into his work is peppered with such clues as I have described. The general tone of the colour and detail in the *The Deluge* seems also to suggest an element of sadness, a final attempt to encapsulate a message, the meaning of which he feared would be lost on his death.

In *The Shepherds of Arcadia* the colours and symbolism are not the only set of clues to the significance of this work. For within its rustic scene is a geometry shared with other works. Much has been made of the curious arrangement of lines that can be drawn linking various figures and features. Some authors and researchers have gone to great lengths to make them fit their theories.

In *The Shepherds of Arcadia* the isolation of the geometry is in fact fairly simple once we have established who the characters we are looking at are and, more importantly, how they relate to one another. The three male figures are carrying staffs. Most notable are those carried by the Pan and Jesus figures, Poussin's veiled reference to the duality of the spirit and the flesh. First we follow the line of the staffs held by Jesus and Pan and extend them towards the bottom until they come off the edge of the canvas and meet. If a line is then drawn from the heel of Pan to the heel of Jesus, both of which are rather distinctly painted – Jesus even having a somewhat luminescent white sandal as a clue – and exactly parallel to the bottom edge of the painted canvas, we find that this line, despite the perspective of the work, is exactly horizontal. It requires only two further lines to be drawn from each of the heels to the top of the opposite staffs and we are presented with a pentagram which, in this case and importantly, extends out of the lower edge of the painting. This is the first time that an extended pentagram has been discovered in this work. Whereas others have found pentagons, the importance of the pentagram is paramount.

Pentagram theory, in keeping with the background of Kabbalist knowledge upon which the painting is based, has two important forms of these five-pointed 'stars'. One is the closed pentagram, where all five points can be connected within and touch a circle drawn around them. The other is the active pentagram, where one or more of the points breaks the circle and extends beyond it. The pentagram itself is these days mostly seen in 'schlock-horror' films where the aim is to evoke images of witches, devil worship and the like to scare the wits out of a willing audience. When mentioned now it is spoken of in the same breath as chalk diagrams on the floor with lighted candles at each point to protect those standing inside them. However, the pentagram has been an important symbol from the time of Euclid, Pythagoras and Plato through to Templar and subsequently Masonic usage. For the alchemists and Babylonians, this was the symbol of wisdom and knowledge.

In this painting we have an open, 'active' pentagram which connects two figures in the work, Pan and Jesus, yet further confirmation of the duality as represented in the picture by the ever-battling twins. Interestingly, the intersection of the lines which come down from the tops of the staffs towards the heel of each man occurs at the centre of the top of the head of the John the Baptist figure, affirmation perhaps that this is a representation of the Baptist and his grisly decapitation. In ancient times the open pattern of a pentagram implied the ability of spirits to enter or leave at will. As we are dealing with the figure of Jesus, this is doubly important, especially when we consider our third important picture.

In Luca Signorelli's *The Education of Pan*, there is also an easily discernible pentagram. Commissioned by Lorenzo de' Medici, who spent an enormous part of his wealth in an effort to discover the original truths of the Golden Age, and painted in 1492, the scene depicts the central figure of Pan seated on a stone throne surrounded by his elders, who are in the process of instructing him. The elders themselves are depicted as being dead, and this is signified by the eclipsed moon which rises above Pan's head like a pair of horns, visible through the raised arm of the elder who stands on Pan's right-hand side. In the background we see two identical temples, side by side, each of which has in front of it a single rider mounted on a horse. While one rider has a dark horse, the other is astride a pale mount, and they are riding away from each other in what can be read as a depiction of the duality of good and evil. The temples may themselves be seen as a representation of the two pillars of the Kabbalah, Jeroboam and Elaphim (on which I shall later elaborate), while the eclipsed moon would also appear to symbolize the advent of a new beginning, a time when Jesus ascends to eclipse the old world of Pàn. The reclining youth at Pan's feet is connected by hollow reeds to a female figure, either blowing life into the young man, as some commentators have suggested, or whispering the secret prayer of life into his mouth. This idea is directly derived from the Sumerian and Akkadian religions, where prayers were whispered into the right ear of a bull in Sumer and into the left ear of a bull in Babylon.[2] Again this work is clearly rich in symbolic metaphor. We see the two-headed bull representing the two-in-one, and at Pan's feet there is an eye on a stalk, the all-seeing eye. This is also a common Templar symbol and may be related to the two horsemen, for Templar art frequently depicts two riders back to back, facing in opposite directions and seated on one horse. Pan, cloven-hoofed, is entirely naked save for a shawl or cloak wrapped over his shoulders. This shawl attracts the eye as it is covered in what at first sight appears to be a random collection of stars. However closer inspection reveals that the arrangement of the stars is far from indiscriminate for they are aligned exactly in the same configuration as those in the constellation of Gemini, the twins of mythology. This would seem to indicate that we are indeed dealing with the twins of the physical and spiritual worlds. As we know the seated figure to be Pan, king of his earthly domain, it follows that his twin and opposite is the recumbent figure, Jesus. Is the female then the Virgin Mary, linked to Jesus and giving him life?

As this much earlier work seems to follow the same rules of coding that Poussin subsequently used, it would seem reasonable to expect that there may also be a hidden geometry at work, especially when we remember the background of the man who commissioned the painting. Excitingly, I believe this does prove to be the case.

Taking lines from the top of the staff held by the elder to Pan's right, down to the bottom of the staff held by the Magdalene figure and the bottom of the staff on which is leaning the elder at Jesus's feet, we see the same shape being formed that we have already discovered in Poussin's picture. If a line is then drawn from the tops of each of these staffs to the bottom of their opposites and then completed with a simple line which connects the tops of each staff, we can see that a simple pentagram has been formed. However, this differs from the first in that it is a closed one, all five points held within the circumference of the circle, implying that whoever or whatever is inside this pentagram is locked there. Given our understanding of Pan and his state of permanence in the mortal world, it is rather apt and surely not accident but conscious design on the part of Signorelli. (Pan's banishment to an eternal life of mortality stems directly from the Egyptian mythology of Isis-Serkh, who bound Sut, the Pan precursor and god of the mortal earth, with invisible chains.)

Further, there is another and most surprising aspect to the pentagram in *The Education of Pan*: it is a direct match for that found in one of the parchments discovered by Bérenger Saunière in the church, dedicated to Mary Magdalene, in Rennes-le-Château.

As I have said, much has been made of Poussin's *The Shepherds of Arcadia*, and *The Deluge* has proved to be no less fascinating. But my sense is that it is the hidden knowledge within another painting by Poussin which confirms that we are on the trail of something remarkable. What is more, it was also commissioned by Cardinal Rospigliosi.

A Dance to the Music of Time was painted in 1638. Currently in the Wallace Collection in London, it also bears a pentagram. Very significantly, it interlocks with the other two. This is highly important. For where the other two pentagrams represent the Jesus figure and Pan, this definitely connects them with a female element. Through it we are able to establish a male/female partnership both in heaven and on Earth and between heaven and Earth, and it is one which symbolizes the poles upon which the Earth spins.

The painting depicts Hermes playing his lyre – music was his method of communication between the two worlds – and a group of earthly figures dancing to his celestial tune. On the left-hand side of the work is a column on which is mounted a carving or sculpture of two heads facing away from each other. In Egyptian mythology this is the double-headed Horus. In this case, one of the heads is clean-shaven while the other is heavily bearded, evoking the different images of Jesus and John the Baptist in the same way that we see them in *The Shepherds of Arcadia*. There is a second column on the right-hand side of the work, another reference to the stone and brick columns of Elaphim and Jeroboam. In the foreground are two cherubim, one blowing the bubble of creation through a thin reed while the other holds an hourglass containing the sands of time. The dominating feature of this work, however, is the impressive portrayal of Orion on his bountiful sweep across the skies in his chariot. Drawn by four immense horses and surrounded by supporters, he stands in the chariot with his arms outstretched to touch a golden ring. This is a direct reference to the *zodiakos kyklos* (circle of animals) of the Greeks, and confirms that the scene is meant as an astrological reference, with Orion playing a central role in the story. When I first acknowledged this I was unaware that only later would its full import be revealed.

However, the central focus of the painting is the group of dancers in the foreground. Again the colour coding that Poussin used in both *The Deluge* and *The Shepherds of Arcadia* is used to great effect here in order to show to those viewers who have the knowledge to understand that they are looking at more than an Ambrosian revel. The key figure is the woman who is centrally placed on the canvas. Again a clue is the gold of the skirt she wears, which leads us to suppose that she has in some way borne the harvest, the fruit of the gods. The second most important figure is the woman with whom she is holding hands and who is dressed in red and blue. As we have seen, red is used to signify the Horus figure, thus implying a connection with Christ. This is borne out by the blue shawl she also wears.

In Catholic iconography the Virgin Mary is almost always shown dressed in red and blue. She is holding hands with the golden-skirted woman, giving them a physical connection. Are we to assume that here is the Virgin, together with a woman who has continued the holy line by giving birth to Jesus's son? We have already seen the concept of Jesus's having a son depicted in the *The Deluge*. There is, however, another element of confirmation. Within this painting another pentagram can be isolated from the curious geometry which Poussin has given the idyllic scene.

Having established that Orion, at the head of the picture, is central to it, it is a simple matter to take a line from the head of Orion to the bubble being blown by the cherubim at the bottom left-hand side of the canvas and another to the centre of the hourglass being held by the cherubim on the bottom right-hand side. The next part of the pentagram follows the eyeline of the bearded head on one of the columns to connect with the highest corner of the column on the right-hand side. Lines drawn from each of these points to the opposing cherubim then complete the pentagram. It confirms some of the relationships we have already established from the colours. The centre of the pentagram is focused on the character we have determined to be the bride of Jesus; the intersection of the lines falling at the position of her womb seem to confirm her role as the mother of his child.

The pentagram that this gives us, like the one hidden in Signorelli's *The Education of Pan*, is a closed one. This is a work concerned with the earthly, physical world, unlike *The Shepherds of Arcadia*, which is specifically concerned with the spiritual and the passage of spirits to and from this world. This earthly quality could be seen as an indication that the fatherhood of Jesus is not a spiritual allegory, but was believed by those who conceived this painting to be a physical reality.

Another painting which I have already mentioned is Leonardo da Vinci's *The Virgin of the Rocks*. Leonardo, as we have already seen, was employed by Lorenzo de' Medici before he left Florence for Milan, where he worked under the patronage of Ludovico Sforza. He is known, however, to have painted only thirteen works in oil himself, another seven being collaborative pieces or works from his studio. The only work he duplicated was *The Virgin of the Rocks*, which varies from one version to the other.

It is known to art historians that Leonardo was fascinated, to the point of idolization, by John the Baptist. Some have seen this as being due to the early separation of his parents and his isolation from his mother. Leonardo was born illegitimately and his father abandoned his mother Caterina, who entrusted him to a local family. In his early years John the Baptist was given up by his mother Elizabeth and survived in the desert on locusts and honey. The painting which Leonardo executed of John the Baptist, considered by some to be one of his finest works in oil, is also one of only two paintings which he never made available for sale and would not part with, keeping it by his bedside until his death. (The other was *The Virgin and Child with St Anne and a Lamb*, a work which he never completed.)

Further, one of the theories to explain the *Mona Lisa*'s enigmatic smile hinges on the possibility that she carries a subtle masculine overtone, a reference perhaps to Leonardo's attempt to portray the spiritual and sexual duality of John the Baptist. This was a concept he was familiar with from his knowledge of the Kabbalah and one which was also depicted on the beautiful bronze doors of the Florence Baptistery by Lorenzo Ghiberti and Andrea Pisano in 1424. This duality is also thought to be symbolized in his drawing known as *The Vitruvian Man*. The human figure in a circle not only demonstrates Leonardo's knowledge of the golden mean, but through its showing two bodies sharing one head or mind is also thought to continue the John the Baptist theme. A further Baptist connection is thought to arise from research conducted on the Shroud of Turin. Although this is popularly considered, and in many cases hoped, to be the shroud in which Jesus was wrapped when he was removed to the tomb at the Garden of Gethsemane, recent work has resulted in a theory that this may have been an early attempt at photography by Leonardo and that the image, rather than being of Christ, is in fact of Leonardo himself in the role of John the Baptist. To the minds of some researchers this idea is confirmed by the fact that the head on the image is separated from the body, and is lent more credibility by a radiocarbon dating test which places it at the same time that Leonardo was active. Interestingly, despite the enormous amount of effort that has been invested in establishing the true nature of the shroud and how the image on it was formed, very little effort has been made to establish its whereabouts before its discovery in Chambéry in France in 1532. There it was nearly lost in a fire which resulted in the scorch marks which we can see today.

Both versions of *The Virgin of the Rocks* show a peculiar motif. The paintings, the first of which was completed in 1483 and the second in 1508, show the Virgin Mary and the infant Jesus with Elizabeth and her child, John. Elizabeth is portrayed with the wings of an angel. This signifies not only that she is mortal (it being only mortals who can become angels, but not divine) but also that her child, the young Baptist, was already conceived before he received the holy spirit. Accordingly, Mary does not have wings, as her conception was immaculate and she is therefore divine.[3] Set in a harsh, rocky landscape, they are grouped together in the foreground of the work. The overall scene differs little between the two versions, but there are some important variations of detail which have exercised the minds of many art historians. In the first version the figure of the Virgin Mary, recognizable as we have seen before from her blue and gold clothing, is kneeling on the ground and has her arm draped protectively around the shoulders of the infant John. He has the palms of his hands together as if in prayer and is looking across the work directly at Jesus. While Mary's clothing is brightly coloured and richly textured, Elizabeth is even more extravagantly clothed in what appears to be a green silk and red velvet shawl covering an under blouse that is so finely painted that it gives the impression of having been crafted of lace. Not only does she leap off the canvas, the red being the only vivid colour in an otherwise autumnally shaded work, but the position of her head is such that she is almost looking out of the painting at the viewer. She is also making physical contact with Jesus, her left hand gently pushing towards John. The gesture she makes with her other hand is interesting and has been the cause of much fascinating artistic and academic debate, for her right hand is raised and she is pointing with her forefinger at her son John. We may assume that this mystifying gesture is meant to have some symbolic meaning, but what that might be has never been satisfactorily resolved. The child Jesus who is seated on the ground beside her is making the sign of blessing with the two fingers of his right hand raised as if in benediction, apparently directed at John. The overall impression of the work is that Elizabeth is the most important figure and is meant to be suggesting something of great gravity to the viewer, something that is related to the fact that the child John is making an act of obeisance to the child Jesus, who in turn is blessing him. Given Leonardo's views on John the Baptist, he seems to be indicating that he was aware of the importance of John and that this importance was recognized by Jesus.

More interesting aspects are brought to light through our

being able to compare this first version with the second version, which is now in London's National Gallery. The same four characters appear in much the same positions as in the first version of the work. However, the most noticeable difference is that Elizabeth is now given much less emphasis in the work. While she is still in the same position on the canvas, she has been made much smaller, so that although she is slightly more in the foreground than Mary, it is the mother of Jesus who dominates the work and towers over her. Indeed Elizabeth's head has been painted almost no larger than those of the children. This demotion is reinforced by the changes made in her clothing. Gone are the lush fabrics and rich colours of the earlier work, replaced here by drab browns and rougher-textured materials. Mary too has altered somewhat in this work, her gold and blue robe being replaced with the blue and red in which she is more usually adorned in Catholic churches today and indeed it is *her* clothes which seem to radiate now, giving her an extraordinary dominance over both the painting as a whole and the figures within it.

The image of the child Jesus has altered little from the first rendition save for one important distinction: not only is his hair a little shorter but he now has a halo (shown off well by the shorter hair). Indeed this is the most immediately noticeable difference in the work, for Mary, Jesus and John all now have haloes; only Elizabeth does not, this detail again reinforcing her dramatic downgrading in importance from the first work. The image of John has also changed. Whereas before it appeared that he was in the midst of an act of reverence towards Jesus, it now seems that he is the one bestowing the blessings. This is not due to any dramatic redrawing of him, but more the result of subtle changes in his body posture, the expression on his face and the fact that he now has a cross looped through his arms and resting on his shoulder. This seems to be a direct reference to the pictures of John on the Florence Baptistery doors, where he is depicted as a child carrying a cross as he goes into the wilderness. Interestingly, the panel on the bronze doors which shows this scene has him walking between two pillars in order to make his way from his home into the desert to prepare for his ministry. This is repeated in the earlier version of *The Virgin of the Rocks*, where the two pillars featured in the background of the work bear features distinctly similar to those of the bronze panel. These may well be a reference to the two pillars of Jeroboam and Elaphim.

These then are the main differences between the two works. But why are there two copies? It is known that the first version was borrowed from Louis XII, who had purchased it from Leonardo for one hundred ducats, and that it was kept at the French court in Milan in order for the second copy to be made. The first version had been originally commissioned by the Church, but the authorities would neither pay Leonardo for his work nor explain why payment was being withheld. After a long legal battle the Church commissioned the second version, the first having been taken by Leonardo and sold to the French king. However, there has been no adequate explanation for the enormous changes in the portrayal of Elizabeth. Could it be that the emphasis on her in the first version was deemed to be too reactionary for what is, after all, a devotional work, created to hang in a church? Or is there an alternative explanation?

Much effort has been spent on analyzing the differences between the two paintings. But what if we focus on the similarities? Are the differences a smokescreen, set to put us off the trail of the painting's importance. Leonardo was a great lover of secrecy and codes. His papers, with their famous engineering diagrams of weapons of war, a bicycle and even a helicopter, are peppered with copious notes written in his own hand, writing from right to left in a script that is easier to read in a mirror. That he revelled in the ease with which he could read and write in this fashion is well documented and we can only assume that he took as much pleasure from the difficulty that others had in deciphering the texts. Perhaps in these, the only duplicated works in his oeuvre, he has also concealed something that would be easily missed by those whose eye is focused on the more noticeable differences.

To me the most significant feature is the rocky landscape in the background of the paintings. Supposedly showing the cave which one tradition recounts miraculously opened in a mountainside to shelter the Virgin and her son, the rocks and boulders are virtually identical in the two works. Indeed they are so close a match that not only is one landscape an almost exact replica of the other, but it is inconceivable that such accuracy could be the result of a simple desire to replicate. It is a very precise rendering of the same scene, especially in the light of the other differences. But why expend such effort in reproducing a fictional landscape that is supposedly a mere background to a much more important religious scene? My answer to this question is found in an almost insignificant image at the top right-hand side of both versions. While most of the background landscape is formed from columns of rock which either rise out of the sea on the left side or the land to the right, there is a strange configuration which looks rather like a rock bridge with a curious diagonal cross member. The structure of this is so exactly reproduced from one version of the painting to the next, the two large slabs of rock forming the same sideways 'V' shape, that I do not think it can be anything other than a motif of some significance. And indeed it is a motif that we also see in another work, Poussin's *The Shepherds of Arcadia*.

There is an X-ray image of this painting which was taken by the Louvre in an effort to determine how much alteration

Poussin had done to the work during the course of painting and whether there had been any major restoration work which had subsequently altered the image. This shows up two main points, the first of which was pointed out by Henry Lincoln in his work *The Holy Place*[4] while the second connects it with the work by Leonardo.

In the painting the figure in red, Poussin's representation of Jesus, wears a laurel wreath which conceals part of the top of the staff that he is holding and resting on. One might reasonably expect the staff, which is in front of the tomb, to have been painted afterwards and over the form of the tomb. However, this is not the case. In the X-ray we can see through the leaves of the wreath and the paint of the tomb and it becomes apparent even to the amateur observer that the staff was painted first. That part of the staff which is visible above the tomb in the painting stops where it joins the horizontal line which is formed by the top of the tomb – that is, the tomb bisects the line of the staff rather than the staff cutting across the line of the tomb as one would expect. Why would an artist of any calibre, let alone the skill of Poussin, feel the need to draw what was surely intended as a fairly simple and insignificant staff before the far more important tomb? If my theory is correct, the answer is simple. Poussin was taking great pains to establish the underlying pentagram geometry in the work, before painting the artistic details of the picture. What is more, in the X-ray the top of the staff, the bough of the tree that is behind the tomb and the top of the tomb itself form exactly the same triangular image as in both versions of Leonardo's *The Virgin of the Rock*.

The repetition of such an image by two painters separated by 200 years seems unlikely to be pure coincidence. Yet if the two artists were aware of the same information they could both have been working to incorporate it into their art.

I have shown that there are indeed geometric designs in the two works by Poussin and one work by Signorelli and that in each of these three cases the design is a pentagram. The X-ray of *The Shepherds of Arcadia* would seem to suggest, if not prove, that such geometry is the result of an act of will by the artists rather than the spurious and coincidental outcome of the 'searcher finding what he seeks in everything he sees'. The underlying premise that a secret design is held within these works is given yet more credibility by the analysis of the colours employed in the clothing of the figures portrayed. This not only indicates that the artists had knowledge of the ancient Egyptian practice of ascribing colours to gods, but that they understood how those gods were represented in the Christian Church. We have made the link between the artists who painted the works and the personalities who commissioned them – in the case of Cardinal Richelieu he even specified elements he required to be included in the work – and we have also seen that there is a connection between these historical personalities, the Roman Church and a quest for knowledge that was hidden or lost.

All these factors seem to imply that there is something behind the enigmas that these paintings present which required an encoded secrecy, about which the holders of the keys to this code could not be open and aspects of which, in the case of Poussin, the artist himself was afraid would be lost for ever on his death.

But what are we to make of these pentagrams and their relationship with the painting's subject matter? I have shown that they are far from being merely innocent exercises in geometry, and that they could not have been placed there purely by accident. On what fund of knowledge were both the painters and the patrons drawing, that led them to create these artistic and spiritual conundrums?

CHAPTER THREE

BABYLON, EGYPT AND
THE KABBALAH

☆

Babylon, the 'oldest culture in the world', exerts far more impact today than most of us realize. Our superstitious impulse to turn back when we see a black cat cross our path, the twelve divisions of the clock face, the term 'shock' for a unit of sixty, all stem from this culture which existed up to 6,000 years ago and whose power endured until 539 BCE.

The country of Babylonia covered most of what is now southern Iraq, from Baghdad to the Arab-Persian Gulf, and was drained by the rivers Euphrates and Tigris, alongside which evidence of the earliest settlements has been found. The population is known to have been mixed, with the non-Semitic Sumerian texts which dominate the literary record in the third millennium BCE gradually being replaced by Semitic Akkadian texts in the second millennium, which in turn were displaced by Aramaic texts in the later first millennium.[1]

Babylonia's political structure was, until the fifteenth century BCE, one of warring city states, some of which, Agade (2340–2200 BCE), the Third Dynasty of Ur (2100–2000 BCE) and Babylon (1760–1595 BCE) succeeded in dominating their rivals. From 1595 BCE onwards, however, Babylonia formed a territorial state with Babylon as its capital.

This city, the ruins of which lie in the vicinity of modern-day Hillah, some fifty miles south of Baghdad in Iraq, became politically important under Hammurabi between 1792 and 1750 BCE. However, it reached the pinnacle of its splendour as the capital of the Neo-Babylonian Empire between 605 and 539 BCE, from which period most its more famous buildings date. The empire was founded by Nabopolassar, who from 626 to 609 BCE fought back the Assyrians under whom the country had been controlled since the eighth century BCE. During the rise of the Empire the country extended from Palestine to the Iranian frontier and was ruled from Babylon, most famously by Nabopolassar's son, Nebuchadnezzar II (604–562 BCE), who was responsible not only for the extensive rebuilding of the country's cities but also for the sacking of Jerusalem in 587 BCE.

The many surviving records show the high level of inter-national trade upon which these empires relied. Iron from Asia Minor, timber from the Lebanon and silver from the mines at Amanus in south-eastern Turkey all made their way to Babylon and Nimrud, as did the skilled craftsmen and unskilled labourers from many neighbouring nations who came to seek work. Indeed there were highly active trade routes that extended not only from Mesopotamia into Syria, Asia Minor and the lands of other middle-eastern potentates but also through what is now Iran from as far afield as the Indian subcontinent and China. The recent discovery of what appear to be tartan-clad Caucasian corpses in graves in the middle of this vast area adds further to the mystery of what actually happened here before it was 'discovered' by the West.

The high degree of culture that existed in this civilization is attested to by the tenacity of Babylonian learning, writing, cultic, legal and literary traditions, which survived the increasing use of the new languages of Aramaic, Persian and Greek. Indeed Babylonian cuneiform texts have been unearthed which date from as late as 78 CE. Both the Greeks and the Romans perceived Babylonia as the source and origin of all astronomical and astrological knowledge and, as some of the later cuneiform texts show, astronomy and mathematics were a highly important and well-developed aspect of Babylonian scholarship. For example, some of the oldest astronomical documents are clay tablets inscribed with three concentric circles divided by twelve radii. In each of these thirty-six divisions is the name of a constellation together with a series of numbers, making these the first examples of astrolabes in the human record. Even the Greek astronomer Ptolemy, in the second century CE, reports using Babylonian records of lunar eclipses which dated from 747 BCE to aid his own studies.

The degree to which this educated people influenced the explosion in scientific knowledge among the Greeks remains a source of hotly argued academic debate. But what is not questioned is the fact that it was the Sumerians, in the third and fourth millennia before Christ, who first looked at the night sky and named the constellations, thereby formalizing the basis of astronomy.[2] Indeed the distinction we make today between astronomy and astrology is a relatively modern one. Formerly astrology was the term which described what we now call astronomy and was subdivided into 'natural astrology', which was specifically concerned with calculating the movements of the heavenly bodies, and 'judicial astrology', which studied the supposed influences of those bodies on human life and destiny, in much the same way that modern astrology does.[3]

In 1872 George Smith, a banknote engraver with a keen interest in archaeology, made an extraordinary discovery. Born in 1840 in Chelsea, London, Smith was a self-taught man who spent his evenings after work studying some of the first publications on Assyriology. At the age of twenty-six he pub-

lished some commentaries on a number of cuneiform characters whose meaning was a matter of some uncertainty. In doing
so he attracted the attention of many professionals in the field,
which in turn led to his being made an assistant in the Egyp-
tian-Assyrian department of the British Museum. This new
career resulted in his deciphering a number of clay tablets
which had been sent to the museum by Hormuzd Rassam, who
had assisted Sir Austen Henry Layard at the excavation of
Nineveh, where the tablets had been unearthed. As Smith
pored over the texts, translating the wedge-shaped symbols, he
was aware that he was reading a most extraordinary tale
describing the great deeds of a character called Gilgamesh the
Strong. Translating more, he became absorbed by the stories:
of Engidu, the man of the woods, who was brought into the
city by a priest's whore to subdue Gilgamesh; and of the
violent battle of these heroes, which ended in a draw and
resulted in Gilgamesh and Engidu becoming firm friends and
working together to accomplish many great deeds. As Smith
laboriously translated, the story continued, describing the
death of Engidu through sickness and his mourning by Gilgamesh, who, to avoid a similar fate, set out to find immortality.
While on his quest, Gilgamesh meets Uta-napishtim, the pri-
meval ancestor of mankind, who had survived intact with his
family when the gods had visited great punishment on the
wicked human race and who had been granted immortality as
a result. Uta-napishtim then tells Gilgamesh the whole story
of his miraculous escape.

Smith read this legend with great interest. He knew he was
looking at some of the earliest texts known to man and that he
was quite possibly the first to read them for nearly four and a
half thousand years. But there was more to it. He was engaged
by the characters and as he continued his translation he was
aware that there were increasing gaps in the narrative flow of

the tablets that had been sent by Rassam. His sense of frustration increased when he realized that the most important part of the story, the conclusion, was missing. It was with the assistance of England's *Daily Telegraph* that the problem was resolved. The newspaper had announced that it would offer the sum of 1,000 guineas to anyone who was prepared to go to Kuyunjik, where the mound that buried the remains of the ancient city of Nineveh was sited, and find the missing inscriptions. Smith accepted the offer and went to Mesopotamia to conduct the search, a task that can quite legitimately be compared to looking for a needle in a haystack. What is most extraordinary is that this bookish man, who had hitherto not set foot outside England, travelled the thousands of miles to the baking-hot, dusty site in what is now the middle of Iraq and succeeded in pulling off one of the most remarkable discoveries in the history of archaeology. He actually found the missing tablets of the Gilgamesh story, and after only five days in the field.[4]

The 384 fragmentary clay tablets with which Smith returned to England allowed him to finish the translation of the story that is now known to us as the *Epic of Gilgamesh*, called in Akkadian after its first line, 'ša naqba imuru', or 'who saw the deep'. This collection of epic tales, which were originally written in Sumerian but have survived through the extant copies in Akkadian and the later languages of Hittite and Hurrian, cover a wide variety of subjects, including man and nature, love and adventure, and friendship and combat. They are the earliest record we have of written epic literature and as such are of enormous interest and value. However, these extraordinary stories, recorded by the laborious method of pressing the end of a cut reed into tablets of wet clay, also have another role, for they are the proof that religious thought has its roots in early Babylon.

The ziggurats – stepped pyramids or temple towers; the stories of Tiamat, the Great Mother who appears in these epics and who was one of the first figures to be constellated in the night sky; the legends of the god Marduk and the legendary land of Dilmun, are all testament to the highly formalized spiritual life that this great civilization led and which can be seen as a precursor of the more developed religious thinking which followed it.

However, the *Epic of Gilgamesh* dating from around 3000 BCE, also tells for the first time the story of a Great Flood, remarkably similar to the later version to be found in the book of Genesis in the Old Testament. There are flood stories in almost every ancient folkloric tradition, but the *Epic of Gilgamesh* specifically describes a forerunner to Noah. In one part of the epic the friendly god Ea reveals in a dream to her protégé Uta-napishtim the intention of the gods to punish the human race and as a result Uta-napishtim decides to build himself an ark:

> What I had loaded thereon, the whole harvest of my life
> I caused to embark within the vessel; all my family and my
>   relations,
> The beasts of the field, the cattle of the field, the craftsmen, I
>   made them all embark.
> I entered the vessel and closed the door . . .
> When the young dawn gleamed forth,
> From the foundation of the heaven a black cloud arose . . .
> All that is bright is turned into darkness,
> The brother sees his brother no more,
> The folk of the skies can no longer recognize each other,
> The gods feared the flood
> They fled, they climbed into the heaven of Anu,
> The gods crouched like a dog on a wall, they lay down . . .
> for six days and six nights
> Wind and flood marched on, the hurricane subdued the land.

When the seventh day dawned, the hurricane was abated, the
    flood
which had waged like an army;
The sea was stilled, the ill wind was calmed, the flood ceased.
I beheld the sea, its voice was silent
And all mankind was turned into mud!
As high as the roofs reached the swamp! . . .
I beheld the world, the horizon of sea,
Twelve measures away an island emerged;
Unto Mt. Nitsir came the vessel,
Mt. Nitsir held the vessel and let it not budge . . .
When the seventh day came,
I sent forth a dove, I released it.
It went, the dove, it came back,
As there was no place, it came back,
I sent forth a swallow, I released it;
It went the swallow, it came back,
as there was no place, it came back
I sent forth a crow, I released it;
It went, the crow, and beheld the subsidence of the waters;
It eats, it splashes about, it caws, it comes not back.[5]

This is a theme we see repeated much later in the Old
Testament deluge story, down to the duplications of specific
events – the freeing of the dove and the crow, for example –
and it is now accepted that this is the progenitor of the biblical
Flood story. Indeed there is now widely accepted geological
evidence that such an inundation actually occurred.

The poem also recounts that Gilgamesh, in his quest to
consult Uta-napishtim and find the secret of immortality, has
to cross the Abyss and is advised by Siduri, the innkeeper who
lives by the shore:

'At no time O Gilgamesh has there been a crossing
And whoever since olden times has reached this point has not
    been able to cross the Abyss.

The valiant Sun-god does indeed cross the Abyss but who but
    the Sun-god can cross it?
The crossing is arduous; the way it is arduous
And in the middle part the waters of death are channelled on
    its surface'

Gilgamesh is advised to go to the forest and cut 120 punting
poles which he and the ferryman, Urshanabi, when they
encounter the waters of death, may use to propel their boat
forward. The reason for the large number becomes clear, for not
a drop of the water must touch the hands of Gilgamesh, and
each pole, when it has been thrust into the water, must be left
behind. The analogies with many of the classical traditions
which we have inherited, notably the crossing of the River
Styx and the figure of the ferryman, are obvious.

Gilgamesh is not the only epic from these times. Recent
work on the Sumerian epic *Atrahasis* has indicated that it may
predate *Gilgamesh* and may even have been used as a source for
parts of it, especially as it also contains a similar and highly
detailed Flood story. The *Epic of Adapa*, like the *Epic of
Gilgamesh*, concentrates on the possibility of mankind acquiring
immortality and is perhaps the origin of the Old Testament
stories of Adam.

The mythical land of Dilmun, which features so largely in
the Epics, may also have actually existed in the barren desert
land of modern-day Bahrain, where there are the remains of
some 10,000 burial mounds. Recent excavations have shown
Bahrain to have been the site of an ancient city, known as the
'Island of the Dead', where walls, houses, pottery and tools have
been found dating the site back to about 4000 BCE.[6] There is
even growing evidence that Gilgamesh himself may have been
a historical king belonging to the first dynasty of Uruk in the
Early Dynastic III phase, between 2650 and 2550 BCE. The

Epics credit him with the building of two temples and the construction of the city wall of Uruk, which recent archaeological excavations have confirmed as real structures.[7]

The last of the great kings of Babylon, Nabonidus, technically ruled from 556 to 539 BCE, although he did so from the desert, leaving his son Belshazzar to rule in his stead, as regent, from one of the city's palaces. As we know from the Old Testament book of Daniel, during a banquet Belshazzar (or Balthazar) dared to use the gold and silver vessels that had been taken from the Temple during Nebuchadnezzar's sacking of Jerusalem and in doing so incurred the wrath of God – the words 'Mene, Mene, Tekel, Upharsin' ('numbered, numbered, weighed and divided') appearing on the wall as a warning that Belshazzar was about to lose his kingdom. The writing was indeed on the wall for Babylon, for in 539 BCE Cyrus the Great took the city and Babylon became part of the Persian Empire. Even Alexander the Great could not restore it to its former glory after its partial destruction in 482 BCE by Xerxes, and by the time the Roman Emperor Septimus Severus (193–211 CE) visited, it was completely deserted and derelict.

Yet while Babylon lost its political dominance, its legacy of law and religion was to continue, in various forms, even to the present day. The Code of Hammurabi, the Babylonian king and law-giver (c. 1792–1750 BCE), which was found engraved on a black diorite stele and is now in the Louvre, is known to be the text which inspired the Hebrew code of law – most notably the principle of 'an eye for an eye and a tooth for a tooth' – in turn the basis for modern Western law.

At a time when the inhabitants of Britain had yet to make the transition from Neolithic to Bronze Age culture, the ascendancy of the great Egyptian dynasties saw a sharing with Babylon of many of the ideas and concepts of religion. This is not to say that the Egyptian religions were borrowed versions of the Babylonian, or vice versa; the fact that these two civilizations developed at about the same time is paralleled by the similarities in many of the rituals and beliefs of both. Indeed among the cults of pre-dynastic Egypt the oldest was that centred on the stars, and yet, masterful astrologers though they were, the Egyptians never became astronomers as the Babylonians did.

The Western tradition has also inherited much from the civilization of the Egyptians, whose knowledge of mathematics and geometry and the spectacular use to which they put it is well documented. However, the echoes of their highly developed sense of the more arcane sciences also endure today. It is thought that the Egyptians were the first to use astrology fully, both in their daily lives and in their rituals for the dead, having refined the knowledge of the Babylonians. While the Greeks first coined the term *zodiakos kyklos* from which we derive our word 'zodiac', the division of the night sky into twelve bands of thirty degrees, each with its own constellation, name and story, is thought to be Egyptian in origin. The signs for the Egyptians were the Lion (Atum), the Scarab (Khepera), the Twins (Set and Horus), the Bull (Ptah/Osiris), the Ram (Amen), the Fishes (In-tiu), the Water-Bringer (Menat the Nurse and later Hapi the Nile), the Goat (Mendes), the Archer (Set or Shu), the Scorpion (Serquet), the Scales (Maat) and the Virgin Mother (Neith or Isis).[8]

Interestingly, although the Greek 'circle of animals' is dominated by the seven animal-based signs, together with four human representations, the one inanimate constellation, Libra (the scales or balance), is an anomaly. It is thought to be derived from the original astronomers noticing that when the sun passed across this collection of stars, it did so at a time of year when day and night were of equal length – that is, during what we now call the autumn equinox.

Contemporary Judaism and Christianity are also rich in correlations with Egyptian theology. The most obvious link is the word 'amen', which Christians intone at the end of a prayer. While this is generally thought to be derived from the Hebrew word for 'certainly', it is equally possible that it derives from an invocation of the name of the Egyptian God Amen-Ra, whose religion was so important that Tutankhamen (Tut-ankh-Amen) changed his name from Tutankhaton (Tut-ankh-Aton) to reflect his obeisance.

Judaic culture actually migrated, as early as the late third to the early second millennium BCE, through Mesopotamia to Egypt. Indeed it may even have originated in that other great centre of urban, literate civilization, the Indus Valley. The effect that Egyptian thinking had on early Jewish faith can also be seen through the deeper knowledge we have acquired of the Egyptian way of life from the hieroglyph record. The strongest of these connections, and certainly that best known to Christian churchgoers, is the history of Moses, law-giver of the Jews and the Western world, who was probably brought up in the court of Ramses (or Rameses) II, pharaoh from 1298 to 1232 BCE. As we have already established, aspects of the Babylonian legal code, the Code of Hammurabi, found their way into the Judaic legal tradition, and the same is true for much of Egyptian legal practice.

When a comparison is made between the religious imagery and stories of the Egyptians and those of the Canonical Gospels, the impact of nearly 3,000 years of Egyptian culture on our modern Western religions is perhaps most fully revealed. These similarities inform almost every aspect of the canon of Christian and Judaic teaching. The story of the Flood and Noah's Ark also appears in the Egyptian tradition in the guise of the ark of Nnu or Nun, the master of the celestial water. Indeed the inscriptions of Thatmes at Thebes reveal that this deity of the

Deluge and the Ark was adopted as the god Num, lord of the inundation of the Nile.

Our early understanding of the religious beliefs of ancient Egypt was largely derived from the work of Vicomte E. de Rougé, who stated that the Egyptians believed in one self-existent, supreme, eternal, almighty God, a belief which prompts comparisons with the God of the Hebrews. It was largely through the mistaken conclusion that the *Book of the Dead* was a theological treatise that this error was made, and the Victorians came to believe that this text would prove in detail the identity of the old religion of the Nile Valley and that of the Hebrews.

From the Ani, Hunefer and Anhai papyri held in the British Museum, we know the *Book of the Dead* to be a book of prayers. The forerunners of these papyri texts were the Pyramid Texts found at Saqqara in the rubble of the pyramid of Unas, who ruled in the late third millennium BCE. These, some 453 prayers or chapters which were engraved on the walls of the pyramids, were the collated funerary texts of an indeterminate number of Egyptian theologians. The *Book of the Dead* itself is a vast liturgical canon, comprising divine rites, embraces and nearly 200 incantations, invocations, psalms, formulae, prayers and rubrics, its purpose being to guide the dead spirit along the hazardous journey through the Twelve Regions of Duat-n-Ba, that part of the night sky more commonly known as the 'Netherworld of the soul'.

The religion on which the book is based is centred on the god Ptah, the creator of the gods and of Egypt. Ptah spoke the divine words at the beginning of the world 'so that the gods would know of their existence' and it is beneath this 'god of gods' that the pantheon of Egyptian deities existed.

Anubis is seen as the light, the one who protects and purifies the souls of men, the bookkeeper of movements, spaces, forms, numbers and planets. Sut or Set is the embodiment of the principle of evil, personifying all that is dark and forming the black half of the Horus-Set conflict of good and evil. Horus, in any of his twenty different aspects, is one of the greatest of the Egyptian gods. The Pyramid Texts recount the struggle between the hawk-headed Horus and Set, telling how Set was emasculated and Horus lost an eye, but that for his pursuit of evil Horus is respected by the dead, for he represents the light which opens their eyes. Then there is Osiris, who, like Anubis, protects the dead and is the symbol for all that is born, and who is both the consort and the brother of Isis. Osiris was also seen as a god of the underworld, but was betrayed and killed by Set. Set wanted the beautiful Isis for himself and ordered the killing and dismemberment into thirteen pieces of Osiris in order to remove his competitor for her attentions. Isis, on hearing of the death of Osiris, set about searching for his scattered remains, assisted by the wife of Set, Nephthys, who disapproved of her husband's actions. These two goddesses found all but the phallus of the poor god, but Isis rejoined him and made him whole, using an artificial member, with which she conceived their son Horus. Later in the story she has an affair with Set which infuriates Horus, provoking him to do battle with the god of the underworld, who appears as a black pig. As we have seen, this conflict led to Horus's losing an eye when it was gouged by the tusk of Set, the sign of the Eye of Horus later becoming valued by the Egyptians for its talismanic properties.

Horus is, in his many actions, associations and sayings, almost exactly identifiable with the Jesus figure. Indeed even the term 'Messiah', usually associated with Jesus as 'the anointed one', may be derived from the old Egyptian '*mesu*', meaning 'to anoint'. But there are also great similarities between the stories of Osiris and those of Jesus. The supposedly

Christian concepts of virgin birth, baptism, shared meals as sacred rituals and resurrection, to name but four, have so many similarities with the 'pagan' beliefs not only of the Egyptians but also of the Babylonians, Greeks and other cults that had gone before, that it is easy to assess Christianity as an amalgam of any number of earlier 'dying god' religions.

A number of writers focus on the concept of Jesus as a magician, the master of ancient arts. His actions were hailed as miracles, but they could well have been Egyptian in origin. In his book *Jesus the Magician* Morton Smith[9] points out that the Talmud, the Jewish book of holy sayings, does not state either that Jesus came from Nazareth or that he was a resident of Galilee. Indeed it states quite unequivocally that he came from Egypt, and goes even further to point out that the reason for his arrest was that he was charged specifically with sorcery and was an initiate of Egyptian magic.

Smith also points out that early Christians, and especially those who were practising in Egypt, where there were a number of Christian settlements, did practise magic.[10] Indeed some of the earliest Christian artefacts are amulets which bear both an image of Christ and written spells indicating that to his earliest followers Jesus was accepted as a magician figure.[11] There are texts dating from as early as the second century CE which support this. In 160 CE Justin Martyr wrote quoting Trypho the Jew, who had called Jesus the 'Galilean magician', while in 175 CE the Platonic philosopher Celsus wrote that although Jesus grew up in Galilee, he worked in Egypt, where he learned magic.[12]

Not only was the practice of magic well established in dynastic Egypt, but it was a fundamental part of the religion, the mysteries, magic and the cult of Osiris forming the three main features of the belief structure. Some of the chapters of the *Book of the Dead* are concerned exclusively with 'great mysteries'. One of these chapters, named 'The Book of the Lady of the Hidden House', is described as containing 'very great secrets' which its reciter is ordered to 'allow no one to see it for it is an abominable thing for an outsider to know it and it must be hidden'. In the text the spell is described as offering 'very, very great protection' and was not to be recited except in the presence of a priest.

The connections between Jesus and Osiris are highly revealing of the similarities between Egypt and the early Christian faith. The story of the wedding at Cana, where Jesus turned water into wine, has been shown to have its origins in a Dionysian, and thus specifically Osirian, ceremony and the Eucharist has its origins in Egyptian texts which are uncannily analogous, not only in the sentiment of the bread and wine ritual but even in the words supposedly uttered by Jesus himself. Even the cross, that enduring sign of Christianity with all that it signifies, is derived from the Egyptians, for whom it was an ancient Osirian symbol.

These, and a catalogue of other affinities between the two traditions and their central characters, led Picknett and Prince to conclude that Jesus not only drew heavily on Osirian imagery when forming his own brand of Judaism but also took the basis of the Osirian tradition as the template for both his work and teachings and the life he led with Mary Magdalene. The basis for this view is the extraordinary similarities between the death and resurrection of Osiris, who, killed on a Friday, rose again three days later through the magical intervention of Isis, and that of Jesus. (It is worthy of note that the three-day timescale, so important in both Christian and Egyptian tradition, is directly derived from the Babylonian *Epic of Gilgamesh*, where Inanna is crucified for three days 'on a stake' by the seven Anunaki judges of the Underworld.)

Even the words that are spoken by Isis are almost identically repeated by Mary Magdalene when she speaks to the 'gardener' – who is in fact Jesus – in the Garden of Gethsemane after finding the tomb empty. Picknett and Prince's theory even goes so far as to interpret Jesus's cry from the cross as being *Helios! Helios!*' ('O Sun! O Sun!') which they then link with the death of Osiris, frequently portrayed as a black sun or a 'forsaking of the light'. This, they claim, is thus related to Jesus's words 'O Sun! O Sun!, why hast thou forsaken me?', spoken immediately before darkness descends upon the Earth.[13]

The concept of a magical secret inner doctrine which works within a mainstream religion is not a new one. The rituals of the Egyptians were reserved and practised only by initiates, those who had studied and proven themselves worthy practitioners of the more esoteric branches of the religion. The idea of many levels of knowledge has echoes in many of the Eastern religions, while in the West it is evidenced in practices ranging from Freemasonry to any number of modern-day cults. But the most famous secret doctrine of all is that of the Kabbalah.

Called in Hebrew QBLH, which derives from the Hebrew root 'qbl', meaning 'to receive', the Kabbalah[14] is a Judaic tradition which is defined from the point of view of the receiver of knowledge.[15] Kabbalism is known to have begun to flourish in first-century Palestine, where its main concern was the ecstatic and mystical contemplation of the divine throne or '*merkava*' that was seen in a vision by the prophet Ezekiel.[16] Originally the term 'Kabbalah' referred to this tradition in general, but it became common to use it when referring specifically to the Halakhic rules, for which there was no defined scriptural texts and which were said to be either a 'kabbalah from Moses on Mount Sinai' or according to some texts 'the word of God himself taught to a select company of Angels. After the fall from grace of the Angels, they communicated their doctrine to the disobedient children of the Earth.'[17]

The basis of the Kabbalah is as the dominant form of Jewish mystical theology and it focuses mainly on the idea that there is a completely hidden and utterly inaccessible Godhead (*Ein Sof* – literally the infinite but actually signifying the hidden, mystical, divine nothingness) which manifests itself in a complex structure of ten emanations (the *sefirot*). One of the more important aspects in this complicated and esoteric teaching is the female character of the tenth *sefirah*, the Shekinah, and the view that the unity of the Godhead is consummated by the union of the male and female elements within it. The human, being male and female, is therefore in the image of God by virtue of its analogy to the *sefirot*. This concept of the duality of human existence is at the very core, not only of Kabbalist thinking but, as we shall see, many later traditions. Indeed while the Kabbalah is accepted as being specifically Judaic, its origins are strongly grounded in many of the traditions of both the Babylonians and the Egyptians.

There have a been a number of phases of development of the Kabbalah. The twelfth-century *Sefer ha-Babir* or *Book of Brightness* represents the earliest stages of the tradition and forms the basis for the concept of the *sefirot* and the importance of the feminine in the divine world. It is also the first introduction into Judaism of such concepts as the transmigration of souls or '*gilgul*' and strengthened the foundations of the Kabbalah by imbuing it with a highly developed mystical symbolism. The second stage of development took place in an area renowned as a centre for a variety of religious developments, Provence in France.

Why a peculiarly Judaic, hidden and closely guarded tradition should undergo a revival in this part of southern France during the twelfth century has never been satisfactorily explained and remains a mystery to this day. However, the renaissance of Kabbalism was very much a part of life in Provence during this period and there were many Kabbalist schools founded in the area around the figure of Yitshaq Saggi Nahor or 'Isaac the Blind'. From here the tradition continued to grow, spreading to Gerona and Castile in Spain until, in the late thirteenth and early fourteenth centuries, it reached its peak. It was during this period that Mosheh de León wrote the numerous Kabbalist treatises which became known as the *Zohar* and his colleague, Yosef Gikatilla, wrote some of the most influential Kabbalist works. The *Zohar* is generally recognized as the single most important work in the Kabbalist canon. Written partly in Aramaic and partly in Hebrew, it is a collection of mystical interpretations of biblical passages, Kabbalist interpretations of the commandments and prohibitions of the Torah (the first five books of the Old Testament or Pentateuch) and many other writings on subjects as diverse as mystical traditions, theurgies, anthropology, psychology, poetry and mythology. There is a strongly erotic quality to the *Zohar*'s descriptions of the holy union of the male and female aspects of the deity, which echoes the theory behind the relationship between Simon Magus and Helen and even a potential relationship between Jesus and Mary Magdalene, and which instils in the reader a sense of the importance of duality and balance. What is more, the *Zohar*'s basic premise is that there is a complete connection between the lower and the upper worlds, that actions here below can educe a response above – in effect, that deeds and prayers can have a cosmic significance.

The development of the Kabbalah in the thirteenth and fourteenth centuries took place above all in Spain. During this time the *Sefer ha-temuna* or *Book of the Image* was produced, which concentrated on advancing the idea of the existence of cosmic cycles, each a separate interpretation of the Torah according to a divine attribute. This showed Judaism not as a religion of permanent truths but as one for which each cycle was said to have a different Torah.

In 1492 the Jews were expelled from Spain and Kabbalism returned to being somewhat of an underground movement. However, in the mid-sixteenth century a renaissance took place in Safed in Galilee, which became the centre of all Kabbalist teaching. It was here that one of the greatest Kabbalists, Isaac ben Solomon Luria, spent the last years of his life developing the doctrine which was to become known as the Lurianic Kabbalah. Complicated even by Kabbalist standards, this work was based on the development of the concepts of the 'withdrawal' or '*tzimtzum*' of the divine light, thereby creating primordial space, the sinking of luminous particles into matter ('shells' or '*qellipot*') and the 'cosmic restoration' or '*tiqqun*' that can be achieved by Jews through an intense mystical life and the struggle against evil. This branch of Kabbalism, perhaps less overtly mystical than the versions from which it originates, became not only the justification for the seventeenth-century Jewish Messianic movement of Shabbetaianism, but also profoundly influenced the doctrines of Hasidism, the Judaic social and religious movement which started in the eighteenth century and which is still flourishing in many countries today.

The essence therefore of the Kabbalah is that of a hidden tradition, one which in its early days was transmissible only by word of mouth and which, like various aspects of the Egyptian religious tradition, involved stages of initiation by a personal guide. What is more, its claims to be of mystical and esoteric value heighten the sense of mystery which surrounds it, a sense which is further increased by the warnings of danger which early initiates received when inducing mystical experiences without their guide.

I have already shown that the basis of the Kabbalah is the

balance between male and female aspects of the Godhead. But there is another dualist principle contained within its doctrine which is perhaps even more important. Part of the Kabbalah's expression of duality focuses on that which is created by man and which is therefore imperfect, and that which is God's creation and which is both perfect and permanent. This is represented at the most symbolic level by the two pillars Jeroboam and Elaphim (or Elohim in some sources).

Jeroboam is the pillar made by man of brick and represents the ever-coming but impermanent sun, both the pillar and the bricks of which it is made having to be constantly renewed and replaced. Elaphim is the pillar made of stone, divinely created and therefore permanent beyond anything that can be created by man. Jeroboam can be seen as a representation of Horus, or in Christian terms Jesus, both of whom represent the light, while the divinely created stone pillar of Elaphim represents the spirit of the hidden God, the Egyptian Sut, or blackness. The twofold existence of these pillars, in Kabbalist terms, represents not only the cosmos but also the flesh and the spirit, the two legs upon which mankind stands and the duality of earthly embodiment and its inextricable link with spiritual existence.

As the Kabbalah developed it became increasingly associated with the use of certain symbols. A wise man, a hermit, a child, a king and a sacrificed god were among those symbols that used representations of the human form. Some of the more arcane signs were the truncated pyramid, the cross of roses and the three-dimensional cube, the Kabbalist use of which is now shrouded in mystery. Many originally Kabbalist emblems are still used in various branches of Freemasonry but perhaps most famously the truncated pyramid, together with the Eye of Horus, endures on no less a document than the legal tender of the United States of America. Nor is it merely the symbolism of the Kabbalah which survives. Threads of Kabbalist thinking are interwoven with many strands of European history. The Grail romances of Chrétien de Troyes – who took his name from the town of Troyes, a centre of Kabbalism – in the late twelfth century; the unfinished *Le Conte de Graal; Perlesvaus* in the early thirteenth century, a Christianized version supposedly written by a monk at Glastonbury; and the bizarre *Parzival* by the Bavarian poet Wolfram von Eschenbach, are all imbued with strongly Kabbalist imagery fused with astrology, alchemy and esoteric symbolism.

As recently as 1984, Joy Hancox, a music teacher from Manchester, England, was researching the history of her house when she discovered a hoard of more than 500 papers that had been collected by a John Byrom. Byrom, who lived between 1691 and 1763, had not only been a leading light in the Jacobean movement that had been set up with the express intention of restoring the Stuarts to the throne of England, but also was a Freemason and a fellow of the Royal Society and as such numbered among his friends and acquaintances the most highly respected scientists, philosophers and intellectuals of the day. He was a member of a group known as the Sun Club, also called the Kabbala Club, which met in a building in St Paul's churchyard. The Byrom Collection, as it is now known, is an impressive catalogue of documents on sacred geometry and architecture, including diagrams of the designs of such buildings as the chapel of King's College, Cambridge and the Templar Church in London, and explains the continuity of the knowledge which underlies the way that such buildings are both planned and executed. Indeed it confirms that, in the case of King's College Chapel, the design was thought to be derived from the fourteenth-century cathedral at Albi, France, based on the Kabbalah's 'Tree of Life'.[18] The value of this collection of papers, however, is not only its focus on the Kabbalist,

Hermetic, Masonic and alchemical symbolism with which it is mainly concerned, but the fact that it shows that such luminaries as John Dee, Robert Boyle and Robert Fludd were preoccupied with them.

From its ancient beginnings, the Kabbalah had survived to exercise the minds of a group of seventeenth- and eighteenth-century intellectuals. But its long and distinguished history is also apparent. We can suppose that, as a rabbi, Jesus would have been initiated into the Kabbalah, and that many of the concepts upon which it is based, those early themes which originated with the Babylonians and the Egyptians, would have been far from alien to him. Indeed it is through such tracts as the Dead Sea Scrolls and the Nag Hammadi gospels that we see the Kabbalah's concept of duality reiterated in the reported words of Jesus himself. The Essenes, the Qumran sect widely thought to be the authors of the Dead Sea Scrolls, were highly Kabbalist in their thinking and while Jesus may or may not have been a member of this group of ascetics, he would have been aware of their influence in his world. Indeed not only was the Essenes' own mode of theology dualist in underlying principle, but they had a stated intent of seeing the restitution of one of the line of David to the throne of Palestine. This has led some scholars to believe that many of the passages in the New Testament are the result of projections of what was expected of the coming Messiah, and which were woven into Jesus's own life in order to fulfil their own prophecies.

There is another aspect of the Kabbalah's legacy which was to have wide ramifications in Europe. As we have seen, there was an explosion in Kabbalist thinking centred on France and Spain during the fifteenth and sixteenth centuries. But long before that time its dualistic essence had found its way into another belief, one that Jesus himself alluded to in many of his teachings: Gnosticism.

CHAPTER FOUR

GNOSTICISM

☆

First-century Palestine was a crossroads between ancient Greece, the Roman Empire and the Persia of antiquity. Persia had seen the birth of Zoroastrianism, a faith which regarded the Earth as the field of battle between the dual and interlinked forces of good and evil. Indeed the Parsees of the Indian subcontinent follow a religion based on Zoroastrianism, and it is thought by some scholars that the biblical Magi, the three wise men, were Zoroastrian sages.

Zoroaster or Zarathustra, the son of a pagan priest who lived in Persia from 660 to 583 BCE[1] had, at the age of thirty, a religious experience during which the one god, Ahura Mazda or 'the Wise Lord', gave him the duty of reforming the polytheistic and sacrificial beliefs which were prevalent in Persia at the time. This he did, not by banning the multiple gods who had hitherto been the focus of Persian religious attention, but rather by absorbing them into a new religion as assistant deities to Ahura Mazda. Although Zoroastrianism is among the earliest of developed monotheistic religions, it is its inherent duality which makes it of interest to us. For it is specifically this religion which is responsible for the idea of a good spirit of God and an evil spirit of God, the light and the darkness, the two equal but diametrically opposed demiurges. The ideas first formulated within the structure of this highly developed early belief system have informed much of later religion. The concept of dualism, albeit covert, can be discerned in the Christian adversaries of God and the Devil. Zoroastrianism was also to have a profound effect on the Jewish, Christian and Islamic beliefs in the afterlife, for although not a mystical religion, it did offer an eschatology which embraced the concepts of heaven, hell and resurrection, ideas already developed in Egypt. Zoroastrianism also placed emphasis on fire as a symbol of God's power and purity, had high moral ideals and, unlike so many of the monotheistic religions which followed it, considered women as equal with men. When Islam became established in Persia during the seventh century CE the majority of Zoroastrianism's followers moved on to India. Today seventy-five per cent of India's Parsees are practising Zoroastrians.

Gnosticism, from the Greek *gignoskein*, or 'to know', has, like Zoroastrianism, as its basis a concept of a duality. It considers there to have been a dual creation in which the divine cosmos was divided from the lower world, the Earth of man. God's angels created human existence but the result of their handiwork was deemed to be less than satisfactory, for man had turned out to be inherently evil. Only with the intervention of God could the light of the cosmos, the divine spark, enter into the human soul and body. The Gnostics believed that intercession was attainable during a lifetime, granting the recipient 'gnosis' (understanding), which guaranteed the immortality of the soul and salvation from the evil of the human condition. This resurrection at death meant that the soul left the body to enter the divine cosmos, a direct parallel with the resurrection of Jesus, although to Gnostics the idea of a physical resurrection is by and large unnecessary. In much of Jesus's teaching there are strong elements of Gnosticism, which promotes the path of respect for the individual and self-determination, in the belief that gnosis is achievable through self-fulfilment.

The Christian Church today remains silent on the question of the Gnosticism of Jesus, and indeed most of its adherents are completely unaware of the Gnostic influence on their faith. It was not until the discovery in Egypt in 1945 of the Nag Hammadi scrolls that the Gnostic Gospels revealed that for many Christians the road to Roman Catholicism had not been a matter of choice. In the second and third centuries the Christian Gnostics believed that Jesus was a divine being, filled with the spark of the cosmos, which allowed him to instruct others on the path to communion with God. To the Roman Church, however, this was heresy of the first order, questioning the status of Jesus as the physically resurrected son of God. The Church had severely narrowed its options for future change by heavily promoting the concept of bodily resurrection, incorporating it into the ritual of the Mass, together with the transubstantiation of the bread and wine into the body and blood of Christ. To maintain credibility, especially if the Church was to maintain its strong and growing influence through this universal sacrament, Catholicism had to make itself more attractive than Gnoticism. The path it chose was to include that powerful human emotion, guilt, into the heart of its teaching. By offering followers confession with a modest scale of penance as a way of alleviating guilt, Catholicism allowed sinners to be fully absolved and requalify for admission into Paradise. This guarantee of absolution at any time, regardless of the degree of sin, proved enormously popular, a simple step to the eradication of guilt. It also put the Catholic Church in the incredibly powerful position of knowing who was doing what and to whom, opening the path for what might be seen as the most widely spread and successful example of moral blackmail of all time.

To the early Christian movement, Gnosticism was the first

and the most dangerous heresy and one which fuelled the burning theological debates which were to rage for many hundreds of years. Among the first protagonists in the struggle were the writers Irenaeus, Justin and Hippolytus, who in their refutations of this 'heretical' mode of thought defended the doctrine of the Church against the threat of the 'evil of Gnosticism'. However, it was no less an individual than Paul who was perhaps the first to recognize the supposed dangers that Gnosticism held for the developing Christian Church. Understanding that Gnosticism was, and is, a 'knowledge' religion which claims to have an insight into the inner true meaning of life, he viewed it as a parasite which used other religions as its carrier. Christianity fitted the role of host extremely well, with its tradition of a mysterious founder who had conveniently disappeared, leaving his message in the form of parable and sayings, some of which were public, some of which would have been secret. Paul feared that Gnosticism would in some way cannibalize Christianity and fought hard, fuelled in part by his disappointment at seeing even well-educated Christians reducing Jesus to a mythical character, to see it eradicated as a threat to the religion he was working to establish.[2]

Gnosticism offered radically different and much more personal challenges to the individual. It espoused a doctrine of self-determination and due penance rather than blind obedience to the written word and the priesthood. The Church of Rome required followers to await the return of Christ on the Day of Judgement in order for them ascend into heaven. If Christ had not resurrected there could be no return and any religion that alluded to this possibility was a great threat and the prime reason why Gnosticism, from the time of Christ to the Cathars in the eleventh and twelfth centuries and beyond, was quelled with such extraordinary fanaticism by the

Roman Church. The liberty of the followers of Gnosticism to determine their own paths to God, the emphasis on self-administered penance and the extraordinary devotion of many Gnostics all fuelled the hatred that was developed against this peaceful, pastoral creed. A tract from one of the Nag Hammadi Gospels, the 'Apocalypse of Peter', describes a discussion between Peter and Jesus and seems to presage these politico-religious debates:

> Now then listen to the things which they are telling you in mystery and guard them. Do not tell the sons of this time, for they shall blaspheme you in these ages since they are ignorant of you ... And they will cleave to the name of a dead man thinking that they will become pure. But they will become greatly defiled and they will fall into a name of error and into the hand of an evil and cunning man and a manifold dogma ... and there will be others of those outside our number who name themselves bishop and also deacon, as if they have received their authority from God. They bend themselves under the judgement of the leaders, they are dry canals.[3]

It is interesting to note that the Vatican has never publicly commented on the Nag Hammadi scrolls.

The fact that, to the Gnostics, man was not a lowly creature, as he was to the all-powerful God of the Christians, but was instead a walking miracle, filled with the divine spark and able to live fearlessly and with a level of confidence that can only be the result of the freedom that self-determination offers, was not the only threat that the Christian Church felt from the Gnostic movement. Tied in with the ethos of self-responsibility was the idea that women were spiritually equal to men and therefore had a valid voice. To the Christian Fathers this idea was a complete anathema, Christian female imagery having been carefully constructed around the extremes of women as either virgins or prostitutes with very little in between.

The first recorded anti-Gnostic work was written by Justin, who was martyred in Rome around 165 CE. His *Syntagma* or *Compendium against all Heresies* has not survived the passage of time and it is known only through references in other works. In the early 1960s a French scholar attempted to reconstruct this text through the third-party references to it, but the undertaking proved unsuccessful and was abandoned. It is therefore largely through the works of Irenaeus, the Bishop of Lyon (*c.*140–200 CE), that proof of the anti-Gnostic intentions of the Church exists. The *Adversus haereses* ('Against heresies'), a work in five volumes, was written by Irenaeus after he was persuaded by a friend to explain the teachings of the followers of Valentinus, a particularly important Gnostic school which was expanding among the inhabitants of the prosperous Rhône valley and into areas of Provence. As Bishop of Lyon, Irenaeus had become concerned by this growth of a faith which was in direct competition with his own for adherents, and so took up the challenge with the express intention of attacking it. With his own wide knowledge of the Valentinian School, the texts of which he had read and studied, he believed that he was able to trace the origins of this supposed heresy to its very roots. According to Irenaeus, the heretic of all heretics was Simon Magus, from whom all heretics had received their instruction through a succession of various Gnostic schools and teachers. Now recognized as one of the more precious sources of early Gnostic antipathy, Irenaeus's *Adversus haereses* derived its importance from his undoubted knowledge, not only of the Valentinians but also of Ptolemy and of Marcus.

The second important work (it is interesting to note that until the discovery and translation of the Nag Hammadi scrolls, most of the information available on early Gnosticism was derived from those works that opposed its thinking) was that written by Hippolytus of Rome. Hippolytus lived and wrote at the beginning of the third century, when theological controversy and debate in the Roman community was the norm. His ten-volume work *The Refutation of all Heresies*, written in Greek and also known as the *Philosophoumena*, revolves around the basic theme that all heresies are actually nothing more than adaptations and developments of the original, so-called pagan religions. The first four books in this work are therefore entirely devoted to explaining pagan beliefs, from magic and philosophy to astrology. Hippolytus's use of primary sources makes this work still valuable to scholars today.

While these two works represent the earliest in the propaganda war raised by the nascent Christian Church against the Gnostics, their authors were by no means the sole participants. Tertullian, who lived from about 150 CE to 225 CE, was almost rabid in his attacks on the Gnostics in general and the Valentinians in particular. It is through his works, and especially his attempts to prove that faith is superior to reason, that the effect the struggle against Gnosticism had on the Roman Church of the second and third centuries can most clearly be seen. Clement of Alexandria, however, took a more lenient stance. In his *Stromateis* there is even evidence that he was attempting to incorporate some of the more basic Gnostic ideas into the thinking of the mainstream Church. He opposed the ideal of 'false gnosis', replacing it with the concept of the true gnosis of the Christian faith and stating that 'through good, healthy living, knowledge of the principles of faith and growth in the spiritual dimension, the Christian is able to achieve the status of a true Gnostic, of one who aspires to know God through the Son'.[4] Indeed Clement's writing in particular shows that in the areas which were most hotly disputed by the two schools of theological thought, he is extremely familiar with the writings and beliefs of his opponents.

The stream of anti-heretical writers, and especially those who were anti-Gnostic, reads like a *Who's Who* of second-, third- and fourth-century literature. Origen, perhaps the greatest thinker and most important Greek writer of the early Church; Eusebius of Caesarea, who wrote the *Ecclesiastical History*; and Epiphanius, who was to become the Bishop of Constantia and wrote the *Panarion* or 'Medicine Chest' from which were dispensed the words that were to act as a soothing balm to those who had been stung by the acid of heresy – all played their roles in establishing the belief that non-Christian heretical thinking was the most insidious and evil disease of the day and yet paradoxically, in their efforts to quash such leanings, they also leave us with a most valuable early record of the existence of Gnostic thought.

Before the discovery of the Nag Hammadi[5] canon, the only works known to be Gnostic in origin were some Coptic documents discovered at the end of the eighteenth century. One of these was the *Codex Brucianus*, named after its Scottish owner, J. B. Bruce, and now in the Bodleian Library, Oxford. This work contains the *Two Books of Jeu*, which use magical formulae, mystical signs and symbols to gain access to the divine mysteries. The other document, known as the *Codex Askewianus* after the Englishman Dr Askew, was brought into the public domain in 1778 by C. G. Woide and is now in the British Library. This work found great fame as, compiled in the fourth and fifth centuries, it also contains the *Pistis Sophia* ('Faith Wisdom'), which originates from the third century CE. The papyri that form this, one of the earliest Gnostic canons, were found in Upper Egypt by James Bruce and were deposited in the British Museum in 1785. They are a curious collection of some five documents, some of which are incomplete, while others survive only in fragments.

These two codices represented almost the entire literature of the Gnostics until the discovery of the Nag Hammadi canon. However, that is not to say that the Gnostics were less than industrious in committing their doctrines to paper. In fact it is known that the opposite is true and that there were many writers and thinkers who contributed to a vast library of Gnostic texts. Unfortunately, however, the material upon which they wrote, papyrus, was extremely fragile and unless properly stored and preserved it became very brittle and therefore hard to handle. It was generally only through the repeated renewal of texts by copying on to new papyri that the survival of information was ensured. This process favoured the anti-heretical works of the growing Christian Church with its expanding resources and larger number of scribes, rather than the besieged Gnostics with their declining numbers and poor resources.

The reputations of some Gnostic writers have survived intact, even if their work has subsequently perished. Among them are the second-century Saturninus and Basilides, who were reputedly pupils of Menander, the disciple of Simon Magus, and who worked at both Antioch and Alexandria. It is through the work of Basilides, preserved through quotations in the anti-heretical work of Irenaeus, that the heresy of all heresies came to light. For Basilides is the first record we have of an alternative view of the events surrounding the crucifixion. He concluded that Simon of Cyrene replaced Jesus on the cross, a claim that was to be repeated as late as the seventh century in the Koran.[6] Perhaps most famous and influential, however, was the Egyptian Valentinus, whose reputation in Rome around 150 BCE was unequalled.[7]

It is the *Pistis Sophia* from the *Codex Askewianus* which

formed the basis of pre-1945 knowledge of the Gnostics through their own words. At times rambling, this work consists of what are supposedly conversations between a post-resurrection Jesus and his disciples, many of which centre on discussions about fall and redemption, interspersed with many revelations from Jesus to his followers. The main thrust of this work is its preoccupation with the question of who, at the finality, will be saved. Its conclusion is that all those who are to be saved must renounce the world completely and follow the strict ethic of pure love and compassion. This will then allow them the ultimate honour of being aligned with Jesus and becoming rays of the Divine Light. However, the importance of the *Pistis Sophia* to Gnostic scholars has tended to be overshadowed by the background to one of its English translations. Its translator, G. R. S. Mead, was a leading light in that particular brand of late-Victorian theosophy[8] which was so heavily promoted by Madame Blavatsky and her Theosophical Society. His heavy emphasis on the spiritualistic – as opposed to spiritual – and mystical makes his translation virtually useless for serious academic research. Amélineau's French version of 1895 suffered from a similarly subjective translation and as a result was widely ignored by the more objective commentators. Thus, until the discovery of the Nag Hammadi texts in 1945, there was little opportunity to perceive the Gnostics as objectively as if we were reading their own words, for in effect this is what the collection of codices allowed for the first time in more than 1,500 years.

The Gospels were discovered in the sands of Nag Hammadi in Upper Egypt at a bend in the Nile between Luxor and Assiut. In December 1945 three brothers were out digging for *sabakh*, or bird lime, beneath the high cliffs of the Jabal al Tarif just outside the village of Hamra Dūm. The cliff contains some 150 natural caves, many of which have been subsequently found to have been painted and used as tombs from the Sixth Dynasty, 4,300 years ago.[9] Near a large boulder which had fallen from the cliff, Abū al Majd, the youngest of the three, unearthed a jar which his older brother, Muhammad, then took responsibility for. Muhammad's story is perhaps best told in his own words:

> I found it at the Hamra Dūm mountain in the December of 1945. By six o'clock in the morning when I started my work . . . all of a sudden I found this pot. And after I found it I had the feeling that there was something inside it. So I kept it, and because it was cold this morning . . . I decided that I would leave it and come back again for it to find out what's inside it. I came back in the same day in fact and broke this pot. But I was afraid at the beginning because there might be something inside it – a 'djinn', a bad spirit. I was by myself when I broke the pot. I wanted my friends to be with me. After I broke it I found that it was a story book. I decided to bring my friends to tell them about the story. We were seven and we realised immediately that this had something to do with the Christian people. And we said that we don't really need it at all – it was just useless to us. So I took it to the ministry over here and he told me, well we don't really need it. It was just rubbish for us. So I took it back home. Some of them were burned and I tried to sell some of them.[10]

What Muhammad and Abū had in fact discovered was to become known as the Nag Hammadi library, a collection of fifty-one texts bound into books which contain between two and eight works each. They are made of papyrus strips and bound in simply tooled covers, some of which bear crosses. The contents of these works aside, the most extraordinary thing about them is their age, for they were written in and around 350 CE and many of the gospels they contain claim to report the actual words of Jesus Christ.

Less well known than the discovery itself is the somewhat more tortuous path by which the find became available to scholars. Following the brothers' discovery, the bound texts found themselves at the centre of a blood feud. The father of the boys, who was employed as a nightwatchman to guard the irrigation system which took water to the fields, had one night some months earlier caught a thief and in the ensuing struggle had killed him. As local custom dictated that only his own death could atone for such an action, he was in turn murdered. This would have been the end of the affair had it not been for the fact that some months later a completely innocent molasses dealer – in some accounts called Ahmed – was passing through the village, where he fell asleep while sheltering from the midday sun in the shade of Muhammad's house. A neighbour is then said to have informed Muhammad that this man was the murderer of his father, which resulted in Muhammad rallying his brother and his mother and setting about the unfortunate man, literally tearing him limb from limb. This violent and horrific chapter of the story had the unexpected benefit of causing the police to issuing a warrant for the arrest of Muhammad.

Warned that he was to be the object of police interest, Muhammad hid the papers he and his brother had found with the Coptic priest in the village. Priests of the Coptic tradition, much like Anglicans, can marry, and the wife of this priest had a brother who was a teacher of history and English in the local schools associated with the Coptic Church. When shown the documents by his sister, the teacher immediately recognized their historical value and persuaded his brother-in-law, the priest, to let him borrow one. He took this work, which became known as the Codex III, to Cairo, where he showed it to a friend, an academic studying the Coptic languages, who in turn took it to the Department of Antiquities, and in October 1946 the work was purchased for the Coptic Museum in Cairo.

The fate of the other volumes was a little more desperate. Muhammad's mother, mistaking them for worthless papers, burned some while others were sold to local Muslims, neither vendor nor purchaser being aware of the value and historical importance of the goods they were trading. One of the buyers, however, passed his purchase on to a gold dealer at Nag Hammadi who subsequently sold it in Cairo, a fate that was to befall the great majority of the codices which were bought by a one-eyed criminal called Bahy Ali. With the assistance of an antiquities dealer, Ali also took them to Cairo, where he used his friend's contacts and knowledge of the market in Egyptian antiques to ensure that he was able to maximize his profit. The collection of codices that they were offering for sale was, after a number of false starts, sold to Phocio Tano, who in turn passed them on to the Department of Egyptian Antiquities.

Codex I, which is now known as the Jung Codex, had a completely different path to public exposure. This found its way into the hands of a Belgian art dealer called Albert Eid, who was visiting Egypt. Concerned that the Codex would be confiscated from him by the Egyptian government, he smuggled it out of the country and subsequently offered it for sale to the Bollingen Foundation in New York and then to the Bibliothèque Nationale in Paris. However, Eid died during the negotiations, leaving an extremely complex legacy of ownership and inheritance problems. It was only with the dogged work of Gilles Quispel that the deadlock was broken and in 1952 the documents were acquired for the Jung Institute, which published it. The entire Codex has now been returned to the Egyptian authorities and the collection can be seen in the Coptic Museum.

In its entirety the Nag Hammadi library comprises fifty-one works, most of which are written in the Sahidic dialect of Coptic and which are apparently translated from the original

Greek texts. Their importance is that, as a collection of biblical texts with a specifically Gnostic character, they now form the bulk of our knowledge of Gnosticism. Indeed many of them can claim an authority which is on a par with that of the Synoptic Gospels themselves. Unlike the latter, however, these were written not for a Roman congregation but an Egyptian audience, and were therefore not subjected to the usual high level of Roman censorship and amendment. Further, there are those who have stated that these Gospels may well be the result of first-hand accounts and eyewitness versions of events relayed by Jews, perhaps even those who were personal acquaintances of Jesus himself, who were fleeing the Holy Land and who could afford to be honest in their recounting of events in a way in which the Synoptic Gospels could not.[11]

In particular the relationship between Jesus and Mary Magdalene is reported quite differently, especially in the Gospel of Mary and also in the Gospel of Philip. And a passage in one of the codices, the 'Second Treatise of the Great Seth', echoes the theme first mentioned by Basilides, that of the substitution on the cross of Jesus for another:

> I did not succumb to them as they had planned . . . And I did not die in reality but in appearance, lest I be put to shame by them . . . For my death, which they think happened (happened) to them in their error and blindness, since they nailed their man unto their death . . . It was another, their Father, who drank the gall and the vinegar; it was not I. They struck me with the reed; it was another, Simon who bore the cross on his shoulder. It was another upon whom they placed the crown of thorns . . . And I was laughing at their ignorance.[12]

We have already seen that the basic creed of the Gnostics was one of self-determination and self-reliance. This difference from the heavily proscribed doctrine of the Christian cult makes it easy to see why Gnosticism had such appeal, even though the emphasis on personal responsibility for one's own actions did not necessarily make it an easier option. We are now also aware of two separate and distinct branches of Gnosticism which originate from two original sources, Hermetism and Mandaeism. The *Corpus Hermeticum* is a collection of texts which, attributed to Hermes Trismegistus, or 'Thrice Greatest Hermes', were translated from Arabic into Greek during the second century CE.[13] Hermes is also identified with the Egyptian god Thoth, who in the Egyptian pantheon of gods was believed to be the inventor of all writing. As scribe to the gods Thoth became the patron of all arts which relied on the written word. The works of the Hermetica, the Hermetic library, are a range of revelations on occult, theological and philosophical subjects and take the form of debates between Hermes and a group of disciples, these dialogues falling into two main classes: 'popular' Hermetism, which is chiefly concerned with astrology, the sciences and occultist knowledge; and 'learned' Hermetism, which takes as its main themes theology and philosophy.

Recent study of the Hermetic library has shown that popular Hermetism predates the learned form and not only reflects the ideas and beliefs which were widely held throughout the early Roman Empire but also draws heavily on its Egyptian heritage for much of the imagery it employs. Indeed during the Hellenistic Age there was a growing mistrust of the old school of Greek rationalism and the hitherto firm and fixed boundary that separated religion from science became far more blurred. It was against this background that Thoth-Hermes became a source of inspiration for those who required a divinely revealed source of knowledge and the Hermetic writings became a quasi-gospel. During this time the Hermetica was also enlarged to include works on medicine and alchemy, the most famous of which was the 'Emerald Tablet', upon which were supposedly inscribed the words of the magus, Hermes Trismegistus himself, and which was the origin of the hermetic phrase 'as above, so below'.

Learned Hermetism, with its theological and philosophical focus, is chiefly concerned with the themes of the nature of the Supreme God, the cosmos, disorderly and irrational matter, and the relationship between the elements and between the cosmos as macrocosm and man as microcosm. While these were not necessarily new or original themes, the discussions between Hermes and his group of pupils show that their speculation and debate is based on a deeply held religious sentiment, a yearning for a deeper understanding of the nature of God and man and the same level of religious piety, which coupled with knowledge, is at the very heart of Gnostic theology. These works, with their emphasis on the physical world as the epitome of evil and the quest of the individual for a state of gnosis, represent perhaps the purest form of Gnostic writings, as yet uninfluenced by Christian influences.

The second branch of Gnosticism is somewhat more physical. While we know little about the personalities or lifestyles of the individuals involved with Hermetic Gnosticism, we know substantially more about the Mandaeans. This group is also the world's sole surviving Gnostic sect, with a history which can be traced back to the time of Jesus and possibly before. Essentially they form a branch of baptism-practising Gnostics who produced an enormous catalogue of Gnostic literature in the eastern Aramaic Semitic dialect and who have managed to survive the ravages of history. They live on the banks of the rivers Tigris and Euphrates in what is now Iraq, and their writings show a mythological world and mode of theology derived from mainstream Gnosticism but which has been blended somewhat with Zoroastrianism. However, it is their discipleship of John the Baptist and their strict practice of

baptism in flowing water that makes them particularly interesting within the context of early Christianity. Indeed the Mandaeans are cited in the Koran, like the Jews and the Christians,
as 'People of the Book'.[14] In terms of trade and profession they
were, in the earlier part of the twentieth century, highly
regarded in the souks of Baghdad and Basra as some of Iraq's
finest gold and silversmiths and those living in the marshy
southern regions of the country were equally famous for their
boat-building abilities.

The Mandaeans first came to Western attention when
seventeenth-century Jesuit missionaries returning from the
regions of the Euphrates and the Tigris brought with them
stories of a group of people whom they called 'St John's
Christians'. However, as more became known about their
customs and practices it became clear that they were not
Christians in the accepted sense, not least because they
regarded Jesus, whom they called both Yeshu Messiah and
Messiah Paulis, as a false prophet who had taken his disciples
away from the true path of a religion which in their framework
had been continued, not founded, by John the Baptist.

Among the library of texts which the Mandaeans hold
sacred are the *Ginza*, also known as the *Book of Adam*, a
cosmological treatise thought to date from the seventh century;
the *Sidra d'Yahya* or *Book of John* or *Book of Kings*, which
describes the activities of John the Baptist; the *Haran Gawaita*,
which is specifically concerned with the history of the sect; the
Book of the Zodiac, a collection of magical and astrological texts;
and the *Baptism of Hibbil Ziwa*, which is concerned with the
purification of the heavenly saviour of the Mandaeans. Little
was known about this closed and secretive community until, in
the late 1930s, Ethel Stevens, who published under her married
name of Lady Drower, made public her studies of the group.

The name Mandaean is thought to be derived from *Manda-*

yya, meaning 'having knowledge' in the Mandaean language, a term which, as Mandaiia, generally refers to the laity but is equally applied to the entire community. The priests are known as Nazoreans, a term which is also applied to Jesus, although it is historically interpreted in his case as 'one who is from Nazareth'. But we now know that the Nazoreans were a group who regarded themselves as the guardians of the true faith of Israel, and who seem to have been in existence for anything up to two centuries before the birth of Jesus. This usage of the term 'Nazorean' has been described by Hugh Schonfeld[15] as a reason for believing that the heirs of the pre-Christian Nazoreans are the present Nazoreans of the lower Euphrates, a fascinating possibility that has yet to be the subject of serious academic research. Much of what we know about the Mandaeans is through the work of Lady Drower, who, in the time that she spent with them, was not only permitted access to their history and doctrines but also trusted enough to be shown the nature of their beliefs and even secret scrolls bearing their sacred texts.

To the Arabs the Mandaeans are generally known as 'Subbas', while in the Koran they are referred to as 'Sabians', a term which was also used to denote the school of Hermetic and Egyptian philosophy centred on Harran in Mesopotamia. This group was extremely influential in the development of the Sufis, the sect of mystical Muslims who were to have such an influence on the culture of the Knights Templar. Indeed this connection has led such authors as Picknett and Prince to question whether or not the Mandaean emphasis on John the Baptist was passed down to the Templars, whose own reverence of the Baptist may be the result of instruction in some secret knowledge of him. The Mandaeans' Johannite tradition is encapsulated in their *Book of John*, where John the Baptist is referred to as both Yohanna, which is specifically Mandaean, and Yahya, the Arabic name under which he appears in the Koran. In the *Book of John* it is the latter name which is used more frequently and this has often been cited as a reason for dating the work after the Muslim conquest of the area in the mid-seventh century. However, the subject matter it deals with far predates this and the fact that the Mandaeans themselves appear in the Koran is today generally accepted as proof that both the people and their writings were in existence before the beginning of Muslim rule.

The basis of the Mandaean tradition is a belief in a system of male and female gods who are divided into those of the light and those of the dark. The supreme God was responsible for the creation of not only the universe but also the 'five beings of light' and their equal but opposite counterparts, the 'five beings of darkness' or archons, these ten demigods being responsible for creating the Earth and Mankind. There are Mandaean versions of Adam and Eve, called Adam Paghia and Hawa Paghia, who also have their opposites, Adam Kasya and Hawa Kasya. A devout people for whom religion is an important part of everyday life, the Mandaeans regard Sunday as their main holy day, and this is when the priesthood carry out the main sacrament, while the laity are responsible for other religious duties. Mandaean baptisms are a fundamental part of both marriage and funeral ceremonies and are carried out in pools which are especially made on the banks of a river which is called the Jordan. Highly ritualistic, the baptismal aspect of Mandaean services is augmented by a series of complicated handshakes conducted between the officiating priesthood and those undergoing baptism. A peace-loving people, the Mandaeans embrace a faith which expressly forbids war in general and the shedding of blood in particular. Celibacy is also deemed to be sinful, causing those men who are unfortunate enough to die unmarried to be reincarnated, the only reference in the religion to any concept of rebirth.

The funeral practices of this highly developed religion centre on the return of the departed soul to the world of light from whence it originally came. The ceremony, with its multiplicity of incantations, prayers and rites, has been shown to be largely based on the funerary traditions of the Ancient Egyptians and, unlike the Falashas, the Ethiopian Jewry about whose origins very little was known until recently, the Mandaeans uphold an insistence that while their sect has its origins in Palestine, their forebears came from Ancient Egypt. Further evidence of a possible Egyptian origin is found in the sacred scrolls of the sect, heavy with depictions of gods bearing more than a passing resemblance to those on Egyptian magical papyri and their name for the demigod who rules over the Earth and who created mankind – Ptahil – uncannily similar to that of the Egyptian god Ptah, creator of the universe and member of the Memphite triumvirate. As Lady Drower was the first Westerner to discover, the Mandaeans consider their religion to be parallel with that of the Egyptians, one of their texts stating that 'The people of Egypt were of our religion'.[16]

In Palestine the Mandaeans claim that they lived alongside Jews as part of the Gnostic Nazorean sect which had John the Baptist as its leader. While John was only one of a long line of leaders that came both before and after him, it was he above all others that they honour as a prophet and leader. This would seem to indicate by implication that John the Baptist was himself a Gnostic. This is supported by the fact that Simon Magus and Dositheus, founders of the two most powerful Gnostic sects, are known to have been disciples of John.

The Mandaeans state that their original home was a mountainous region which they call Tura d'Madai, where they lived among people who had come from Egypt. It was from here that they arrived in Palestine which, according to the *Haran Gawaita*, they fled in 37 CE for Mesopotamia and the city of Harran, now in Turkey. When and where exactly the bulk of their sacred writings originated remains unclear, but the emphasis they place on John the Baptist and the light in which they cast Jesus is fascinating. It is in the *Book of John* that some interesting points are revealed, for it tells in essence the story of John and Jesus from a specifically Gnostic standpoint. The birth of John to an elderly, childless couple, Elizabeth – called Enishbai – and Zachariah – called Zakhria – is foretold in a dream and then confirmed when a star hovers over Elizabeth. During his childhood the Jews seek to kill him and for safe keeping he is placed in the hands of Enoch (or Anush) who hides him in a secret and holy mountain where he remains until his return at the age of twenty-two to be the leader of the Mandaeans and a gifted healer.[17] The chronicle of his life then becomes even more interesting, for while it notes such details as his taking a wife, Anhar, the *Book of John* makes absolutely no reference to his decapitation at the hands of Herod. It seems to focus instead on foretelling his death as a peaceful event in which his soul is led away, having taken the form of a child. This anomaly remains unexplained by the academic community, but as Picknett and Prince point out, it may be that the answer to this lies at the heart of the Mandaean mystery tradition.

Jesus does not fare so well in the Mandaean history. Sometimes referred to as Christ the Roman, he is painted as being a disciple of John the Baptist's who, once accepted, proceeds to both pervert the words of John and effectively steal his thoughts, motives and religion.[18] The Mandaean texts do not mince their words when describing Jesus and his actions. The *Ginza* states:

'Do not believe him because he practises sorcery and treachery'[19]

and:

'When Jesus oppresses you, then say: We belong to you. But do not confess him in your hearts, or deny the voice of your Master, the high King of Light, for to the lying Messiah the hidden is not revealed';

while the *Haran Gawaita* is even more specific:

'He perverted the words of the light and changed them to darkness and converted those who were mine and perverted all the cults.'[20]

In another parallel with the religion of the Egyptians, the Mandaeans look forward to the coming of the god Enoch, who they trust will:

'accuse Christ the Roman, the liar, son of a woman, who is not from the light . . . unmask Christ the Roman as a liar, he will be bound by the hands of the Jews, his devotees will bind him, and his body will be slain.'[21]

The Mandaean emphasis on Jesus as a false Messiah only serves to highlight the reverence they accord to John the Baptist, although why this is so remains unclear. The Mandaeans' claim that their sect was in existence long before John became one of their leaders may remain unproven but their insistence that they are descendants of John's original followers is at least in part borne out by the origins of some of their sacred texts. It has long been argued that some of the New Testament Gospel of St John originated from writings by followers of the Baptist, commentators claiming that similarities between the Christian Gospel of John and the Mandaean *Book of John* show them to have come from the same original source material. This idea has even been taken one step further with the suggestion that the Christian ceremony of baptism is drawn from the Mandaean baptismal rite.

Even today the Mandaeans use a language and a script that is directly traceable to the time of Christ. Aramaic is the Semitic language which gradually replaced the widespread usage of Akkadian as the lingua franca of Mesopotamia and the Holy Land. It also replaced the use of Hebrew among the Jews, some of the books of the Old Testament, those of Daniel and Ezra in particular, being written in Aramaic rather than Hebrew. Spoken Aramaic was the language of Jesus and John the Baptist and was divided into two distinct dialects: West Aramaic, which included Nabataean, Palmyrene, Palestinian-Christian and Judaeo-Aramaic and is still spoken in some villages in the Lebanon, and East Aramaic, which had a number of sub-dialects, including Syriac, Eastern Neo-Assyrian and the Aramaic of the Babylonian Talmud. The Mandaean language today is a derivation of a dialect of East Aramaic.

It is sad to recount that this fascinating people, one of the few remaining physical links with the time of Jesus and with a history which, still not fully understood, would undoubtedly reap the rewards of serious research, is today one of the most persecuted and diminishing populations of the world. Largely settled in the marshy southern region of Iraq, they have become embroiled in a pogrom at the hands of Saddam Hussein against the Ma' dan or Marsh Arabs since before the Gulf War in 1991. This plight brought them to the attention of the world's media and as a result of the campaign of bombing, chemical and biological warfare and even draining of the marshes themselves – a premeditated ecological disaster unrivalled in modern history – that he continues to conduct against them, it is feared that we shall never know the true origins and secrets held by this enigmatic, fascinating and peaceable people.[22]

There have been a number of other groups throughout history who have also maintained a continuation of Gnostic themes. The Manichaeans were followers of the Gnostic teacher Mani, who lived from around 216 to 276 CE and was brought up in a sect called the Mughtasilah, another baptismal group whose origins are now thought to be directly related to the Mandaeans, possibly from the time of their exodus towards southern Iraq. It was long thought that Manichaeism was another Christian heresy, but it is actually a dualistic religion which offers salvation through special inner knowledge of spiritual truth – in essence the idea that lies at the very heart of Gnosticism. Although the religion became extinct during the Middle Ages, some of its scripts and texts were found in Chinese Turkistan and Egypt in the twentieth century and it is through these and other commentaries that we know of the existence and beliefs of its followers.

Mani was born in southern Babylonia and was 'annunciated' at the age of twenty-four, when he was 'ordered by heaven' to manifest himself publicly and to proclaim the doctrines which formed the basis of the new religion. He thought of himself as the continuation of a line that began with Adam and came through Buddha, Zoroaster and Jesus to himself, the carrier of the true word of a universal religion that would eventually replace all others. Through vigorous missionary activity, the religion did indeed see an explosion in growth, westwards through Egypt into North Africa (where even Augustine briefly became a convert) and reaching Rome in the early fourth century. Churches were subsequently established in Spain and, to a greater extent, southern Gaul. However, both the Church as a body and its adherents as individuals were vigorously attacked by both the Roman State and the Christian Church and it had disappeared completely from western Europe by the end of the fifth century. In the East Manichaeism found footholds in the Persian Sassanian Empire, albeit under the constant threat of heavy persecution. But with the reopening of the caravan routes after China's conquest of East Turkistan it blossomed, both in East Turkistan, where it remained the state religion until the Mongol invasion in the thirteenth century, and in China, where an edict allowed the religion's followers freedom of worship within China's national boundaries.

In its practices the religion has distinct echoes of Mandaeism, the basis of its theology being that the soul is fallen and becomes entangled with matter, which is of its essence evil, but then becomes liberated by the spirit. In effect the story has three stages: the past, where there was a fundamental separation of the opposing forces of light and dark, good and evil, spirit and matter; the present, which mixes the two sides; and the future, where the original duality will once again be restored. A rigorously ascetic religion for its strict adherents, it held that at death the soul of the truly righteous person will be restored to Paradise. For the non-righteous, however – the fornicators, meat-eaters, procreators, wine-drinkers and anyone who tills fields, cultivates, harvests or who owns possessions – the future was less bright, for they were condemned to be reborn in a succession of bodies, presumably until they got it right. It must be said that only a portion of the Manichaean faithful followed the more austere lifestyle, the communities tending to separate into the elect, who pursued the religious proscription rigorously, and the hearers, who supported the elect with alms, donations and work.

Perhaps the most widespread of the Gnostic religions during its time, Manichaeism adapted itself according to the region in which it was being practised. Thus we see different branches of the mainstream form reflecting aspects of Buddhism, Taoism, Christianity and the Iranian and Indian religions, and this interaction may be responsible for the echoes of Gnosticism which are still felt in some of these religions.

No brief discussion of Gnosticism would be complete without mention of the Essenes. At the heart of the Dead Sea

Scrolls debate, it is known that the Essenes, a sect which was of similar importance to the Pharisees and the Sadducees, clustered in monastic communities throughout the Holy Land and its neighbouring regions. Within these communities, which were largely male-dominated, property was held in common and the details of daily life were strictly regulated by officials. Like the Pharisees, the Essenes were strict observers of the laws of Moses, setting aside the Sabbath as a day of prayer and study of the Torah, practising ritual purity and wearing their highly identifiable clothing of white robes, distinctive for their rarity at that time. They also professed belief in immortality and the punishment of sin; however, unlike the Pharisees, the Essenes did not believe in the resurrection of the body and shunned temple life in favour of their ascetic, secluded existence, which focused on manual labour.

Joining the Essenes was in itself good training for the strictly religious life. After one year's probation the proselyte could receive his Essenian emblems but was not permitted to participate in common meals for another two years. Those who subsequently qualified for membership swore piety to God, justice towards men, hatred of falsehood, love of truth and the faithful observance of all other tenets of the Essene sect. Only after this act of initiation were new converts permitted to take their noon and evening meals with other members and even then only in silence.

When the Dead Sea Scrolls were found at Qumran it was, quite reasonably, assumed that they had been written by the Essene community who were known to have lived there. This was further confirmed by the dualist theology expressed in the texts, which had much in common with not only that of the Essenes but also the teaching of Jesus, who it is thought would have been aware of the community and may have spent time there before embarking on his ministry.

More modern scholars, however, find that there is no evidence to prove that the Dead Sea Scrolls are of Essene origin at all. One highly regarded academic, a specialist in Jewish history, is of the firm opinion that the Scrolls are in fact none other than part of the Temple Library and had been hidden there during the Jewish Revolt in 70 CE.[23] Nevertheless, it remains clear that the Essene community was as responsible for maintaining a tradition of Gnosticism as any of the other groups we have mentioned here.

Having come to understand that there are strong similarities between the beliefs of the Gnostics and the teachings of Christ, and being aware of some of the arguments that have been put forward linking Jesus with Gnosticism in general and connecting him with some of the Gnostic sects in particular, I realized that perhaps here lay the key to the powerful suggestions I was detecting in the symbolism and inherent geometry of the paintings I had been studying.

As with the early research on the Gnostics, in the absence of any direct evidence much insight can be gained by focusing on third-party references to a subject. I knew that I had uncovered what appeared to be a repeating image, a recurring code in a number of paintings, and that the personalities behind these paintings had a fascination with both the teachings of the ancients and the absolute truths of existence. Given the power of the men who commissioned these works, the exalted positions that some of them reached and their close associations with the Church, it seemed logical to me that they may have uncovered a secret now encoded in these paintings. Could this secret have been one regarding the origins of that Church? If so, the secret itself would take on the importance of an absolute truth. The parties involved would have needed to use a code to both protect that secret and insulate the Church, on which their careers and reputations were dependent, from it.

I fully realized that I was dealing with nothing more than supposition at this stage, but, in the light of some of the hints in the available Gnostic writings, as well as in the Koran, it was to the origins of Christianity and the life of one man that I turned my attention.

CHAPTER FIVE

THE CRUCIFIXION MYTH

☆

The life and teachings of Jesus of Nazareth are, if one accepts the standard biblical version, well documented. However, the scriptures of the New Testament abound with contradictions and errors. For example, at the time of Jesus's birth there is no record on any Roman map or document of a village or town called Nazareth. Flavius Josephus, the most highly regarded chronicler of the period, who commanded troops in Galilee and who listed the province's towns, makes no reference to a settlement called Nazareth. Why then do we refer to Jesus as Jesus of Nazareth? The most commonly accepted explanation is that the term 'Nazareth' originates from a mistranslation of the original Greek version of the New Testament in which he is referred to as 'Jesus the Nazarene'. This term itself is a derivation of Nazoreans or Nazorites, one of the many small religious sects and sub-sects whose beliefs and aims have become muddied by the passing of time. In fact Samson, many centuries before, is said to have been a member of the Nazorites.[1]

Even the term Messiah has become corrupted, imbued with a false meaning that has accreted through the ages. At the time of Jesus it meant purely 'anointed one' and was used in general reference to a king. Its meaning subsequently developed to describe a king who would also be a liberator, the term having taken on a distinctly political overtone. It was this secular interpretation of the phrase that was applied to Jesus: Jesus the Messiah, or Jesus Christos in Greek. This, when contracted into the contemporary Jesus Christ, takes the originally purely functional title and distorts it into a proper name which has subsequently become synonymous with the Christian 'Son of God' idea. For Jesus and his contemporaries, however, the concept of a 'divine' Messiah would have been nothing short of laughable.[2]

These two examples alone demonstrate that much of the contemporary idea we have of Jesus is the result of mistranslation or corruption of the original information. It is worthy of note that the Apocrypha, a collection of books and writings which were left out of the original compilation of the Bible, include many such observations which seem to run contrary to the biblical message which the compilers wished to disseminate. Among these writings are clues which point towards the true nature of the crucifixion itself. To develop a more realistic view, both of the man and the background to his extraordinary rise, we have to take a close look at the political and religious landscape in which Jesus lived and preached.

Palestine during the time of Jesus was split into three distinct areas. To the north was Galilee, situated on the western shore of the Sea of Galilee, and to the south, separated by Samaria, was Judaea, the spiritual and secular capital of the province. There was also a smaller region of Jewish settlement, Peraea, close to the old Hellenistic city of Philadelphia.

The majority of the population of Palestine was Jewish. Only Samaria had kept itself separate and made no room for Jews who were faithful to the temple at Jerusalem. Indeed the existence of Samaria, placed as it was like a wedge between the two centres of Jewish settlement, was a thorn in the side of the Jews, although there are some records which show that both Jews and Samaritans worked hand in hand in the struggle against the rule of the Romans.[3]

Judaea, the seat of both political and religious power, was under the direct rule of Rome through the offices of the Roman Procurator, the Emperor's representative. It was through the Procurator that the full weight of Roman rule was administered. Frequently autocratic and generally brutal, it relied on heavy taxation to maintain its power and engendered an atmosphere of dread among the general population. The relationship between the Jews and the Romans was not improved by the Romans' plundering and defiling of the Temple and their frequent use of torture. Indeed any prospect of a relationship based on harmony had almost certainly been dispelled when the Romans had assumed direct control of Judaea in 6 CE and had summarily crucified 3,000 rebels.

The Jews themselves were a factionalized race embracing various modes of religious and political thinking. The Sadducees were the wealthy landowning sector of society, who, to the horror of their fellow Jewry, collaborated with the Roman oppressors. The Pharisees were responsible for much of the reform of Judaism and positioned themselves firmly, although largely passively, in opposition to Rome. The third major sect were the Essenes, a group whose beliefs were more predominantly mystical and who based much of their activities on their understanding of the Kabbalah, the secret inner sanctum of Judaic thought that was derived from the more 'pagan', Egyptian beliefs. The Zealots, about whom much is written in the Testaments, drew their membership from both the Pharisees and Essenes and were highly political. It is the activities of the Zealots which resulted, in 66 CE, in the whole of Judaea rising up against the Romans, a revolt which culminated some seven years later in the siege of Masada and a mass exodus of the Jews from the Holy Land. However, there was still a large enough population for another rebellion to take place in 132 CE. In 135 CE the Emperor Hadrian expelled all Jews from Jerusalem and it became the Roman City of Aelia Capitolina.

While Judaea was the seat of local government, dispensing the law according to the Emperor, Galilee was a northern trouble spot. It was ruled over, virtually by proxy, by a line of puppet kings who had been placed there by the Romans and who were answerable to the procurator in Judaea. The procurator during the time of Jesus was Pontius Pilate, but first we shall deal with Herod, the tetrarch of Galilee, whose actions during his reign are much misrepresented in the Bible and who on closer examination has a far more interesting story and one which is key to understanding the reality behind the supposed death of Jesus.

On the death of Herod the Great in 4 CE, his descendants ruled over an extraordinary number of the principalities of Galilee and elsewhere during the first century CE, extending their power northwards into the Lebanon and eastwards into the Transjordan. Thus parts of Ituraea in Lebanon were ruled by Herod's son Philip from 4 BCE to 34 CE and by his grandson Agrippa I from 37 to 44 CE. Another grandson, Herod, ruled a separate kingdom of Chalcis, also in the Lebanon, from 41 to 48 CE as did Agrippa II, son of Agrippa I, from 50 to 53 CE. Agrippa II was transferred in 53 CE from Chalcis to a kingdom which encompassed the whole of the former tetrarchy of Philip, including part of Ituraea, together with some parts of Galilee, Peraea and the neighbouring areas. It was only on his death in c. 93 CE, long after the Jewish revolt of 66–70 CE, that this territory was incorporated into what we now call Syria, an indication of the regard in which he was held by the Romans.

The transition of power on the death of Herod the Great was not a smooth one. Jewish antagonism spilled over into a series of revolts, only to be suppressed by Varus, the governor of Syria. Succession was disputed largely because of the sheer number of Herod's sons, itself a result of the number of wives he had maintained, commonly regarded to be five,[4] although some authors cite more. It was only with the intervention of the Emperor Augustus that the matter was resolved and Herod's kingdom was divided among them. As a result of the division, there was to be no overall king. Instead Archelaus was to be ethnarch of Judaea, Philip tetrarch of a region to the east of Galilee and part of the Transjordan and Herod tetrarch of Galilee itself. While the reigns of Philip and Herod were to endure, that of Archelaus only lasted ten years. In 6 CE he was removed from power and, at the instigation of his subjects and the Governor of Syria, was sent into exile to Vienne in Gaul. As a result, the Herod family lost any say in the running of Judaea, power having been ceded to a 'prefectus of equestrian rank', termed procurator.[5]

Herod, son of Herod the Great and his wife Malthace, thus became the tetrarch of Galilee and Peraea, reigning from 4 CE until 39 CE. Before this time he had been resident in Rome and on his return found Galilee ravaged by war. He embarked on a period of reconstruction, rebuilding the cities of Livias and Sephoris and later founding a new capital city, calling it Tiberias in deference to the Emperor. While generally considered to be a good ruler, much less aggressive than his father had been, he was nonetheless adept at controlling the population and suppressing any signs of insurrection, more by uttering threats than taking any direct action. He also seems to have lacked any personal political ambitions. The moves he made to gain the whole of his father's kingdom seem to have been inspired by his wife Herodias. Indeed it was her ambitions for her husband which seem to have been the main cause of the troubles that Herod encountered, most notably his execution of John the Baptist.

The story of John the Baptist will be well known to anyone who is familiar with the Scriptures. John's place in history, as baptizer of Jesus, masks the ministry that he had conducted throughout Palestine before Jesus embarked on his relatively short period of preaching. The essence of John's teachings was centred not only on the act of baptism but also on his proclamation of the arrival of an expected Messiah. However, less well known is the fact that he, like Jesus, was a Jew, and yet he is cherished by the Christian Church as a martyr when, in point of fact, is was not for his faith that he died.[6] One of the reasons John was so successful as a prophet and preacher was that he was the first to expound the view that through baptism one's sins could be forgiven and the 'slate wiped clean'. In fact he was the first to popularize the theory that God, far from the Old Testament image of a vengeful, jealous God, so beloved of the Jews, could be a forgiving, loving God.

Spreading the word of events that were due to happen, as foretold in the Scriptures, events that would lead to the salvation of the people, while at the same time leading a life of frequent self-imposed solitary confinement in the desert, led John to accumulate a wide audience and a large band of followers. Most of these were drawn from the common people, his messages of hope inspiring a population burdened by the oppression of the Roman yoke and suffering extraordinary deprivation. This aspect of John's teaching and the effect that it had gave him a role which was increasingly political and brought him to the attention of those in power. Thus when he openly criticized Herod over the nature of his second marriage, the act that led ultimately to his decapitation, he was doing so with the will of the people behind him.

Already married to the daughter of the Arab king Aretus, Herod had met and wanted to marry Herodias, a noblewoman of the Hasmonean line. Herodias, however, was already married to Herod's half-brother Herod Philip, who by this time had failed in his ruling of the lands he had inherited from the death of Herod the Great and had moved to Rome, living as a wealthy private individual. The life of obscurity, albeit surrounded by the trappings of fortune, did not suit the ambitions of Herodias, who, most authors agree, entered into an adulterous relationship with Herod, securing from him a promise that he would divorce his wife. As a Hasmonean, she would not have wanted to share a household with an Arab, a representative of the long-standing enemies of her own dynastic heritage. It is also probable that she would have wanted to avoid the household troubles of her grandfather, Herod the Great, caused by the constant rivalries between his wives and their many sons.[7]

Whatever the family political background, Herod did divorce his wife, an action that was later to come back to trouble him when Aretus and he went to war. On marrying Herodias, he then installed both her and her daughter by Herod Philip, Salome, in the royal residence at Machaerus on the eastern shore of the Dead Sea. This marriage, already a source of general disgust to Herod's family and to the Jews in general, was further criticized when Salome herself was to marry Herod's other brother, also called Philip.[8] John the Baptist was one of the more outspoken critics of Herod's strange adulterous and incestuous union. Whether the latter heard about John's views as a result of a direct denouncement by him at the court of Machaerus or through intermediaries is now impossible to tell. However, it is clear that Herod did hear of the very vocal denunciations of him by John and was concerned by them, not least because of John's hold on the rank and file of the population over which he was meant to be ruling.

It is highly probable that Herod was already taking an active interest in the work of John, for John's preaching had taken on a distinctly political tone. His announcement of the imminent arrival of the Messiah would have been of particular interest to Herod, as it was the supposed function of this Messiah to put an end to the rule of a foreign government in Israel. Perhaps even more insidious was John's emphasis on baptism, which could easily have been construed as the rite of initiation into the Messianic community, then a highly treasonable act.[9]

The events surrounding John's execution are well known. Following Salome's dance at a feast to celebrate Herod's birthday, her request for the head of John the Baptist, a wish primed by her mother Herodias, was granted by Herod. John was beheaded. The length of time between his incarceration and his death has been the subject of much learned debate over the years, but no scholar has been able to establish a clear picture. What is generally agreed upon is that it was Herodias who was the advocate of John's demise. Herod himself seems to have had a large amount of respect for him. Despite the fact that John posed a considerable political threat to his rule, Herod is reported as holding him in high regard. There are accounts which seem to indicate that John was in many ways a spiritual adviser to Herod. Perhaps for this reason the tetrarch seems to have been content with merely imprisoning John to contain his influence, while it was the hatred of Herodias that led to John's gruesome and untimely decapitation. Indeed the Gospel of Mark states that Herod not only kept him safely but kept asking him questions, and although perplexed by the answers John gave, was intent on hearing him.

The death of John was to have a profound effect on Herod

and seems to have haunted him for the remainder of his days. When his forces were defeated in the battle against King Aretus, he ascribed it as being due to his slaughter of John. He knew that John had been a 'just and holy man'[10] and it is likely that his sense of guilt at the slaying of an innocent prophet, albeit at the behest of his manipulative wife, was a major factor in determining Herod's role in Jesus's trial.

A further intriguing aspect of the life of Herod is his relationship with the Romans. We know that he was in great favour with both the Emperor Tiberias and those who surrounded him. Indeed the permission granted him to marry Herodias would almost certainly have been through the relationship of Berenice (Herodias's mother) and her closest friend, Antonia (sister-in-law to Tiberius and mother of the future Emperor Claudius). His relationship with Pontius Pilate is a little more difficult to determine, although the general impression is one of some amity. While Herod, tetrarch of Galilee, was under the direct control of Pontius, the Emperor's representative, the two would have had frequent cause to discuss matters of regional political interest both in their own dominions and in Rome.

Pilate is something of an elusive character and little is known about his early life. Indeed, the Gospels aside, the only real evidence for his existence is a fragmentary stone inscription, a few coins and the remains of an aqueduct.[11] His name, Pontius, suggests that he was of Samnite origins and it is known that he was a knight or 'of equestrian rank'. The Samnites, a tribe of peasant fighters who were often at war with the Romans, were eventually disbanded and disappeared from history. But there are at least two other supposed backgrounds for him. One is that he was a Spaniard and more specifically a resident of Seville, an origin which would have automatically granted him the right of Roman citizenship. Another theory proposes that he was born a German in the Rhine city of Mainz. Whatever his early life may have been, in 26 CE he came from the household of Tiberius through the influence of Sejanus, a favourite of the Emperor, to become the procurator of parts of the imperial province of Syria. This included the areas of Judaea, Samaria and Idumaea and he ruled over these for ten years. He quarrelled incessantly with both the general Jewish population and their leadership, possibly to gain favour with Sejanus, his sponsor, who, unlike most of the Caesars, is said to have disliked the Jews and to have made no secret of his feelings towards them.

During his period of power Pilate seems to have incurred the wrath of both the Jews and Tiberius. Finding the Jews a troublesome people, he was so irritated at their general behaviour that at one stage he raised golden shields on the temple walls at Jerusalem which bore the image of the Emperor. An act designed to reinforce the mastery of the Romans, it backfired when the Jews rioted in protest at the wilful desecration of their holy place and the subsequent quelling resulted in the death of two to three hundred of them. In the aftermath a complaint was made against Pilate and he rapidly found himself out of favour with his Emperor.

This problem was compounded by Pilate's appropriation of temple funds and treasures to build an aqueduct bringing water to the city. Although intended as an act of patronage to the city over which he ruled, this further enraged the Jewish population of Jerusalem, who, when he entered the city, were extremely vocal in their dissent. Pilate, however, had foreseen that he ran the risk of inciting civil disturbance and had ordered disguised soldiers to mingle in the crowd.[12] On a signal from him they subdued the rioting and, although they were forbidden to use their swords and were restricted to batons and clubs, many Jews died.[13]

In 36 CE Pilate was recalled to Rome to face Tiberius, but before he arrived Tiberius died and instead he faced Caligula, who condemned him and his wife Procula (or Procla according to some texts) and banished them to Vienne in Gaul, where he committed suicide.[14]

It is partially through the differing accounts in the various Gospels that today we have such an ambiguous view of Pilate. What is clear is that his attempts to maintain a peaceful equilibrium in Palestine were made with very little understanding of the peoples over whom he ruled. This gives rise to the opposing opinions of him: 'inflexible, obstinate and merciless' according to Agrippa and 'weak, vacillating and feeble' according to some of the authors of the New Testament.

It is for his role in the death of Jesus that Pilate is most deeply inscribed in history and yet when we look more closely it appears that his actions differ radically from the account of them which the Gospels would have us believe.

When Jesus is first brought before Pilate by the Sanhedrin, the council of Jewish elders, he states that he wishes him no harm and refers him to Herod. This apparently simple act probably hid a number of political considerations. First, Jesus, the supposed 'King of the Jews', should properly be judged by the true King of the Jews – the tetrarch of Galilee, Herod. But this also seems to have been a reciprocal peace-making gesture between Pilate and Herod, for it was the latter who had warned Pilate that the abuse of the temple funds for the construction of an aqueduct was becoming a matter of dissent among the Jews. Herod took no further action in this matter, simply informing Pilate and hoping that he would put his own house in order discreetly. The ensuing massacre was an embarrassment to Herod and there was a cooling of the two men's friendship after this event. Pilate's sending of Jesus to Herod could easily be read as a peace-making gesture, a return of the compliment.

Further, Jesus actually had no crimes against the Roman Empire to answer to, so Pilate had no cause to try him – especially not at the request of the Sanhedrin, for whom he had little time and virtually no respect. (Difficulties had arisen between Pilate and the Sanhedrin throughout most of his period of command. One particular incident was his minting of coins which bore a representation of the Jewish sacrificial ladle, an act which illustrates his complete misunderstanding of Jewish sensibilities and which further alienated him from the Jewish elders.)

Even when Jesus was summoned before Pilate to answer the charges laid before him by the Sanhedrin, several incidents illustrate the tense relationship between Pilate and the Sanhedrin. Pilate had commanded that Jesus be brought before him, normal tribunal protocol dictating that a messenger be sent to bring him before Pilate. However, the messenger, on seeing Jesus, paid deference to him, treating him with a level of respect which the Sanhedrin felt was inappropriate, and they duly complained that this behaviour was insulting to them. The situation was further exacerbated when Jesus entered to see Pilate. The ensigns who lined the way with the standards of the Emperor dipped their flags as Jesus passed, an act of respect further incensing the Sanhedrin, who once more made representation to Pilate to voice their displeasure. Pilate did make an effort to appease them, but in vain, and the trial proceeded. Pilate had no wish to try Jesus, going so far as to declare three separate times that he could find no fault whatsoever in him.[15]

When it had come to Herod's attention that there was another Galilean who was preaching a similar message to that of John, his interest was piqued. He was keen to meet Jesus, to have a private audience with the man who was being hailed, at the very least, as a great preacher and a man worthy to follow in the footsteps of John the Baptist. He was undoubtedly aware that Jesus and John were viewed as spiritual brothers and, given the reputation that Jesus had already gained for incredible acts, hoped that Jesus would show him a sign to satisfy his curiosity.[16]

However, the gospels tell us that Jesus, a man known for his amazing powers of oratory, remained remarkably silent before Herod. This could have been viewed by the tetrarch as an act of utter disrespect. But he took an opposing view. He found Jesus, although taciturn, to be engaging company and no threat to his kingship. He was apparently not even concerned that Jesus has been dubbed the 'King of the Jews'.

The apocryphal gospels of 'Abd al-Jabbar, written in 995 CE in order to establish that Muhammad was a true prophet, make some extraordinary claims about the relationship between Jesus and Herod. Hearing from the Jews about the supposed misconduct of Jesus, they state that it was Herod who had Jesus arrested and brought before him. However, on hearing him, the tetrarch sees that the accusations brought against Jesus by the Jewish Sanhedrin are invented and he refers him to Pilate, who also has no quarrel with him and returns him to Herod, who imprisons him at the demand of the Jews. In an echo of the Gospel of Peter, 'Abd al-Jabbar also states that it was Herod who washed his hands of the blood of Jesus.

For the Sanhedrin, however, Jesus was an embarrassment. Proclaimed King of the Jews, although not by himself, he was spreading through his ministry the sacred word of the Jewish faith to those who were not the rightful tribal members of Judaea. Fiercely protective of their sacred heritage, they were appalled to hear that Jesus was allowing the non-righteous into their secrets. Although they recognized him as a prophet, they were not prepared to accept his action and wanted him quieted.

Given that neither Pilate nor Herod could find adequate reason to try Jesus, let alone crucify him, why then was he supposedly condemned to hang on a cross? Given the forceful personalities involved, it is not unlikely that some sort of deal was struck to satisfy all the parties. The accepted biblical account of the crucifixion could well conceal in its telling a much deeper truth which could have as far-reaching a legacy as its more orthodox interpretation.

The life of Joseph of Arimathea is shrouded in mystery. A wealthy merchant, he is described by various writers as being a secret disciple of Jesus, a member of the Sanhedrin and to have had access to Pilate. Indeed the Gospel of Peter, one of the apocryphal gospels first mentioned by the Bishop of Antioch in 180 CE, a copy of which was discovered in a valley in the Upper Nile in 1886, states that Joseph was no less than a close friend of Pontius Pilate. He is thought to have been born some eight years before Jesus, in the town of Arimathea near Sophim on Mount Ephraim. This town, also called Rameth or Ramula, was allotted specifically for the residence of the Levites and here Joseph's father, Matthias, was said to have held a position of authority. Joseph is believed to have gone away at the age of seventeen to learn the customs of the three sects of the Jewish nation in order that he might choose between them, and eventually he forsook the Pharisees and Sadducees in order to align himself with the Essenes. He is said to have been taught by a holy man called Malachi, who lived in the desert and clothed and fed himself solely with what nature could provide. Joseph apparently stayed four years with Malachi before returning to Jerusalem at the age of twenty-one.

History does not recount the basis of the rest of the life of Joseph, until his appearance in the crucifixion story. He is variously described as a wealthy merchant and a noble senator, along with many other titles. What is clear is that Joseph had accumulated a level of wealth and with it a degree of power and friends in high places. His role as a secret disciple of Jesus appears to have begun on his return to Jerusalem from his time in the desert with Malachi, perhaps only becoming a secret on his election to the Sanhedrin.

His role in the crucifixion of Christ we shall deal with shortly. However, there are also interesting aspects of the later life of Joseph. A work which purports to be a history of his life states that after the death of Christ, Joseph led a solitary life for about six months before making contact with the Apostles. He was then recruited by St Peter to become one of the seventy-two disciples and was sent to Rome in order to determine why Tiberius Caesar was so against them. *En route*, via a shipwreck in the Adriatic, he became acquainted with a Jew called Baliturnus who was able to introduce him to Tiberius's wife, Poppeia, in the Eternal City. Through her, Joseph procured the liberty of those Christians who were held in bondage and on returning to the Apostles he was bestowed with honour, ordained and appointed to preach the Gospels in England.

After sailing from Joppa, it is told, he arrived at Barrow Bay in Somerset, from where he proceeded some eleven miles inland to Glastonbury. Here legend recounts that he planted his staff in the ground, where it took root, 'just like Aaron's rod which blossomed flowers when there was a contest between him and other learned Jews for the priesthood'. It presently turned into a blossoming thorn which survives to this day and is called the 'Glastonbury thorn' (*Crataegus monogyna praecox*), which is said to flower only on the morning of Christmas Day, the flowers withering by the evening. Another version maintains that he arrived in the West Country with twelve disciples of his own, before being granted twelve hides of land (an area large enough to support one family for one year with one plough) in Glastonbury; while yet another suggests that Joseph arrived with Jesus, a theme which William Blake used as the basis for *Jerusalem*, one of the poet's 'Prophetic Books'. In the *Annales Ecclesiasticae*, written in 1601, no less a figure than the Vatican librarian, Cardinal Baronius, recorded that Joseph first went to Marseilles in 35 CE – an act that is supposedly confirmed much earlier by the sixth-century chronicler Gildas III in his *De Excidio Britanniae* – before heading for Britain to preach the Gospel.

Eusebius, Sozousenes and Ruffinus, three ecclesiastical writers of the Middle Ages, all recount that Joseph held baptisms in the city of Wells, supposedly converting as many as 18,000 people a day. They also credit him with the conversion of King Ethelbert and his company of noblemen. Indeed it is said that he spent a total of forty-two years in Glastonbury until his death at the age of eighty-six. He was supposedly buried in the chancel of Glastonbury Abbey and a tombstone was said to bear the inscription: 'Here lies the body of that most noble disciple, recorded in Scripture by the name of Joseph of Arimathea, and noted by the four Evangelists, St Matthew, Mark, Luke and John, for his begging the body of Our Blessed Saviour, when crucified to redeem lost men from Eternal Destruction, and burying it in a tomb of his own making. He died AD 45, aged 86.'

We know from the Bible that Joseph provided Jesus's tomb. Could it be that he played a larger role in the crucifixion and the events which led up to it – a role that was expunged from the Bible's account? Given his position, he could well have acted as go-between for the interested parties. We know that he could move freely between the court of Pontius Pilate, where he would be recognized as a friend of the procurator and a successful and wealthy merchant, and the palaces of Herod, where he would have been received as a respectful member of the Sanhedrin. We know that neither of these two important figures had any reason to execute Jesus and would perhaps have been interested in any solution to the problem with which they had been confronted at the request of the Sanhedrin. Given this scenario, it is possible to portray Joseph as the man who offered such a solution. The confusion surrounding the decision taken by Pilate, who seems to shrug off the judgement that the Jews were clamouring for him to make, may even allude to this. Pilate, having asked, 'Shall I crucify your King?', delivered Jesus 'unto them to be crucified. And they took Jesus, and they led him away' (John xix:16). In other words, Pilate did not condemn Jesus or order him to be crucified, but merely delivered him to the Jews. If Joseph had the ear of the procurator and was able to provide a solution which allowed Pilate to be seen to do justice and at the same time not incur the wrath of the Jews, then surely he would have taken it. If that solution involved handing responsibility of Jesus to the Jews themselves and in doing so permitting Joseph, as one of their leaders, to handle the affair, then so much the better from Pilate's point of view.

The Gospels locate the site of the crucifixion at Golgotha, 'the place of the skull', which only later was supposedly identified as the hill to the north-west of Jerusalem. It is the Gospel of John which, more explicitly than the others, states: 'now in the place where he was crucified there was a garden; and in the garden a new sepulchre wherein man was never lain' (John xix:41). Received images of a thousand years of artistic interpretation aside, it would appear that the crucifixion took place in or near a garden, in which was a private tomb. The Gospel of Matthew is yet more precise, naming Joseph of Arimathea as the owner both of the garden and of the tomb. Indeed it has recently been argued that the actual site of the crucifixion was the garden of Gethsemane, and had this been owned privately by a secret disciple, it would go some way towards explaining the free use of it that Jesus made during his lifetime.

The crucifixion, far from being conducted publicly with a crowd of both followers and barrackers milling around the foot of the cross, is described by all three of the synoptic Gospels of Matthew, Mark and Luke as having been witnessed by most people from 'afar off'. Thus we have a private crucifixion in a private garden with a new and private tomb nearby. If Joseph of Arimathea had been able to orchestrate a ceremony which could only be witnessed from a distance and on land that he owned, then surely the possibilities for organizing an event to give the impression that the troublesome prophet was no longer a threat, while actually sparing him, are self-evident.

Indeed the very nature of the act of crucifixion itself has to be brought into question, for the general image which is promulgated by both the Catholic and Protestant Churches would seem to have little basis in the act of punishment that was prescribed by Roman law.

Crucifixion was a specific punishment for a specific set of crimes and in practice was generally reserved for those crimes which were committed against the Roman Empire. This fairly broad brief meant that it was meted out to all manner of thieves, criminals and a number of self-proclaimed Messiahs before Jesus. It was carried out according to an exact formula laid down in Roman law which demanded that the victim be flogged on the back and then fastened with leather cords around the wrists to a horizontal beam which was placed across the neck and shoulders. The victim would then carry this beam to the place of execution, where it would be raised on a vertical post. He would then be left hanging from his wrists. More latterly the punishment was refined and the feet of the victim would be fixed to the upright post, allowing him to support himself and relieve the pressure on his chest, which would otherwise collapse the lungs, causing suffocation. Supporting the feet would prolong the agony after the flogging and the victim would usually die of dehydration, blood poisoning or sunstroke. The act of breaking the victim's legs, which in Jesus's case was expressly forbidden by the Sanhedrin – they gave explicit orders against the breaking of any bone in his body – was generally considered to be an act of mercy, a coup de grâce, rather than a further method of torture. In breaking the legs the weight of the victim's body would collapse the ribcage and bring about death by suffocation. To a victim who had endured many hours, if not days, of exposure this would seem to come as welcome relief.[17]

A further, and somewhat key, element of the crucifixion was the method of fixing the victim to the cross beam. The generally accepted view is that Jesus was nailed to the cross, an image that has spawned a whole genre of devotional art through the centuries. But there are many pointers which seem to indicate that the practice of nailing the victim to the cross was exclusively retained for punishments under Roman martial law, and more specifically for soldiers and officers of rank who had transgressed that law. There is very little real evidence to suggest that Jesus was attached to the cross in this manner. There is much stronger evidence that binding with cords was the general practice for attaching both the hands and the feet to the wooden framework.[18] Three of the Gospels actually mention neither cords nor nails in their accounts of the act, whether for the crucifixion of Jesus or for the two robbers who were either side of him.

It is therefore highly likely that the true crucifixion would not have resulted in the death of Jesus. Most scholars agree that the maximum amount of time Jesus could have spent on the cross is six hours: the Jews were preparing not only for a Sabbath but also the feast of Passover, and were strictly forbidden to let a corpse hang overnight. Even under normal circumstances a body was meant to be buried and the service concluded before the sun went down. We know that the trial and punishment began on the third hour and can suppose that the sun set around 9pm. Given that Jesus was bound to the cross and not nailed, and that his legs were not broken, we begin to see that while certainly traumatized and bleeding from the flogging, he could have remained alive. It would actually have been possible for him to have survived two to three days in this position. (There is a sect of devout Filipino Catholics who every year test their faith by being nailed to a cross and left to hang there for twelve hours before being brought down.)

There are also some doubts as to whether the cross on which the act of crucifixion was committed was as most of us imagine it to have been. There is a long heritage of fixing criminals to vertical posts of various designs which goes back much further than the Romans. These range from the simple post, a line of which, each bearing a victim, was termed a *palisade*, to the early form of cross, which was of a 'Y'-shaped construction and was called a *furca*. Some authors, most notably Scaliger, contend that it was this which was employed on Calvary as the Jews never used the cross, as we now know it, for legal punishments. Indeed the Christian symbol that it has become is a comparatively modern religious affectation. Justin Martyr, writing in 150 CE, states that Christians made the sign of the Greek letter *khi* 'to denote the first power of God'. This letter was written like the algebraic sign '+' and can be seen on works as early as the Sigeian stone, which dates from 500 BCE.[19] Dating from even before this time there are representations of what we now consider to be the Christian cross on Egyptian murals, where it can be found alongside the ankh, the Pharaonic holy symbol which is a cross surmounted by a loop and which signifies 'life'.

What historical research also makes clear is that the image

that we have of Jesus being mounted on high, on a tall scaffold which makes the surrounding crowd have to look up to see their Lord, is likely to be completely erroneous. Evidence of other crucifixions bears witness to the fact that the victim, when raised on the vertical post by the cross member, was lifted up just high enough to prevent the feet from touching the ground. The crucified Jesus may have been raised only a matter of inches, and as we have established, the 'surrounding crowd' was limited to viewing the scene from 'afar off'.

So we have a crucifixion where Jesus was bound, not nailed, to a cross by his hands and feet and where his legs remained intact and able to support the weight of his body on the express orders of the Council of Jewish Elders – of which Joseph of Arimathea was a member. We must also remember that as the Romans had no particular quarrel with him there would have been no recrimination from the authorities for bringing the body down from the cross.

In contemporary terms, however, the act of removing a body from a cross would have been almost inexplicable, the main point of crucifixion being that the victim's body was left on the cross to rot or be picked apart by carrion birds or other scavengers, leaving the remaining family with nothing but bones to inter. Thus it is surprising that, when Joseph of Arimathea went to Pilate to request the body of Jesus, Pilate entertained the idea at all. What is even more strange is that Joseph, who was not a family member and had absolutely no claim on the supposed corpse, was granted permission for the removal of the body. Even more bizarre is the dialogue between Pilate and Joseph which led to this. When approached by Joseph, Pilate expressed surprise at Jesus's rapid death and questioned a centurion on the validity of Joseph's statement. However, the original Greek version of the Gospel of Mark states that Joseph, in asking for the body of Jesus, asked for his *soma*, the word for a living body. When Pilate replies, however, he is quoted as using the word *ptoma*, meaning a corpse. Pilate could have been unaware of what Joseph was doing at this stage, hence his reference to a corpse; alternatively, he could have been collaborating in a stage-managed affair. Whether or not money or favours were exchanged, Joseph, who was, according to the Gospel of St Peter, 'a close friend of Pilate's', would have been best placed to effect such a scheme.

After its removal from the cross, we know that the supposedly dead body of Jesus was removed to a tomb in the Garden of Gethsemane, a tomb owned by Joseph, who had commissioned it. A tomb that was new and unused. Adricomius states that 'the glorious sepulchre of Our Lord is a new monument situated about one hundred and eight feet from Mount Calvary and one thousand paces from Mount Sion'. Indeed it seems even more natural that Jesus was removed to here if the theory that the crucifixion itself took place in a garden that was owned by Joseph is correct. It would then follow that a nearby new and unused tomb was not the result of chance but rather of some careful planning by Jesus's secret disciple and powerful, well-connected friend.

The Gospels state that Joseph, having laid Jesus in the tomb and covered him with the new linen shroud, returns to the tomb over successive days, bringing with him aloes and herbs. The Gospels go even further and put a precise weight on the amount of aloes that are brought to the tomb, stating it to be one hundred Roman pounds, or thirty kilograms. Many theories have been put forward regarding the use of this herb, but one seems particularly apt in this context. As any herbalist will confirm, aloe, a genus of shrubby succulent plants related to the lily, is even today renowned for its ability to relieve and aid the healing of heavy bruising and the effects of physical trauma.

We have established that it is not only entirely possible, but in fact extremely likely, that Jesus was alive when he was brought down from the cross. We know from the Bible that he was then secreted from public view in a private tomb, situated in the confines of a private garden. If he had not died, he could have been restored to health. Thus we have a Jesus who, according to eyewitnesses, is thought to have died but in fact has not, shortly afterwards appearing to his disciples, who believe him to have risen again.[20]

It is now that another aspect of Jesus's story comes into play. John the Baptist, as we know, was the baptizer of Christ and the man who, in Jesus's own words, 'paved the way for my coming'. Indeed even the Gospels allude to the almost private joke as to who should baptize whom. When Jesus later heard of John's decapitation from his disciples, he retreated to the desert, where he saw Moses and Elijah in a vision. Swearing his followers to secrecy, saying that what they had seen and heard of his vision was not for mortal man, he then embarked fully on his ministry, becoming the charismatic prophet. What is implicit in this development of Jesus's role is that the spirit of John the Baptist 'entered' the body of Jesus Christ.

Whether or not one acknowledges that Jesus may not have died on the cross, this concept of a duality in one man harks back to the Egyptian concept of the double Horus, the two prophets standing back to back, seeing two horizons. It also reflects, in Christian terms, the representation of the duality of the spirit embodied in man. Indeed so strongly is this duality principle embedded in the Christian psyche that John the Baptist is often wrongly referred to as Jesus's elder brother, a confusion that arises from the fact that they are brothers in spirit, but not in flesh.

This becomes even more fascinating when set against the context of both Babylonian and Egyptian mythology, where it is only ever one half of the duality which is sacrificed for the betterment of mankind. In Babylonian culture this is expressed in terms of the bull 'Sin', which is ritually sacrificed to pave the way for the coming of the priest-scribe 'Warad Sin' or 'Slave to the Bull'. The role of the priest-scribe is to preach the word and to be the physical embodiment of the spiritual Sin. The analogy with the Christian ideal is plain to see. John the Baptist, whose message predated that of Jesus, was beheaded – itself a ritualistic method of killing, separating the head, repository of the spirit and knowledge, from the body, the earth-bound flesh. This event not only conforms to an ancient rite but also is heavy with the implication that a further sacrifice (that of Jesus the preacher) was not only unnecessary but would be utterly at odds with the ancient beliefs upon which so much of the imagery of early Christianity was based. These archaic laws were common knowledge to all those who were inducted into the Kabbalist Jewish faith. Indeed many modern biblical theorists have come to the conclusion that Jesus was himself aware of this, and manipulated both his teachings and life in order to conform with this knowledge and the ancient Scriptures.[21]

Healed by the ministrations of Joseph of Arimathea and his other close followers, Jesus would have known that it was far too dangerous to show himself again publicly, the whole point of the exercise having been to remove him from the scene for the sake of both the Sanhedrin and the Romans. He would therefore have to have travelled away from the Holy Land, where he would have been recognized. His selective reappearance to the disciples confirms this. But where would he have gone?

There is more than one claimant. A Christian sect in India believes itself to have been founded by Christ after his resurrection, maintaining that he travelled to India with Mary Magdalene and St Thomas. Other tales and legends have him travelling to Kashmir, or continuing his ministry in Ireland and other supposed destinations. There is, however, one place where he could quite credibly have sought sanctuary, where there was a Jewish and Arab heritage, where the Romans exercised enough control for there to be a stable infrastructure and where there would have been potential followers who could help him assimilate into the local society. That place was not so dissimilar from Palestine, in geography, climate and indigenous vegetation. That place was Gaul.

CHAPTER SIX

THE FRENCH CONNECTION

☆

The Synoptic Gospels are of no assistance to us in tracking the whereabouts and movements of Jesus after he showed himself to his disciples. The emphasis placed by them on the ascension would seem to tie the Gospel story up very neatly, removing the possibility of there being any mortal remains and fulfilling the Old Testament predictions that the Saviour would rise. However, in the context of our findings, as he would have been immediately recognizable even in rural Galilee, it is logical to assume that Jesus would have left the country and that plans would have been made to spirit him away as quickly and as quietly as possible.

France, or Gaul as the Romans termed it, was a vital part of the larger Roman Empire. The area of southern France which we now call Provence derives its name from the Roman 'Provincia Romana', the Roman province which formed an important land-trade route bordering the Mediterranean. The south-eastern part of the country around Narbonne, during the time of the Merovingians, was called 'Septimania' after the Roman Seventh Legion, which had been stationed there as early as 125 BCE to protect the vital trade route with Spain, many of its veterans staying on in the area.

The Mediterranean coastline of south-western France around Narbonne, in the heart of what is now the Languedoc-Roussillon region, was the first colony founded by the Romans in Gaul as early as 118 BCE, on the site of Narbo Martius, from which it derived its Roman name, Narbo. The most important Roman seaport in the western Mediterranean, it was also the principal Roman colony in Gaul until the rise of the capital of Lyon in the second century CE. At the time of Jesus Narbo held the largest documented Jewish population outside the Holy Land, totalling some ten per cent of its inhabitants, and was renowned for its tolerance not only of the Jews but also of the significant numbers of Arabs and North Africans for whom it was primarily an important trading centre and subsequently a colony. Indeed so cosmopolitan was the city that, in addition to a number of synagogues, it even boasted a Kabbalist school.

When, in 37 CE, Caligula succeeded Tiberius as Emperor, Herodias became increasingly jealous of her brother Agrippa's close links with the seat of power, a link far outstripping that of her husband Herod. Manipulative and scheming, Herodias persuaded her husband to denounce Agrippa to the Emperor, but Agrippa anticipated Herod's actions and levied charges against him. This open power struggle between the two key branches of the family came at a time when Herod himself had raised an armoury of some 70,000 weapons with a view to rebelling against the Roman yoke. This was also discovered by Agrippa, who had replaced Pilate as Procurator, and gave him further cause to condemn Herod before Caligula. Presented with such damning evidence, the Emperor found against Herod and banished him and his wife to Gaul, allowing Agrippa to add the tetrarchy of Galilee to his domains.

It is known that on arrival in France the couple set up home in a place called Lugdunum Convenarum, which for many years was generally accepted as being the city of Lyon.

However, the original Roman military settlement on the hilly site at the confluence of the rivers Rhône and Saône was only ever known as Lugdunum from the time of its establishment in 43 BCE and the correct location of Lugdunum Convenarum is in fact what is now the small village of St Bertrand de Comminges in the foothills of the Pyrenees. It is known that this was the place, at the time a centre of pilgrimage, where Herod died and was buried in 39 CE, and it is entirely possible that 'Comminges' is a translated derivation of 'Commagene', the area south of the Caspian sea, near Nimrud, which was the ancestral home of the Hasmonean line.

It would also seem that although Herod had been banished from his homeland and stripped of all his Roman offices of state,[1] his position as the titular King of the Jews was still respected enough for him to be allowed to take with him into exile the treasures of the Temple. These included the Dish of the Annunciation, a large dish of beaten and worked gold in which supplicants were anointed, and, perhaps more extraordinarily, the remains of the head of John the Baptist, who was revered by Herod. Although there can no proof for this contention, it is my belief, given the importance of St Bertrand de Comminges at the time and the fact that Herod had been stripped of personal wealth but not of his other holdings, that he would have taken the treasures with him.

The clues that the head may have remained under the guardianship of Herod come initially from the Bible, where it is explained that John's disciples took away the body of John the Baptist but no mention is made of his head. Given that the method of his demise was decapitation, it would be reasonable to assume that any description of the removal of John the Baptist might include the fact that his disciples took away not only his body but his head too.

It would not have been out of character for Herod to have

retained this grisly but important relic. As we know, he was appalled at the role he had played in the death of John, having been entranced by the man and his teachings. We also know that Herod, on hearing of the miracles being conducted by Jesus, believed that he was none other than John resurrected. It is also not too great a leap of the imagination to suppose that Herod would have been perfectly aware that John's untimely and gruesome death would make him a martyr of the growing Christian religion, especially given his role as the baptizer of Jesus, and that as such his mortal remains would take on a special significance in the eyes of those who were aware of the early origins of this faith. Given that this was actually the head of the martyr, the repository of the spirit, the importance would have been even greater, especially with John being, in Kabbalist terminology, the spiritual part of the brotherhood in which Jesus, the physical aspect, spread the word.

Herod and Herodias were not unique in their banishment from the Holy Land to Gaul; indeed the former's own brother, Archelaus, had found himself in Gaul some years before. The son and principal heir of Herod the Great, Archelaus was half Idumaean and half Samaritan and, like his father, was considered to be an alien oppressor by his Jewish subjects. Their repeated complaints against him led to his being tried in 6 CE in Rome, where he was unsuccessfully defended before the Emperor Augustus by the future emperor, Tiberius. As a result of the trial he was deprived of his throne and banished to Vienne, just south of modern-day Lyon. Nor was Archelaus alone as an unwilling political exile. As we saw earlier, Pontius Pilate is said to have been cast out from the inner sanctum of Roman power, to spend his last days in Vienne, like Archelaus before him. Pilate, however, was unable to rebuild his life after this wrench from power and privilege and died 'of his own hand'.[2]

These banishments, although not widely known, are well documented in the historical record. Conversely, the history of Mary Magdalene after the crucifixion is perhaps far better known through legend and oral traditions than in conventional histories. As with Jesus, the movements and whereabouts of Mary Magdalene are not reported in the New Testament once the story of the supposed crucifixion and resurrection has been told.

It is as if she suddenly disappears and is of no further importance to the authors and compilers of these texts; and indeed this absence may have been of major significance to those who were corrupting the facts in order to find easy images to spread. There is no report in the Bible of her death, and yet during her lifetime she is portrayed as one of Jesus's most loyal and favoured companions, her relationship with him being the cause of some resentment among the male disciples.

Mary Magdalene first appears in the New Testament in the Gospel of Luke as the woman 'out of whom went seven devils'[3] and is later described as 'a sinner'. However, Barbara Thiering, in her work *Jesus the Man*, states that the first actual reference to Mary in the New Testament is the story of how, as the daughter of Jairus, she was 'raised' in 17 CE. This 'raising' is taken to mean a symbolic raising from eternal darkness, an elevation to a position of status, which, according to Laurence Gardner's *Bloodline of the Holy Grail*, is similar in meaning to the term used today in Freemasonry rituals, and which, at the time of Mary, was conducted for boys at the age of twelve and for girls at fourteen. If correct, this would suggest that Mary was born in 3 CE, ten years after Jesus, who scholars now believe to have been born in March 7 BCE.

But for the most part Mary's early origins are as obscure as her life after the disappearance of Jesus from the records. It is said that she was the daughter of Syrus the 'Jairus', the chief priest who officiated at the great marble synagogue at Capernaum, and that her mother, Eucharia, was related to the Royal House of Israel, the Hasmoneans, who were the descendants of the Maccabees.[4] The name Magdalene or Magdala is thought to be derived from the Hebrew noun *migdal*, meaning tower, as in Micah iv:8, which mentions the 'Magdal-eder' or watchtower of the flock.[5] It is often claimed that Mary came from a wealthy background, as she follows Jesus and the disciples on their tours of the Holy Land while having neither visible means of support nor any husband. Some biblical scholars have used the theory that Mary was of independent means to explain the survival of Jesus's small sect, drawing the conclusion that it was Mary who effectively bankrolled them all.

The *Legenda Aurea* by Jacobus de Voraigne, Archbishop of Genoa in the thirteenth century, states that Mary Magdalene died in Aix in southern France and was buried there by the Bishop Maximus. Some of her remains were later taken to the French monastery at Vézelay, the church of which was named after her. According to the legend, the adoration of St Mary Magdalene at Vézelay was accompanied by many miracles and it is little wonder that such a widely worshipped saint was offered so many patronages. Indeed many towns in France claim her as their patron saint, Marseilles and Antun among them, but what is most interesting is that it is Provence which seems to be the heartland of a Magdalene cult.

Marseilles is the focus of many Magdalene legends which claim that it was the landing point for Mary after her flight from the Holy Land. There exist in the city today relics which purport to be the remains of her bones and which can be viewed in its museum. In St Maximin, to the east of Marseilles, there are also relics which are supposed to be the mortal remains of the Magdalene. They are said to have been found buried in the crypt of the church in 1279 by Charles II of

Anjou, Count of Provence, who on opening the fifth-century alabaster sarcophagus discovered not only her skeleton but also documents which explain the late dating of the coffin, stating that the body had been removed from its original repository and rehidden to protect it from the invading Saracens.

However, Marseilles is far from being the sole claimant to a Magdalene heritage. All along the south coast of France there are villages and towns which harbour almost more reverence for Mary than for Jesus himself, a veneration usually associated with a legend which claims some connection between her and the town or village in question. Many of these places claim, like Marseilles, to be the place where she first landed in France on arrival from the Holy Land or, like St Maximin, her final resting place. The validity of the legends and the claims for each in the wide range of localities in which they are based is both highly questionable and unverifiable. However, there are some places where the sheer number of claims and connections, coupled with the passion with which they are still held, leads one to think that there may be more to these stories than pure fabrication or desire to outdo neighbouring parishes or areas.

Nowhere is this more so than in and around Rennes-le-Château. The strange church in this equally extraordinary village, bizarrely decorated towards the end of the nineteenth century by its priest, Abbé Bérenger Saunière, is dedicated to Mary Magdalene and was consecrated to her as early as 1059. Along the valley at Rennes-les-Bains there is another connection. This pretty little village, nestling in a steep-sided valley, has been a popular destination since Roman times for those who come to bathe in the warm mineral springs from which it derives its name. But it has also become something of a Magdalene shrine as many deep-seated traditions tell of how Mary Magdalene also used to come to this spa resort to bathe when she lived 'not far away'.

The Gnostic Gospels are peculiar in their references to Mary Magdalene and their discovery has shed light on what is now considered to be a golden string of religious teaching by a small group of people who continued an alternative tradition to the teachings of conventional Christianity. Both Rennes-le-Château and Rennes-les-Bains are in the heartland of the Languedoc, the centre of Gnostic thought in Europe until the first half of the thirteenth century, when the terror of the Albigensian Crusade all but eradicated Gnostic thinking for ever. The Gnostics were a lone voice among eleventh- and twelfth-century religions as, far from reviling the Magdalene as a harlot (the view expressed with much vehemence by the expanding Roman Church), they hailed her and for a number of extremely valid reasons. After all it was Mary who was the first to witness the supposed resurrection, and it was the Gnostics alone who took the trouble to consider what this might have meant both in terms of the equality of man and woman before God and also in reference to any relationship that may have existed between her and Jesus. In the fourth-century Berlin Codex there is a fragment of the Gnostic 'Gospel of Mary' in which Mary rebukes Peter for being too dominant and in which it is stated that Jesus held her in especially high esteem. In the Gnostic 'Gospel of Philip' it is recorded that Jesus used to kiss Mary on the mouth, leading the disciples to question why Jesus loved her more than them and Jesus to answer enigmatically, 'Why do I not love you like her?', implying that Mary had seen the light while the others remained blind. Indeed the reference to Mary having 'seen the light' is an important one, for implicit in this phrase that we may use unthinkingly today is the very essence of Gnosticism. For the Gnostic, the 'Light' is the opposite of the 'Dark', and the dark is the physical world of man and Earth. The light for a Gnostic was the important aspect of life, the place where we come from, the essence of our being. It is not by accident that we today speak of spiritual 'enlightenment', the term being a direct legacy from the Gnostic tradition.

To read of Mary in this context has led many scholars to infer that she herself was a Gnostic, and from this fact, given her proximity to Jesus during his short period of teaching, it can read that the basis of his own teaching was highly Gnostic in character. Indeed the Gospel of Philip is interesting to us for another reason, for it is entirely unambiguous in describing the Magdalene's relationship with Jesus: 'There were three who always walked with the Lord: Mary his mother, his sister and Magdalene, who is called his companion. His sister, his mother and his companion were all called Mary. And the companion of the Saviour is Mary Magdalene.'

In his work *Mary Magdalene in the New Testament Gospels and Early Tradition*, Richard Atwood explores the identity of Mary Magdalene and its relationship with the reverence for her in southern France. He argues that in order for this tradition to have any historical accuracy it is necessary for Mary Magdalene to be the same woman as Mary of Bethany, who was the sister of Martha and Lazarus, and the unnamed 'sinful woman' who is mentioned in Luke vii. Atwood cites the example of the Latin church, which held that all three were in fact Mary Magdalene, and then goes on to explain that it was only as late as the end of the nineteenth century that the possibility that they were three different women became prevalent, and then by a vast majority of Protestant writers. Given his own conclusions, Atwood would appear to be backing the historical truth of Mary Magdalene's having resided in France; but he seems to be unable to commit himself fully to the notion and leaves its legitimacy open to question.

If the two Marys (the Magdalene and the sister of Lazarus) were the same, this might give grounds for Mary's financial independence. Indeed the possibility that Mary was a wealthy woman is alluded to in one of the tracts dealing with Mary's and her sister Martha's origins, which states: 'Martha, hostess to Lord Jesus Christ, was born into a royal family. Her Father's name was Syro and her Mother's Eucharia; the father came from Syria. Together with her sister by inheritance through their mother, Martha came into possession of three properties: the Castle Magdalene, Bethany and part of Jerusalem.'[6]

There are further legends which maintain that not only was Mary Magdalene living in this south-eastern corner of France, but that she actually preached there. In their book *The Templar Revelation*[7] Lynn Picknett and Clive Prince recount the tradition that Mary Magdalene came ashore from the Holy Land at what is now the town of Saintes-Maries-de-la-Mer in the Camargue region. The story tells that Mary preached throughout the region before becoming a hermit in a cave at Sainte Baume where she lived out her days, naked and covered only by her extremely abundant hair. As Picknett and Prince point out, there can be little truth in the story, and indeed even the Catholic guardian of the shrine admits that she was never there. However, they go on to state that Arles, the nearest town of any size, was once the centre of a major Isis cult and the region seems to have been home to any number of goddess-worshipping groups. The idea that Mary may have preached in the region does however have a degree of credibility as historians now agree that Christianity established a foothold in the Provence region during the first century CE and had she been either Gnostic herself or part of a Gnostic group, then the act of preaching would not have been barred to her as a woman in the way that it became within the Christian Church during the Middle Ages. Indeed the Gnostics showed very little misogyny, respecting the different strengths of women and men alike, their understanding of the duality of the human condition matching their acknowledgement of the other dualities of existence.

There is another intriguing aspect to worship and belief which is particularly prevalent in this region of France. In and around Marseilles and south-eastern France there are many statues which have become known as the Black Madonnas or the Black Virgins. These religious works show the Madonna and child image in the usual way except for the fact that the Madonna is depicted as having black skin. Nor is this phenomenon restricted purely to France. Picknett and Prince, in an analysis of Ean Begg's book *The Cult of the Black Virgin*,[8] show that these statues are to be found all over Europe from Poland to the United Kingdom, but that the highest concentration of them is to be seen in the south of France. They also explain that while these statues inspire large and passionate followings, they occur on a purely local scale and are not recognized or sanctioned by the mainstream Catholic Church. They go on to state that there is something 'not quite nice' about the Black Madonnas and cite a reference[9] which explains how, on 28 December 1952, when papers on the Black Virgins were presented to the American Academy for the Advancement of Science, every priest and nun present stood up and walked out of the room.

Indeed Begg's book cites many references where the local priests have denied any knowledge of the statue in what are known Black Madonna sites, some of them even claiming that the statue had disappeared. As Picknett and Prince point out, assertions that the Madonnas are black because they have spent so many years in smoke-filled churches, or because they were brought back by Crusaders from places where people were black-skinned, range from the ridiculous to the downright laughable.[10] However, they have established that there is a recurring link between the various Black Madonna sites and what are known to be the sites of ancient pagan worship. These encompass a whole range of goddesses from Diana to Cybele, both of whom have been depicted as being black-skinned. However, another classical goddess who was the basis of a cult which lasted well into Christian times was Isis. The mother of Horus, the sister of Nepythys and the consort of Osiris, the god of the underworld, she was also worshipped as a Holy Virgin. She was said to have possessed special gifts of magic and healing and was associated with the sea and the moon. The fact that Isis was worshipped as both a mother and a virgin appears not to have been a contradiction in the eyes of her followers as she was never hailed as a virgin mother in the way that Mary, the mother of Jesus, was. It is clear that the early Christians borrowed heavily from the iconography of Isis when formulating the images of the Virgin Mary, who, like Isis, is often depicted standing on a crescent moon or with stars in her hair or around her head. The most enduring image we have of the Virgin Mary, that of the Mother and Child, is also heavily redolent of the Isis cult, from where the Madonna and Child concept originates.

More pertinent still is the undeniable link between the cult of Mary Magdalene and that of the Black Madonnas. Ean Begg has isolated no fewer than fifty sites which are centres of Magdalene legend or worship which also have shrines to the Black Madonna. And of these a high proportion are based in the areas of Provence and the eastern Pyrenees.[11] The repetitions of this link range from the site of the black statue of St Sarah the Egyptian to be found in Saintes-Maries-de-la-Mer (where the Magdalene is said to have first stepped on French soil after her voyage from Palestine) and the Black Madonna in the crypt of the basilica of St Victor outside the underground chapel dedicated to Mary Magdalene in Marseilles, to the two churches in Aix-en-Provence, one the main church and the other consecrated to her, and both of which are close to one of the sites where she is supposed to have been buried. The range and depth of these coincidences and associations would seem to imply that there *is* some basis for the idea that Mary Magdalene lived and preached in southern France.

Most of the versions of her voyage from Palestine claim that she arrived on a rudderless and oarless boat, a motif which not only recurs in these tales but which was also picked up later in paintings and other works referring to this voyage. Once landed at Marseilles, it is usually told, Mary and her party could find no house in which to seek refuge and instead spent the night in what is usually referred to as the porch of a pagan temple. The next morning when the people assembled to sacrifice to their idols the tales recount that:

> And whan blyssyd Mawdelyn dede se
> Mych folk bidder comyn to sacryfyse
> to bere ydols, ryht anoon she
> wyth a plesaunth chere up dede ryse
> And wyth a feyr face in desert wyse
> she hem revokyd from hyr ydolatrye
> and preched hem cryst most stedefastlye.[12]

As Helen Meredith Garth[13] states, there are a wide number of references to this act of preaching by Mary in Marseilles, all of which agree on the beauty and the eloquence of the speaker. Indeed the story in its various guises usually continues with the arrival at the temple of the King and Queen of Marseilles, who came to offer sacrifices and to pray for a child, their sacrifices, according to Bokenham, being made up to the Goddess 'Dyane'. Mary remonstrates with the couple, forbidding them to make these oblations to false gods:

> & prechit bame be cristine fay
> for-bedand bame sadly ay
> til ydolis for mak sacrifice
> bat bame mycht helpe on na wise[14]

However, they pay no attention to her, and she has to resort to using two angels, sent down to her by Jesus. She changes clothes with one of them in order to appear to the royal couple as a radiant vision, thereby converting them to Christianity and at the same time procuring food and shelter for her and her companions. Despite her celestial clothing it takes three nights before the King takes notice of her and even then Mary has to use language which we rarely associate with any of the disciples, let alone the Magdalene:

> She appeared . . . with a frowning and angry visage . . . and said: 'Thou tyrant and member of thy father the devil, with that serpent thy wife . . . thou restest now enemy of the cross, which hast filled thy belly by gluttony, with divers manners of meats and sufferest to perish for hunger the holy saints of our Lord. Liest thou not in a palace wrapped with clothes of silk. And thou seest them without harbour, discomforted, and goest forth and takest no regards of them. Thou shalt not escape so ne depart without punishment, thou tyrant and felon because thou hast so long tarried.'[15]

This storm of abuse from Mary worked. The King had a change of heart and provided food and shelter for Mary and her party while they in return prayed for a child for the royal couple. After hearing Mary's preaching of Christianity the King asked her if she was able to justify her faith and on hearing her explanation he felt compelled to convert.

These works, redolent though they may be with the embellishments of the period, all share one important aspect in the way they tell their stories. They all accept the concept that the Magdalene was in France as a fact and use it as the basis for the differing tales that they tell.

There are, as suggested already, many sound reasons why anyone wanting to leave the Holy Land would make their way to Gaul. The relative safety and security of a country maintained by the Roman Empire, its geographical similarities to Palestine, especially in the south, the existence of Arab and Jewish enclaves in many of the large cities and its southern ports with their active centres of commerce, all make it attractive as a destination of refuge for those who were banished from their homelands, as were Herod and Pilate, or those who sought sanctuary from a possible backlash provoked by their personal association with a discredited preacher, as in Mary's case. Given her complete commitment to Jesus before the crucifixion, it is not unlikely that she would have been at risk after the event. As a woman known to be the companion of Christ, it would have been impossible for her to blend back into normal society after his supposed death at the hands of the state. Gaul therefore would have been a quite natural destination for her to flee to.

There could also be another explanation for Mary's arrival in France. If she would have been unable to re-enter normal society, even with the security of independent means behind her, then the same argument must hold even more strongly for the man who had been at the centre of events. The Gospels of the New Testament may be of no assistance to us when trying to determine what did happen to Jesus after the crucifixion, but other sources offer some surprising confirmation of what, to the Roman Church, is the ultimate heresy: Jesus's survival. The Gnostic Gospels and early heretical writings aside, the Koran is explicit in describing Jesus's life after the crucifixion, stating that Allah exalted Jesus over his enemies by saving him from the death on the cross and the plotting of his enemies to kill him and that Jesus later went on to die a natural death.

The Ahmadi, a sect of non-orthodox Muslims, hold that Jesus travelled to the East to look for the lost tribes of Israel and subsequently settled in Kashmir, and they rely on Western biblical scholarship and Eastern tradition to prove that this is the case. They accept, as all Muslims do, that Jesus was a prophet and interpret Matthew xxviii:38–40, where Jesus says that as with the prophet Jonah, who spent three days and three nights in the belly of a whale, so would the Son of Man be for three days and three nights in the heart of the Earth, as an indication that Jesus would enter the Earth alive and would come out alive – that is, *he would not die*. They go on to assert that as Jesus spent only three to six hours on the cross, he could not have been dead when taken down. They also quite correctly cite recorded cases where individuals survived the ordeal of the cross for one or even three days before being brought down and treated in time to be saved.

Their biblical scholarship has led them to quote that Pilate, who had been warned by God, through his wife, of Jesus's innocence, did his best to save him from death by ensuring that he remained on the cross for only a short time. Also that Jesus was saved, for in the Garden of Gethsemane he prayed tearfully to God to spare him from an accursed death: 'Anyone hanged on a tree is cursed by God' (Deuteronomy xxi:23). They even go so far as to claim that the herbs and unguents used in healing Jesus were in fact the famous ointment Marham-i-Isa or Ointment of Isa and Marham-i-Rasul or Ointment of the Prophet, which are well known in Eastern history and are described in oriental medicinal texts, including the world-renowned medieval *Canon of Avicenna* (Vol. V, Discourse No. 11 on Ointments and Plasters).[16] Further, the Ahmadis' claim that he settled in Kashmir, where he died of old age and was buried in the Khanyar district of the city of Srinagar, is, to them at least, supported by the existence of a tomb in the area which survives to this day.

Indeed there is a large canon of Ahmadi literature which supports these ideas but as most of the authors have interwoven strongly held religious beliefs with strands of historical fact, their works are not immune to criticism. But their persistence in questioning the commonly held version of Jesus's death finds echoes in the works of Western authors as wide-ranging as F. W. Farrar, William Hannah, Ernest Renan, Frederick Strauss and William Stroud, all of whom took the view that the central tenet of Christian religious teaching was based on a fallacious and distorted portrayal of the facts. More recently there have been a whole string of books, of which the most notable is perhaps that by Baigent, Leigh and Lincoln,[17] which have brought this and other theories on the early days of Christianity into focus and which in turn have catalysed an enormous amount of academic research.

This work has been largely enabled by the discoveries of the Dead Sea Scrolls and the Nag Hammadi Library, both of which continue to force us to reappraise the origins of the most successful religion of the past 2,000 years and as a result of which we have begun to see schisms within the Christian Church which seem to illustrate that both the Catholic and Anglican Churches are concerned by the information which is coming to light. One is reminded of the Bishop of Durham, who in the early 1990s courted controversy by saying that it was no longer necessary to believe in the Virgin Birth and the literal resurrection of Jesus in order to be a Christian.

But what does this all point to? I have established that there was a well-beaten path to Gaul which was trodden by the disgraced and discredited seeking refuge and sanctuary from the

Holy Land. I have further shown that there are many legends based on the supposed arrival in France of Mary Magdalene and that these traditions are deeply held, firmly rooted in the local and regional psyche of parts of the South of France and that there are few reasons why they may not be based in truth. Indeed there are many very sound reasons why they may be borne out of fact. I have also illustrated that the belief in Jesus's continued existence after the crucifixion is not only prevalent outside the formal teachings of the Church, but that in at least one case it forms the basis of a separate religion.

However, contrary to the specific belief of the Ahmadi, I feel sure that, far from seeking refuge and continuing to preach in Kashmir, Jesus would have done so somewhat closer to home, in the same part of southern France where the Magdalene is still venerated. It would quite possibly have fallen to Joseph of Arimathea to organize the escape plan, for he alone among those who would have been involved in concocting this act of stagecraft had the necessary funds, contacts and organizational ability.

I do not claim to be the progenitor of this claim. There are many who have written before who have voiced similar views. However, some of them have suggested that it was the dead body of Christ which was spirited away, or that he merely vanished into a life of anonymity. To my mind, however, given the circumstances of the whole crucifixion episode, the most logical action would have been to protect him from further persecution, and the best way to do that would have been to transport him to another country. France would almost certainly have been the preferred option.

There is one other major factor in the choice of destination. The weight of writing which suggests that Mary Magdalene was far more to Jesus than simply a disciple cannot be ignored. Indeed the concept that they were actually husband and wife has been in existence since the third century CE and in all probability before then. The *Pistis Sophia*, of 250 CE, a Coptic recast of an earlier document (mentioned on pp. 82–3), claims to carry the words of Jesus as he told the disciples a great many things about sin and salvation while living with them for eleven or twelve years *after* the Resurrection. And it makes clear the importance of Mary Magdalene, not only as one of the group of disciples, but as a partner of Jesus.

The Gnostic Gospel of Philip is even more explicit in its claim that Mary was none other than the sexual partner of Jesus, an assertion supported by the numerous references to brides and bridegrooms and unions between men and women with which the text is ripe.[18] As Picknett and Prince point out, even in the canonical Gospels Jesus frequently refers to himself as the 'bridegroom'.[19]

This aspect of Jesus's own personal life, so notable in its absence from the New Testament Gospels, is in accord with his role as a preacher. It is commonly accepted that he was a rabbi, a fact borne out by his display of knowledge to the elders in the Temple. However, as a preacher he would have been expected to be a married man, Mishnaic Law stating very clearly that unmarried men may not take on the role of teacher/rabbi. Indeed the idea that he would have spent his adulthood as a single man runs as contrary to the mores of the time as does the concept that Mary Magdalene could have followed him, even as a disciple, as either a single woman or the wife of another man. Neither of these options would have been acceptable in the context of devout Jewish faith or first-century social norms.

The idea that Jesus and Mary Magdalene were married in the modern sense of the word has found supporters both inside and outside the formal structure of Christian doctrine. Their relationship also has a deeper significance than that of human bonding, when one looks further at some of the more esoteric origins of the Christian faith.

We have established the links between Jesus and John the Baptist and the shown that early Christian chronicles marginalized not only John but also Mary Magdalene. However, it is known that John had a large following which survived his death and can be assumed to have been a 'church' in its own right. Indeed there is some evidence, presented in A. N. Wilson's book,[20] that such a church was not restricted to Palestine. As Wilson points out, the author of Acts lets slip that such a church existed until 50 CE. It was assumed that this following was subsumed into the early Christian Church, Paul having been quick to see, when encountering adherents in Ephesus, that such a church would have to be tempered to ensure the dominance of the followers of Jesus.

Another figure does, however, feature in early Christian writings, who may shed further light on the nature of the relationship between Jesus and Mary Magdalene. That person is Simon Magus. Traditionally reviled by Christians as 'the father of all heresies' and a black magician, he is perhaps the only person ever to have lived to have a sin named after him – simony, the act of trying to buy the Holy Spirit.

Simon Magus or 'the First Heretic', was deemed to be beyond redemption.[21] He was overtly Gnostic and, of course, the early Church regarded the Gnostics as heretics. What is known about him is that he came from the village of Gitta in Samaria in the first century CE, was the leader of the Magians of West Manasseh and was renowned for his skill as a magician, from which his title, Magus, is derived. Intriguingly, he was honoured as a God both by the Samaritans and in Rome, where he travelled during the reign of Claudius and where a statue was erected in his honour. His companion on his travels was a woman named Helen, said to have been a prostitute from the city of Tyre and whom he called Ennoia or First Thought, a name derived from the Gnostic belief that God's first thought had been female. As we have seen, the concept of the power of women was normal not only in pagan but also in early Christian traditions, from Isis and Diana to the Magdalene, who incurred the enmity of some of the male disciples. Indeed the power of many male prophets has been ascribed to their links with women and Simon Magus is no exception in this respect. Karl Luckert[22] traces Simon's concept of the *Ennoia* as embodied in Helen, directly back to Isis. There is another apocryphal text, written in about 185 CE, which describes Helen as being 'as black as an Ethiopian' and 'dancing in chains' before stating that 'The whole power of Simon and of his God is this woman who dances'.[23] Indeed no less a source than Irenaeus explains that Simon's priests 'lived immorally'[24] while Epiphanius goes even further and reveals that they practised sexual rites involving sex magic which used semen and menstrual blood.[25]

The impact that Simon Magus had and the life that he led were in many ways similar to those of Jesus. Although the Church Fathers were deeply concerned with the influence that Simon had, they were no fools and were aware that both his and Jesus's preaching were along parallel lines – so much so that they expended great energy in pointing out that the sources of their respective power were very different: Simon's through the magic sorcery that made him a black prophet; Jesus's through the purity and power of the Holy Spirit.

Even more disturbing to the progenitors of the early Christian faith would have been the knowledge that Simon Magus was a disciple of John the Baptist and was named by him as his successor. The evidence to support this claim originates from a third-century text called the *Clementine Recognitions*, which states: 'It was at Alexandria that Simon perfected his studies in magic, being an adherent of John, a Hemerobaptist, through whom he came to deal with religious doctrines. John was the forerunner of Jesus ... of all John's disciples, Simon was the favourite, but on the death of his master, he was absent in Alexandria, and so Dositheus, a co-disciple, was chosen head of the school.'[26]

When Simon returned from Alexandria he took over the leadership of John's Church from Dositheus, who in turn had a sect named after him which also worshipped John the Baptist and like Simon Magus's was in time either assimilated into mainstream Christianity or disbanded.

That there was a discernible link between Simon Magus and John the Baptist would have been enough for the early Church to have wished to find ways to discredit Simon. In their eyes John was the foundation stone of the teachings and power of Jesus and Jesus alone. Anyone else who could lay claim to an association with and, worse, acceptance by, the original Baptist, would have been viewed as deeply threatening. This may explain the zeal with which Simon was 'blackened' by the Church. That he had magical powers, learned from the ancient Egyptian traditions while at Alexandra, would have given his enemies more than enough material with which to do this, whereas the same skills when enacted by Jesus could be reported as miracles. The Church accused Simon of trying to steal the knowledge of the Christians, although as Picknett and Prince explain, such vehemence against him is no more than a tacit admission that his teachings were in fact compatible with those of Jesus and that the two protagonists were even part of the same movement. More revealing in this implication, given the knowledge we have from Epiphanius of the sexual rites practised by Simon and Helen, is the question it raises of whether or not Jesus and Mary Magdalene had the same type of relationship.

If so, this would help to explain both the persistent presence of the Magdalene in the accounts of the Synoptic Gospels and the antipathy directed towards her by Peter and others, as reported in the Gospel of Philip. According to Epiphanius, the Gnostics had a text called the *Great Questions of Mary* which purported to be the innermost secrets of the Jesus movement and which took the form of 'obscene' ceremonies.[27] As Picknett and Prince point out, there is enough evidence to suggest that, far from being the common prostitute that the New Testament portrays, Mary Magdalene was in fact a sexual initiatrix or priestess in the tradition of a temple prostitute or sacred servant, one whose function and power was derived from her ability to bestow upon men the gift of *horasis*, spiritual enlightenment through sexual intercourse.

If indeed this was the case, then her relationship with Jesus would have been far more profound than that of the modern concept of marriage alone. Further, it is virtually inconceivable that they would have gone into exile separated from each other.

But, given the number of traditions which assert that the Magdalene arrived in France, it seems odd that there are no such myths or legends which claim the same of Jesus. The answer to this must lie in the nature of his arrival. Having made good his escape from Palestine with the assistance of Joseph of Arimathea and ensured that his work would be continued through the preaching of the disciples, he would have either understood the necessity of keeping a low profile or had it impressed upon him by Joseph, who, if a deal had been struck to ensure Jesus's survival, would not have wanted to embarrass those who had made it possible. Gaul's religious landscape at that time would have been a mixture of Roman and pre-Roman paganism, with many sites associated with the veneration of Isis and Diana. Against such a background it would have been easy for Jesus to have remained to all intents and purposes a private citizen, leaving the spreading of the word of God to his wife and spiritual partner Mary Magdalene, the disciple he calls 'the Apostle of the Apostles'. It was, after all, the Magdalene who rallied the disciples after the crucifixion, and it was she who was not only the first woman but also the first person to see Jesus when he came out of the tomb.

One source makes the case that Jesus would easily have found passage across the Mediterranean on, for example, one of the many ships which plied their trade from the Holy Land, taking bricks and other cheap and easily made materials across the sea to Gaul. While Marseilles may have been the port at which they first arrived, it would have made a great deal of sense for Jesus and Mary to have moved swiftly on from there once they had adjusted to their new surroundings and made arrangements to find a new home. Even though Marseilles was a large and bustling metropolis, even in Roman times, it would have been quite possible for anyone arriving from the Holy Land, and therefore likely to have known about Jesus's works and subsequent demise, to have come across him and revealed his identity to the authorities or any other interested parties.

In my view, Narbonne would have made the ideal next stop on their journey. Like Marseilles, it was a port town with extremely active Jewish, Arab and North African communities into which they could have assimilated and felt at home. Unlike Marseilles, it is surrounded by a warren of myriad valleys and hills recalling the geography of their homeland. What is more, the Kabbalist school and synagogues at Narbonne would have provided a congregation for the teachings of Mary. Only a few miles away are the warm spas of Rennes-les-Bains, where Mary is reputed to have bathed. Certainly a tradition lived on there: in 1143 Peter the Venerable of Cluny condemned the Jews of Narbonne, who claimed to have had a King residing among them, while Theobald, a Cambridge monk, spoke of the 'chief Princes and Rabbis of the Jews who dwell in Spain [and] assemble together at Narbonne where the royal seed resides'.[28]

Living in Narbonne as husband and wife, Jesus and Mary Magdalene could well have brought up a family. This would have required the complicity of a few trusted individuals to ensure their safe protection, however, and perhaps such help was the last act of Joseph of Arimathea before he embarked on his own ministry. But the knowledge that among the olive groves and arid hills of the Languedoc resided the holy family of Jerusalem would have been the secret of all secrets and the natural focus of a new, protective and growing religion.

The 'mystery' surrounding the nearby village of Rennes-le-Château came spectacularly to public attention following the work done by Michael Baigent, Richard Leigh and Henry Lincoln. Having got this far along the trail and started to understand what were to me incontrovertible suggestions in the paintings I had been examining, the peculiar rise in fortunes of Rennes-le-Château's rural priest that these pictures hint at took on a new significance. I became increasingly certain that there was a connection between the codes in the paintings and the secrets of this village and its surrounds.

CHAPTER SEVEN

A VILLAGE, A MYSTERY AND A
MEROVINGIAN KING

☆

In 1886, in the tiny village of Rennes-le-Château, some eighty kilometres south-west of Narbonne, the local priest, Abbé Bérenger Saunière, embarked on a series of renovations on his church. During the course of the building work four parchments were found concealed in a baluster. Two of these purported to be genealogies of the Merovingian dynasty, the bloodline of the first kings of a united Frankish Kingdom, the precursor of modern France. The other two seemed to be Latin extracts from the New Testaments, supposedly composed by Abbé Antoine Bigou, a predecessor of Saunière. On close inspection these latter two parchments appeared to conceal a variety of codes, and hidden within them a secret geometry.

Saunière saw these codes, took the documents and his discovery to his bishop in Carcassonne and was immediately sent to the ecclesiastical authorities in Paris. What ensued formed the basis for the modern-day investigations into what became something of a mystery. For Saunière, hitherto a poor priest, suddenly and inexplicably became extremely wealthy.

He built a house, the Villa Bethanie, complete with a tower, formal gardens, orangery and zoological garden. He finished the renovation of the church and redecorated it in a unique and bizarre fashion. While the walls are adorned with the expected Stations of the Cross, they depart from the usual Catholic style and not only are they painted in the most lurid of colours but they also bear inconsistencies with the Scriptural accounts. In one there is a child dressed in Scottish tartan, another depicts Jesus's body being taken into the tomb, but at night. Just inside the door is a hideous statue of Pan – or the Devil – bearing the bowl of holy water. And the lintel above the church doorway carries the decidedly strange Latin inscription *'Terribilis est locus iste'* ('This place is terrible').

Saunière also received many significant visitors and seems to have collected some important friends, among them the Archduke Johann von Habsburg, with whom he had opened a number of bank accounts and to whom he made over, for no apparent reason, substantial sums of money. When Saunière was called to account for his sudden wealth he defiantly offered no explanation. His bishop accused him of simony – selling masses – (none other than the sin named after Simon Magus) and a local tribunal suspended him. However, Saunière appealed to the Vatican. Curiously the Bishop was overruled and Saunière was exonerated.

When, on 17 January 1917, Saunière suffered a stroke, a neighbouring parish priest was summoned to hear his final confession and to administer the last rites. On hearing Saunière, the priest is said to have left the room 'visibly shaken' and refused to administer unction. On 22 January Saunière died unshriven and his body was placed on a chair on the terrace of his tower, dressed in an ornate robe edged with scarlet tassels. As the mourners, most of whom were mysteriously unidentified, filed past to pay their last respects, many of them took tassels from the dead priest's robe, a ceremony which has never been explained and which mystified the residents of the village.

At the reading of Saunière's will, and to everyone's aston-
ishment, it became apparent that he had died penniless, leaving
his entire estate to his housekeeper, Marie Denarnaud, who had
shared the house and life of her master for thirty-two years. She
is alleged to have told villagers: 'the people around here walk
on gold without knowing it ... With what the Monsieur has
left we could feed Rennes for over a hundred years and there
would still be enough left over ... one day I will tell you a
secret which will make of you a rich man – very, very rich.'

When she came to sell the house she promised the purchaser, Monsieur Noel Corbu, that she would confide in him
before her death, telling him a secret that would make him not
only rich but also powerful. However, on 29 January 1953
Marie Denarnaud, like her master before her, suffered a sudden
and extreme stroke which left her incapable of speech and she
died shortly after, taking her secret to the grave.

Since that time the area around Rennes-le-Château has
been besieged with treasure hunters. The hill on which the
village stands has become the object of much digging and
tunnelling by those who think the parchments are some form
of treasure map. But the parchments themselves are also the
source of some mystery, as the whereabouts of the originals has
never been disclosed. In the 1960s an organization called the
Prieuré de Sion – the Priory of Sion – allegedly leaked two of
them bearing the Latin texts and it is these illustrations that
have been used by many authors in this field. Another account,
however, has it that the originals are now in the archives of
the Knights of Malta.

The story, outlined above in only the broadest terms, might
have been of no more than local interest were it not for the
publication in 1967 of a book by Gérard de Sede, *L'Or de
Rennes*. De Sede has published many works which, on first
viewing, seem to treat disparate subjects. The Cathars, the

Knights Templar, the Merovingian dynasty, Bérenger Saunière, the Rose-Croix and Rennes-le-Château have all come under his scrutiny and it was he who first intimated that the 'treasure' of Rennes-le-Château may be of a spiritual rather than a financial nature. Some authors have concluded that he is a form of mouthpiece for an organization that is aware of the secrets that are held within the parchments. In fact links have been confirmed between de Sede and the main protagonist for the Prieuré de Sion, which, historically called the Ordre de Sion, is frequently linked with the formation of the Order of the Poor Knights of Christ and the Temple of Solomon – more commonly known as the Knights Templar.

What was it that Saunière actually found? Was it enough to scare the Roman Church into either buying his silence or did he blackmail them by threatening to reveal what he knew? Much work has been done by a number of authors in an attempt to decipher the parchments and discover the secret that led to the riches gained by Saunière. Some have worked hard to establish their origin and yet to this day there are still questions over their validity. Henry Lincoln[1] states that their origin is confusing and questions whether Saunière actually found them by accident while restoring the church, or simply found them because he was looking for them. Pierre de Plantard, the wilfully mysterious Grand Master of the Priory of Sion, is on record[2] as stating that they were 'cooked up' by a Philippe de Chérisey during the 1950s. However, he subsequently altered this to say, 'de Chérisey's confections were closely based upon very good originals'. De Chérisey himself has neither confirmed nor denied any attempt to mislead, remaining remarkably silent on any views he may have as to the parchments' authenticity.

Contained within the script of the parchments are a number of curious anomalies about which much has been made in the past. One particularly possible interpretation of their hidden message jumps out at me, however. It is a rendering of a code which leads us on a very different path from those who have gone before and which implies that their author, whether ancient or modern, had some awareness of certain unrevealed secrets.

The accepted understanding of the codes is that first revealed by Baigent, Leigh, and Lincoln.[3] Of the four parchments that Saunière discovered in 1891 it is those which bear the texts which are of interest to us. On one of these is a Latin text which appears to be an amalgamation of several different Gospel versions of the tale of Jesus walking through the fields with disciples where 'they did rub the ears of the corn and did eat'. Even on first viewing there are several curious aspects to the way in which the text is physically presented. The lines are of uneven length and appear to have no logic, some ending in the middle of a word which is then continued on the next line. There are the curious designs at the top-left and bottom right-hand sides of the page, together with the final two words '*solis sacerdotibus*', or 'only for the priesthood'. And then there are the letters in the text which on closer inspection are slightly raised above the lines in which they are contained. These letters are distributed in no apparent pattern, but when isolated read as follows:

ADAGOBERTIIROIETASIONESTCETRESORETILESTLAMORT.

Previous authors have asserted that, when broken down into its constituent words, this forms the sentence:

A DAGOBERT II ROI ET A SION EST CE TRESOR ET IL EST
LA MORT.

This translates as:

'This treasure belongs to Dagobert II King and to Sion and he is there dead.'[4]

They have then continued, on this basis, to conclude that the Merovingian king Dagobert II was in some way connected with the mystery. In part this theory has been borne out by the existence of the other two parchments, which are genealogies of the Merovingian dynasty.

The Merovingians, often called the 'Long-Haired Kings' took their name from King Merovee, who ascended the throne in 447 CE on the death of his father, King Clodion. In doing so he sowed the seeds of a line of dynastic nobility that was to rule over the early Frankish kingdoms until 750 CE. It has to be remembered that Gaul after the departure of the Romans around 450 CE was not the homogeneous, centrally governed France that we know today, but was instead a collection of fiefdoms and administrative areas with extremely flexible boundaries and borders. Indeed so confused is the general picture of land ownership during Merovingian times that there is no clear evidence of the full extent of land owned by any of the various kings. Many of the Frankish monarchs conferred land on their supporters and followers in return for military or political favours and, as a result, the fluidity of the land pool makes the overall picture highly confused.

What is known is that the early Merovingian kings held many estates and palaces which had been taken over from the Imperial Roman landholdings and were run on their behalf by the *comités* of the palace, agents, referendaries, notaries and so on.[5] Indeed, much as Britain's royal family today has palaces around the country, it was usual for the king to have at least two centres of power.

Merovee was succeeded by Childeric I, who, although 'valiant and ingenious'[6] was such a brutal womanizer that the

Franks expelled him to what is now Germany, where he was received by the King of Thuringia. In his place, the Franks elected Aegidius (or Gillon), a commander of the remaining Roman militia. However, Childeric had left behind his main supporter, Guyeman, who ingratiated himself into the confidences of Aegidius to the extent that he was able to advise him to load the people with taxes. This abuse of the population, directed through the advice of Guyeman at those branches of the nobility and people who were Childeric's enemies, induced the banishment of Aegidius and prepared the ground for the king's return. The chronicles tell us that Guyeman then sent half of a coin to Childeric, the prearranged signal that all was safe for his return. On his restoration, Childeric brought with him the wife of the King of Thuringia, whom he then married (apparently with no regard for her existing marriage) and with her had a child, Clovis. Childeric advanced his territories as far as the Loire and according to some accounts is said to have taken possession of Paris. However, as the Romans were still in control of Soissons, north-east of Paris, there is considerable doubt about the validity of this claim.

On Childeric's death at Tournai, Clovis, aged only fifteen, assumed the throne. He was a warrior king who, in his battles with King Alaric of the Visigoths and against the Thuringians, added greatly to the lands that the Franks controlled and laid the foundations of much of the extended Frankish kingdom. Clovis[7] is also known to any student of French history as the first Christian King of France. His wife Clotilda, who was the niece of Gondebaud, King of Burgundy, had taken on the religion of the Church of Rome partly in defiance of her uncle, who was an Arian[8] and who had murdered her father. Clovis had resisted her attempts to convert him, but he had ceded to her when she had expressed her desire to baptize their first child, Ingomer. Sadly, the child died soon after, strengthening

Clovis's anti-Christian resolve. However, on the birth of their second child, Chlodomer, Clotilda persuaded Clovis that the boy should be baptized, a testament to her religious conviction. When, in 496 CE, Gaul was invaded by a huge force of Alemanni, Clovis mustered a large army and just west of what is now Cologne a battle took place. The Germanic Alemanni were formidable opponents and soon it looked as though the fields of Tolbiacum were to be the site of a Gallic defeat. However, legend has it that Clovis invoked the name of his wife's god, an interesting choice for a royal whose beliefs were more of the Thor, Odin and Frieda persuasion, saying: 'O God of Clotilda, if thou will give me this victory, I promise to thee that I will embrace the Christian religion and that I will bring over to it all my people.'[9]

It appears that the king of the Alemanni then fell in battle, which probably had as much to do with their poor tactics as the sudden conversion of Clovis. However, Clovis remained as good as his word and on his return to his wife was baptized into the Christian faith by St Remigius, the Bishop of Rheims.[10] Later in his life Clovis defended a formidable battle against King Theodoric of Italy, who was the father-in-law of the Visigothic king Alaric. Alaric is said to have been responsible for the sacking of Rome in 410 CE and to have carried off as plunder the remaining treasures of Solomon's Temple, including, it is thought, the menorah, the seven-branched candlestick so important to the Jewish peoples. He was killed by Clovis near Poitiers, and Theodoric intended to avenge his son-in-law's death. He marched an army into Gallia Narbonensis, formed by the regions we now know as Provence, Savoie and the Languedoc, and routed Clovis, forcing him to retreat to the north and leaving the southern part of Gaul under Visigothic control.

Clovis's adoption of the Christian faith began a period

which saw the Merovingians strengthened enormously. Through the subsequent reigns of Chilperic, Clotaire II, Dagobert I, Clovis II and their successors, the hitherto divided Frankish kingdoms of Neustria, Austrasia and Burgundy became a more formally and centrally ruled kingdom, and among the first of the European powers to dovetail the existence of Church and State.[11]

Relatively little is documented about the life or reign of Dagobert II. The main chronicles of the period, the *Liber Historiae Francorum* and the *Chronicles* of Fredegar, have little to say about him. Almost all of any import that we know of him originates from the *Life of Wilfrid* of York,[12] written by the Ripon monk Eddius Stephanus in the second decade of the eighth century. Where authors make reference to him[13] they tend towards over-romanticized accounts of his life.

Dagobert II was born in 651 as the heir to the kingdom of Austrasia. However, on his father's death in 656, the young prince was kidnapped by Grimoald, the Mayor of the Palace, who then engineered his own son Childebert's placement on the throne, claiming that this had been the wish of the dead king, Sigisbert III, Dagobert's father. It appears that the plan had been to kill the young prince. However, Grimoald, lacking the stomach for regicide, instead gave charge of the boy to Dido, Bishop of Poitiers, who exiled him to the Irish monastery of Slane.[14] Before his exile the boy had been tonsured by Grimoald in preparation for his religious instruction, a gesture of utter contempt towards a rightful heir of the 'Long-Haired Kings'. During this time the Celtic Church of Ireland was separated from the Roman Church, refusing to accept its authority. Either while in Ireland or, according to some authors, during a sojourn in York, where he established a residence, Dagobert II formed a friendship with the future saint Wilfrid, who was bishop of the city.[15] Wilfrid is perhaps best remembered for his bringing together the Celtic and Roman Churches at the Council of Whitby in 664 and it may have been his wish to see the potential future monarch of France firmly indoctrinated in the Christian faith so as to consolidate the by now wavering congregation that had been founded by Clovis 150 years before.[16]

Ireland was by no means a small backwater of Europe, cut off from the great changes that were happening both on the mainland and across the Irish Sea. Something of a religious and commercial hub, it had also become a repository for early religious tracts and other documents that were in danger of being destroyed as the Roman Church in mainland Europe gained enough power to dictate what the prescribed teachings should be. There is evidence that during this time both Christian and Judaic apocrypha, together with Nazorean, Nestorian, Gnostic and Manichaean texts, were held within the many monasteries to be found around the Irish countryside. There is also evidence that the *Book of Cerne*, the ninth-century English collection of Roman and Celtic prayers, devotions and Gospel Passion extracts, bound with later material which relates to Cerne Abbas in Dorset, England and part of which is derived from the Nag Hammadi scrolls, found its way here.[17] Ireland was a centre of learning between the early fifth and late seventh centuries, and there is comprehensive evidence that it was also linked by trade with Spain, North Africa and even with the Eastern Mediterranean. Some authors assert that there was a Christian tradition in Ireland as early as 200 CE, but the first real evidence shows that it was not until the early fifth century that Christianity really had a foothold here when Palladius became Ireland's first bishop in 431 CE. It is known that Irish monks were visitors to Egypt, bringing back with them not only travel journals which describe the pyramids, but also religious ideas and concepts that have more in common with the ancients than with the Pauline orthodoxy that the Church was disseminating. The Celtic Church was also influenced by the even more heretical traditions of earlier and more eastern beliefs, among them those of Syria and Mesopotamia. The heresy of the Celtic Church went even further, however.

One aspect of the teachings of the Celtic Church, perhaps more than any other, set it against the Church of Rome. At this time Rome had sidelined, almost to the point of avoidance, not only any reference to the Old Testament, but also, more crucially, adherence to the ancient Mosaic Law. The Celtic Church, however, still adhered to aspects of this tradition. Usury was forbidden, the Judaic Sabbath was observed, Passover was celebrated and animals used for food were killed in accordance with the Judaic requirements. Further, many documents of the Celtic Church include references and excerpts from Judaic books and texts which had long been banned by Rome. When St Patrick consecrated a new church he is said to have left not only copies of the Gospels but also of the Mosaic Law.[18]

These supposedly heretical leanings of what appears to be a free-thinking (St Patrick himself was no proponent of the Virgin Birth) Church with its own strong traditions, came to end with the Synod of Whitby in 664, which saw the Celtic Church dissolved and subsumed into the Roman. This was a relatively peaceful transition, the Roman Church being careful not to openly brand the Irish Church as heretical for fear of alienating its members completely.

It was in this environment that Dagobert II gained his education until, in 674,[19] he returned to his native Austrasia to be installed as king. It should be pointed out here that there is some debate not only as to the exact length of Dagobert II's reign but also as to whether he reigned once or had two separate and distinct periods of kingship.[20] What we do know is that during his short period of power Dagobert II made many enemies, including the Church and local magnates. He was a king who was not prepared to do as his bishops wished and who would make his own way without the counsel of his *seniores*.[21] Indeed his relationship with his bishops and the Church in general was so poor that it put even the life of Wilfrid in danger. When Wilfrid was passing through Austrasia *en route* to Rome in 679, Dagobert II offered him the see of Strasbourg out of gratitude for his youthful protection. Wilfrid declined the offer and continued to Rome. A year later, on his return, he was intercepted by the supporters of Ebroin, a Neustrian mayor and one of Dagobert's greatest enemies, who revealed that Dagobert had been murdered because of his oppressive government. Wilfrid himself was held responsible for the tyrant's rule and was nearly killed as a result.[22]

One of the main reasons why Dagobert II's reign was not popular was his propensity for raising taxes against the people and despoiling the cities of Austrasia. Some have argued that he was aware of the resistance to his rule and that he pulled down city walls in order to prevent them from becoming centres of opposition. It was the strength of feeling among his enemies that appears to have been the cause of his death in 679, near his royal palace at Stenay in the Ardennes. While out hunting in the forests near the palace, he evidently lay down to rest at the foot of a tree near a stream. While he slept one of his household (in some renditions of the story it is his godson), acting under the orders of Pépin, Mayor of the Palace (effectively, First Minister), crept up to him and killed him with a lance though the eye.

What then happens seems rather curious. After his death he was buried first in the Royal Chapel of St Rémy at Stenay, then, nearly two centuries later in 872, he was canonized and moved to a new church that was named the Church of St Dagobert. Even his remains became objects of reverence and although the church was destroyed and the relics scattered throughout France during the French Revolution, there is an incised skull at the convent in Mons that is said to be his.

In a collection of documents lodged in the Bibliothèque Nationale in France called the *Dossiers secrets d'Henri Lobineau*,[23] there is what purports to be evidence that Dagobert II had been married to a Celtic wife called Mathilde. When she died giving birth to their third daughter and on Dagobert's return to France, these documents claim, he took a second wife, Giselle de Razès. It is further asserted by this work that Giselle de Razès was the daughter of the Count of Razès and that the marriage was celebrated at Giselle's residence at Rhedae, Rhedae being one of the names by which Rennes-le-Château was known in antiquity, and that Dagobert lived there for a period until he was able to return to Austrasia and take up his position of king. It is also argued that Giselle de Razès was the niece of one of the Visigothic kings who at the time were in control of the region called Septimania, which extended west of the River Rhône at Marseilles down to the Pyrenees.

This is the accepted link between Dagobert II and the Rennes-le-Château mystery. Further, it ties in with the theory that the whole mystery centres on the existence, through the Merovingians, of a bloodline which can be traced from Jesus Christ through to the present day. But in the course of my research I have found no links between Dagobert II and the village of Rennes-le-Château.

Let us return to the meaning of the coded message in the parchment. It appears that, when breaking the line of letters into its constituent words, another possibility has been overlooked – and one which might have far greater bearing on determining the meaning of this conundrum. During my research into the existence of Dagobert II, it soon became apparent that there was not only a Dagobert I but also a

Dagobert III. A brief amount of time reading the archaic English, Latin and French texts about these three kings reveals that if little is known about Dagobert II, then even less is written about Dagobert III. By comparison, the amount that is known and documented about the life of Dagobert I is relatively large.

An alternative reading of the line of letters reveals that:

A DAGOBERTI I ROI ET A SION EST CE TRESOR ET IL EST LA MORT. In archaic French, in its Latinized form, the name Dagobert is Dagoberti and therefore the king who is of interest is Dagobert I. So the line reads:

To Dagobert I King and to Sion is this treasure and he [or it] is there dead.

Or alternatively:

To Dagobert I King and to Sion is this treasure and it is death.

The obvious implication of this new interpretation is that the supposed treasure of Rennes-le-Château is not only connected in some way with Sion and related to death, but also belongs to King Dagobert I. But does the known history of this king shed light on the mystery?

King Chlothar II, Dagobert I's father, is considered by nearly all writers on the Frankish kings to be the founding father of a near-united France. The sixty years prior to his reign were troubled times for the kingdoms of Austrasia, Neustria and Burgundy and it was Chlothar who was first able to restore an element of stability not only to the various kingdoms and fiefdoms but also to the royal politics of the Merovingian line. Even so, Chlothar's power was distinctly limited as each of these three semi–independent regions had its own laws and was governed by a string of local landowners and magnates who took it in turn to be Mayor of the Palace. However, the mayoralty was answerable to the king and peace largely prevailed. Indeed it was not since the reign of Clovis I that a monarch had had the legitimacy of the title 'King of the Franks', although some had claimed this title. Chlothar's rise to fortune began with his kingship of Soissons in 584, after which he became King of Neustria in 592 and of Austrasia in 613. It was at this point that Chlothar embarked on a new beginning for the Merovingian monarchy after the appalling civil wars that had raged across the country and resulted in terrible deprivation. The Edict of Paris of 613 is perhaps the best-known document expressing this. Popularly thought of as the 'French Magna Carta', it combines a pious expression of Chlothar's wish for law and order with a confirmation of his resolve to continue the taxation policies of his forebears.[24] This edict also deals with the monarchy's relationship with the Church. It is clear from the edict that Chlothar upheld the king's right to appoint the bishopric and the historical record shows that he used this to great advantage. For not only were local magnates involved in the selection and appointment of local judges – the main means by which Chlothar maintained the peace that he had created – but bishops also had a large role in this selection procedure. Further, Chlothar cleverly endeavoured to spread his ideas among the aristocracy by attracting their youth to his court for their education. This cannot have been difficult. For any family to have a member so closely connected with the seat of power would have proved both a useful short-term asset and an excellent investment for the family's future. The result of this court policy can be seen clearly in the mid-seventh century, when a group of young men who had been educated in the royal household became variously the Bishops of Cahors, Rouen, Noyon and Bordeaux and remained active not only in preserving their old friendships but also in protecting royal interests.[25]

Born in 605, it was in this environment that Dagobert I

grew up, amidst learned debate and a level of education which, along with the general environment of peace, was rare in the rest of Europe at the time. Indeed there is much evidence to show that the kings were literate at this time and indeed that some were capable of writing poetry[26] and discussing the finer aspects of theology. The signatures of many of the seventh-century kings survive on charters made during their reigns. These charters also reveal that the major court scribes had a mastery of an extremely complicated form of early shorthand. Known as Tironian notes, after Cicero's secretary Tiro, this shorthand system remains today one of the chief methods of authenticating documents of the period.[27]

In 622 Chlothar created a sub-kingdom for his son Dagobert, which was in effect a reduced part of Austrasia. It did not include the lands which lay to the west of the Vosges and this seems to have become a source of some conflict between father and son.[28] Indeed there is much evidence to show that magnates and bishops alike were frequently called upon to arbitrate in squabbles between Chlothar and Dagobert. However, this was to be Dagobert's first reign and he took up his position, aided and advised by Pepin, under whose influence he was to remain until Chlothar's death. His reign over Austrasia was by all accounts a good one. Dagobert appears to have discharged his duties with an even hand and was well disposed to both the people and the Church. Of a number of stories which illustrate his relations with the Church, one recounts that one day while hunting – he had inherited his father's keen taste for the chase – Dagobert was pursuing a deer near a little hamlet in which some one hundred years earlier St Geneviève had erected a chapel. In this chapel lay the mortal remains of St Denis and two other martyrs. Dagobert's hounds drove the deer through the village, forcing it to seek refuge in the chapel. Some years later, having incurred the wrath of his father, Dagobert is said to have returned to the chapel and spent the night there. While asleep he had a vision of the three martyrs which inspired him to improve and extend the building, reburying their remains under a jewelled cross and dedicating the building to St Denis.

On the death of Chlothar II in 628, Dagobert succeeded to the throne of the Franks and in doing so became overall king, but not without difficulty. Dagobert's mother, generally regarded to be Queen Berthetrude[29] and who was of noble Burgundian descent,[30] died during Dagobert's childhood and after her death Chlothar remarried, this time a woman called Sichild by whom he had another son, Charibert. One of Dagobert's first wives was Gomatrudes, Sichild's sister, a marriage undertaken at the behest of his father, who seemed to be attempting to align himself with her family. On the death of Chlothar a bid for the throne was made on behalf of Charibert by his uncle, Brodulf, a brother of Sichild, who had been involved in many political conflicts during Chlothar's last years. Although this claim for power failed, Dagobert did later grant Aquitaine to his half-brother. Shortly after, Dagobert arranged for the assassination of Brodulf and before long discarded Gomatrude for one Nantechilde. Indeed from most accounts it would appear that Dagobert spent the early months of his reign unravelling himself from the family ties which Chlothar had forced upon him. When Charibert died in mysterious circumstances, in 632, some even held that Dagobert and his supporters were responsible for his death.[31]

Even though there was a relative level of peace within the Frankish Kingdom, the Visigoths had control of the south-western region of Septimania and there were constant skirmishes over disputed territory and boundaries. To the north-east the Thuringians and Frisians were frequently under attack from the Wends. But Dagobert is known to have been in control of Bavaria, south of Thuringia, during his reign and there are records which indicate that he settled a group of Bulgarians there before having them executed. He was also implementary in the writing of the *Lex Baiwariorum*, an early charter outlining the laws of the Bavarian region. Saxony was also subject to Merovingian influence, but during Dagobert's reign as sub-king in Austrasia, there was a Saxon rebellion, and the involvement of his father Chlothar to save him later became the subject of verse said to have been sung by women in the ninth century.[32] Dagobert also had rule over the Bretons through a Frankish overlord and it is known that in 636 King Judicael, the last independent ruler of Brittany, who was to eventually retire to the cloister, came to Dagobert's court to pay obeisance, as did the Gascons a year later.[33] Indeed, when the Gascons came they were headed by their duke, Aighyna. *En route* to Clichy, where Dagobert was installed, they were apparently overcome with fear of the King and sought refuge at St Denis.

Dagobert I is popularly regarded as the last of the Merovingians to have dominated the political landscape. In contrast, those who came after him, including Dagobert II, became known as the 'Rois Fainéants', the 'do-nothing Kings'. It is from the accounts of a particular international foray by Dagobert, however, that our picture of him takes on particular relevance. During a battle against the Visigoths, Dagobert was asked to support Sisenant against the Visigothic King Sumtilla.[34] For raising an army that could assist in overthrowing Sumtilla, Dagobert was promised a gold dish weighing 500 pounds which was part of the treasure of the Goths. This dish had been given to their king, Thorismund, by the Roman military commander and consul Aetius for assistance in defeating the Huns at the battle of the Catalaunian Fields in 451 and was known to be of great importance to the Visigoths, not only for its undoubted financial value, but also for the mystical connections it was deemed to have. After the battle, which successfully seized the Visigothic throne for Sisenant, the Goths objected to this national treasure being handed over and Dagobert negotiated to receive 200,000 solidi in its place. (Another story regarding a large golden dish recounts that Aetius gave such a trophy to his commander, Magorian, having received it as part of the treasure which Alaric had gained from the sacking of Rome.)

A solidus, traditionally weighing 24 *siliquae* (4.55 grams) during the Roman period, had been changed around 575 to become a lighter coin, weighing 21 *siliquae* (3.89 grams). This, the *solidus gallicus*, was generally denoted by the appearance of XXI on it to signify the new weight and had a gold content that ranged from eighty-five per cent to more than ninety per cent, depending on where and by whom it was minted. Coins from Provence usually contained more gold than those from elsewhere. This enormous amount of money helped Dagobert to become personally richer than most of the other Merovingian monarchs. Indeed this one incident has been cited by numismatists as being solely responsible for a marked improvement in the precious-metal content of coinage of the period. It also seems to have fuelled in Dagobert the desire to accumulate even greater wealth.

It is during this period that there is a marked change in the manner in which the activities of Dagobert are reported, even by those who are considered to be authors of the most favourable accounts. It is told that he moved his seat of power to Paris and then embarked on a period of incredible personal excess, surrounding himself with wives and mistresses, forgetting the rule of justice on which his reputation had been built and generally exhibiting a 'total collapse of morals'.[35] What is also intriguing is that he is frequently reported as robbing churches.

For a king who had spent the early years of his life power-broking with the Church in general and endowing generous gifts to one church in particular, this would appear to be a most extraordinary turnaround.

Perhaps there is a certain train of events which can help to explain this. In order to take his army to support Sisenant, Dagobert would almost certainly have chosen the most direct route towards the Pyrenees. This would have been the pilgrim road from the north that passed by the town of Rhedae, or Rennes-le-Château as we know it today, and on to Spain. At the time of Dagobert, what is now a small hill-top village was supposedly a much larger conurbation with a population thought to rival that of Carcassonne. Originally a Stone Age site, it had subsequently taken its name of Rhedae from one of the Celtic Tectosage tribes who had settled there and who regarded it as a sacred place. It was the Romans who drove these Celts out and who extended its importance, the area becoming a thriving Roman community owing in part to the extensive local mining activities and the therapeutic hot springs along the valley at Rennes-les-Bains. The Romans also regarded it as a sacred place and there is archaeological evidence of pagan temples. They were in turn driven out by the Visigoths as they proceeded westwards after sacking Rome and it appears that the town became one of their strongholds. The Visigoths themselves were ousted by the Franks, only to return to the safety of its walls as a defeated population on the run from the Saracen invasion that was sweeping up from North Africa and through Spain.[36]

In passing through Rennes-le-Château Dagobert would have become aware of its rich history, both as a sacred place and as a supposed repository of Visigothic and other treasures. Arguments have even been put forward that the spoils of the sacking of Rome in 410 by the Visigoth leader Alaric the Great had found their way to Rennes-le-Château and its surrounding area. With Dagobert's keen interest in portable wealth, he would have been well disposed to anyone who could lead him to buried hoards of Roman and Visigothic coins and jewellery. Further, given that the area was riddled with caves and mine-shafts, he would naturally have seen it as a rich picking ground. Indeed it is thought to be partly through this early form of commercial archaeology that Dagobert amassed the wealth which allowed him to pay and equip the large army which was the basis of his power.

There is even evidence to suggest that during one of his frequent visits to the area Dagobert found his way to a hillside tomb, stripped it of its treasure and returned to Paris, leaving the bodies he had found in it on the hillside. On his return, his wife, Nantechilde, far from being impressed by the fruits of her husband's labours, became horrified. By all accounts an edu-cated woman, versed in the occult and the Egyptian heritage from which it was derived, she read the inscriptions on the pieces Dagobert had brought back and insisted that he return them to where he had found them. One of the pieces bore an inscription stating that 'anyone removing them from the tomb will be cursed and their line will be cursed also'.

A strange document called *Le Serpent Rouge* appears to contain a direct reference to this defiant act of grave-robbing. Singularly abstruse, *Le Serpent Rouge* comprises a genealogical chart, a plan of St Sulpice in Paris which delineates the chapels to various saints, two maps, dated 511 and 620, and commen-taries showing the boundaries of the Frankish Kingdom during the time of the Visigoths. It also contains a strange collection of thirteen prose poems, each of which is attributed to a sign of the zodiac – a thirteen-sign zodiac which contains the additional sign of Ophiocus, the keeper of the serpent, and which is directly linked to the original Egyptian zodiac. It is a line in the poem ascribed to the sign of Scorpio that makes this work of particular interest: 'But how many have pillaged the house leaving only the embalmed corpses and a number of metal things they could not carry'.

It appears that Dagobert refused to heed his wife's counsel and did not return the various articles of treasure to the tomb. What he did by way of compromise, however, was to agree to visit the monks at the Abbey of St Denis. Abbot Grimo was the leading cleric at the Abbey and the one to whom Dagobert turned for counsel. He had been a recipient of Dagobert's generosity to the point where he owned vast estates which stretched through the Meuse and Moselle valleys and in the Liège and Maastricht areas and was, it appears, one of Dagobert's strongest allies in the Church.[37]

As stated earlier, Dagobert had a close relationship with the expansion of what had hitherto been a small shrine. He is frequently considered by some to be its founder, but the origins of the Abbey of St Denis go back far further than Dagobert. It is known that before there was any Christian shrine there had been a vast Gallo-Roman cemetery on the site, which was then called Catalliacum or Cadalgo. Although excavations on and around the site continue to this day, it is clear that most of the ancient tombs are Roman and pagan.[38] The historical Denis who was martyred and buried there was one of the seven bishops sent from Rome in the third century CE to preside over the cities of Gaul. Denis became the first Bishop of Paris and died during the persecution of Decius around 251.[39] The first evidence of a cult around this martyr is drawn from the life of St Geneviève written in 520, which tells of how she led the effort to construct a church over the remains of St Denis. There is also one legend which recounts that a Christian noblewoman, Catulla, buried the body of Denis and his companions and then erected a small church over the site which was later enlarged by Constantine around 337. Now popularly regarded as the patron saint of France, St Denis was actually beheaded at Montmartre, or Martyrs' Hill, in Paris, along with a priest, Rusticas, and a deacon, Eleutherius. In one of the many legends that surround him, he is claimed as a cephalophore, a head carrier, one of those martyrs who was fabled to have carried his severed head to the place of his burial.

It is natural that Dagobert would have been aware of this history if he became so great a benefactor of the Abbey, investing it with considerable gifts of land, with revenue from the port of Marseilles and instituting for it the Fair of St-Denis. The local taxes that were destined for the Abbey's treasury were collected by a Jewish merchant called Solomon, who made his collections at the Gate of Glaucinus in Roman Paris and bizarrely was baptized into the Christian Church in 629 CE. Dagobert enlarged Geneviève's old building to over twice its original size, added an apse and side aisles, and adorned the interior with rich decorations.[40] Indeed it was here at St Denis that Dagobert himself would be buried, the first French monarch to be so, thus starting a tradition which would transform it into the most important royal necropolis in the history of France. It was also at St Denis that the oriflamme was kept, an image of a flaming ball which was the earliest emblem of France. Mounted on a banner of which the background was reputed to have been fashioned from the blue cloak of St Martin, it was only ever carried out in the presence of the king and was used up until the reign of Louis XI, when it disappeared.

Dagobert showed great devotion not to the embryonic Frankish Christian Church in general, but to one specific Abbey. It is thought that the main reason for this is the meeting he had with the Abbot at the behest of Nantechilde. During this interview he confessed to his act of grave-robbing, explained his wife's interpretation of the inscriptions on the pieces of treasure that he had removed from the site and confirmed that he had left the bodies that he had found there on the hillside. The Abbot appears to have proceeded with great haste to the tomb to bring the bodies back to Paris and subsequently took them on to Rome. After this, not only do we see the enhancement of the power of the Abbey through the lavish gifts of Dagobert, even though he went on to raid many other churches, but also a welter of evidence to show that the Abbey itself, strengthened as it was by royal patronage, was a powerful force in supporting the King. Indeed this strong bond between the secular and spiritual hearts of the nation gave France a political stability that was virtually unheard of in Europe in the early seventh century.

If the discovery and subsequent removal of bodies from a tomb led to the forming of such a strong bond between the Church and the Frankish Kingdom that Dagobert was instrumental in establishing, then we have to look at the significance of the tomb and the identity of the bodies. If, as the Saunière parchments suggest, the mysterious treasure associated with Dagobert I is of a spiritual rather than a financial nature, could one of the bodies have been that of Christ himself? There is the reference to Sion concealed in the code that would seem to allude to this. There would have been no greater religious trophy, allowing Dagobert to raid other churches with impunity, but leaving the Abbey of St Denis unaffected and probably even a beneficiary of the revenue generated. Dagobert's discovery would have led him to question the validity of a growing Christianity, leaving intact only his strong emotional ties with his own personal church and the Abbot and monks who supported him.

*

My attempts to crack the codes presented by the Renaissance paintings that had so fascinated me had led me to establish a deeper understanding of the men who painted them and the patrons who commissioned them. In turn, this led me to an explanation of the esoteric knowledge possessed by these people, and both the roots and the legacy of that knowledge. This brought me to a fuller awareness of the influences on, and the impact of, the Bible stories and their contemporary texts, which in turn took me inexorably to a region of France where a heritage of legend and mystery was long established. Closer examination of the clues that had presented themselves only served to confirm the train of thought now in motion. It also struck me that the heritage of heresy that this region possessed might not be accidental. If indeed Jesus had walked the hills and the valleys of the Languedoc, if Mary Magdalene had preached in the villages, would they not have sown the seeds of beliefs that would flourish long after their demise?

CHAPTER EIGHT

THE HOME OF THE HERESY

☆

In the eleventh, twelfth and thirteenth centuries the Gnostic legacy of the Essenes, the Mandaeans, the Manichaeans and others was not only alive, but flourishing. It had found sanctuary in the hills north of the Pyrenees, in that area of south-western France which we now know as the Languedoc (and which has at its heart the village of Rennes-le-Château). The Languedoc at this time had a great deal in common with classical Byzantium, some historians ascribing this to the fact that the region was not at the time part of the political structure of France but was instead almost an independent principality, ruled by a collection of powerful and wealthy noble families. Education was highly esteemed, a situation far from the norm in the rest of Europe. The study of philosophy, poetry, languages and art all flourished and there was a dedicated quest for knowledge of every hue.

Against this cosmopolitan and educated background, the area also resounded with religious tolerance, the advancement of spiritual knowledge being paramount. Judaism had arrived some one thousand years before and this was now joined with threads of Islam from the Moorish influence. Paradoxically, the Roman Church was not held in high esteem. Roman clerics were notoriously corrupt, there were churches in which masses had not been held for thirty years and many priests forsook their spiritual calling for the secular endeavours of running businesses and estates. Many of the clergy were actually illiterate and even those who had received a level of education were more interested in simony, concubinage and, in at least one case, the compilation of indecent books. In general the orthodox Church was weak, vacillating and staffed by a clergy who were notable only for their ignorance, corruption and indolence. There are records of one Bishop of Narbonne who not once during his tenure even visited his diocese.[1]

It was amid this Christian spiritual poverty that generic Gnosticism flourished under the dual guises of Albigensianism and Catharism. We must bear in mind that Gnosticism was not in itself an institutional religion in the same way that the Roman Church was. The 'personal path' aspect of its creed actually ran counter to the notion of building of vast edifices and strictly organized preaching. It was far more in keeping with the tenets of Jesus's own preaching or instruction methods, in the fields or the homes of adherents. As with pure Gnosticism, Cathars believed that the world was intrinsically evil – indeed that all matter was evil. The universe was the handiwork of a usurper God, the god of Evil, Pan, or, as the Cathars termed him, 'Rex Mundi' or 'King of the World'. Curiously, in one of the parchments found by Abbé Saunière there are eight letters, quite different from the others and slightly raised above the lines of regular text which, read in sequence, spell 'Rex Mundi'.

As a creed Catharism became popular with the inhabitants of the Languedoc, the faith's tolerance attracting nobles and peasants alike. In 1145 St Bernard of Clairvaux arrived in the area intending to preach against these supposed heretics. What he found, however, appalled him a great deal less than what was being carried out in the name of his own Church. He is documented as being clearly impressed by them: 'No sermons are more Christian than theirs . . . and their morals are pure'.[2]

The origins of an organized Cathar faith are to this day unknown. The name Cathar is thought to be derived from the Greek '*katharos*', meaning pure, and the beliefs the Cathars held were shared by the medieval religious sects of the Paulicians, those who followed the teachings of Paul, and the Bogomils in the Middle East and the Balkans, with whom they are known to have had contact. In the first half of the eleventh century various groups of heretics surfaced across Europe in Germany, northern Italy and in Flanders, yet by the end of the century most had disappeared. However, in the early twelfth century there was a revival in the movement, followed by a period of extraordinary growth. Some historians link this renaissance with the reorganization of the Bogomil Church and Bogomil missionaries spreading out to western Europe, but it may also have been the result of western European dualists returning from the Second Crusade after 1149.

During the eleventh and twelfth centuries Catharism and its sister religion Albigensianism became highly popular and even those Languedocians who were not practitioners were extremely tolerant and respectful of its adherents. This was no doubt due in part to the fact that many of the area's noble families were either Cathars or sympathetic to the Cathar cause, making the religion the most widespread in the region. Indeed when the first Cathar heretics arrived in Limousin between 1012 and 1020, they were protected by no less an individual than William IX, Duke of Aquitaine.

By the mid-twelfth century the Cathars had become a fully fledged church with a well-defined ecclesiastical hierarchy, a liturgy, a system of doctrine and, more importantly, a large and growing congregation of believers. In 1149 the first Cathar bishopric was established and the status of the Church as a whole was confirmed during a visit by the Bogomil bishop Nicetas in 1167.

Various groups of Cathars placed differing emphasis on aspects of the basic tenets of the religion, but all were in agreement on the intrinsic evil of matter. To them man was an alien sojourner in an evil world, whose aim must be to free his naturally good spirit in order that it might return to its rightful communion with God. In practice the Cathars were extremely ascetic, there being strict rules governing fasting, sexual intercourse and the eating of meat. This made the religion very much a church of the elect, and given its strictures it is all the more surprising that it found the popularity that it did. Perhaps this was in part due to the way in which the Church was organized into two bodies, the 'perfectii' or 'perfects' and the 'believers'. The perfects were set apart from the main congregation of believers, and were required to undergo a ceremony of initiation called the *consolamentum* or consolation, and a form of spiritual baptism. This was administered by those who had already received it, and granted the recipient forgiveness for all sins upon death, immediate entry into the Kingdom of God and life eternal. The price was high, however. Both those perfects who were single and those who were married had to practise complete celibacy, the latter having to leave their spouses. Aside from a general abstinence from meat, there were long periods of fasting during which eggs and milk were also forbidden. Ownership of property was banned and a vow of pacifism was given. It was from the perfects that the clergy was drawn and formed into three orders: Majors or Bishops, Presbyters or Priests and Deacons.[3]

The second division of the Church, the ordinary members or 'believers', were not subject to such a strict regime. They were allowed to marry and own property, and many were even outwardly members of the Roman Church, receiving the sacrament and obeying Catholic laws. To be considered Cathars, these members were required only to promise to receive the *consolamentum* either in old age or as they lay on their deathbed.

Those practising the religion became known to the local inhabitants of the Languedoc as the '*bons chrétiens*' or the '*bons hommes*' – the good Christians or the good men – and as travelling preachers they moved around the countryside in pairs, helping, healing and spreading the word as they went. Indeed they appear to have led utterly blameless and extremely worthy lives in poverty, chastity and simplicity. And yet they became the object of rabid hatred by the orthodox Roman Church, for even though the basis of their beliefs was Christian, they were seen to challenge fundamentally the doctrine of Rome.[4]

The general beliefs of the Cathars became utterly intolerable to a Church that had decided on a definite and fixed orthodoxy. The dualist principle on which the Cathar faith was founded led to a theology far removed from that which Rome was preaching. In essence the two opposite and equal powers of good and evil formed the basis of everything. To some Cathars the force for evil was a rebellious offshoot of the force for good, to others they were co-existent, while others still believed that the one good God had two sons, Satanal, the rebellious one, and Christ the redeemer. Implicit in these beliefs was the understanding that the Cathar Church was the product of the good god and founded by Christ, while the Roman Church was the product of the evil principle. Man himself was originally a mixture of the two principles, which existed in spiritual form until tricked into a material body created by the evil principle. This idea led to the belief that the soul, which was the product of the good principle, must be freed from its material prison and that this could be achieved by the strictly ascetic lifestyle practised by the perfects. This element of the creed also explains the Cathars' loathing of procreation, their vegetarianism (although apparently they were permitted to eat fish in the belief that they did not reproduce sexually) and that although marriage was permitted by the believers, it was seen by many Cathars as being even more evil than adultery.

However, what really characterized the Cathars firmly as heretics as far as the orthodox Church was concerned was the belief that if all matter is evil, then for Jesus, as the son of God, incarnation was impossible, and his birth, body, crucifixion, resurrection and supposed ascension must therefore all be fictions. As a result, Cathars set no store by the cross – which was seen as a sign of Rex Mundi, the king of the material world – nor by the crucifixion, which was considered by many to be unworthy of reverence because of the sheer brutality of the act. Adding fuel to the fire that was already being stoked by Catholicism in their opposition to Catharism was the accusation by the Cathars that the Church of Rome had lost sight of the original teachings of Christ and was promulgating a dogma and theology far removed from that taught by Jesus himself. The Cathars were also highly critical of the emphasis placed by the Roman Church on the building of vast edifices, the gathering of wealth and the general atmosphere of pomp with which both the wider Church and its individual preachers were surrounding themselves. Catharism's emphasis on the equality of the sexes only increased the tension between the two faiths. While this recognition of the feminine principle in religion manifested itself in the ordination of women as perfects, the Catholic Church of the time was expending much energy in the repudiation of any feminine role in religion. However, perhaps the main force of the Catholic Church's vehemence was targeted at the Cathars' repudiation of blind faith in favour of the highly Gnostic principle of personal and direct knowledge, which could be gained only at first hand, rather than received through the questionable legitimacy of the priesthood. This tenet undermined the entire basis of Roman Catholicism. The Roman Church's defence strategy resulted in acts of atrocity the like of which had rarely been seen in Europe and was all the worse for the fact that it pitted Christian against Christian.

For some time Catholic theologians did analyse and attempt to disprove the central tenets of the Cathar creed, and many held to the conclusions that they reached. More than thirty such tracts are known, most of them written at the end of the twelfth and the beginning of the thirteenth centuries. It is fascinating to read of the pains to which the authors of these works went to sift out for their readership the cheap slanders and ridiculous accusations, which were increasingly directed at the Cathar population, from the serious theological concerns. One example of the Roman Church's attack is the persistent charge of sexual deviancy that it levelled against Cathars as a body. This may have been due in part to the Cathars' association with the Bogomils of Bulgar (from whence derives the word 'bugger' as a term for a sodomite), who, like all heretics, were associated with deviant sexual practices by those had no understanding of their beliefs. It may equally have been a result of the Cathars' use of various methods of birth control (then, as now, anathema to the orthodox Church) and there is some evidence that abortions were also conducted, a practice that may have originated as a result of doctrines that they shared with the Manichaeans.

It was only the serious differences of doctrine that were of interest to these scholars, their work bearing a tone of laudable intellectual honesty. This is certainly true in the *Liber contra Manicheos* by Durand de Huesca, the *Summa quadrapartita* written in Montpellier by Alain de Lilly, and the *Summa adversus catharos* by Moneta de Crémone. Perhaps the best example, however, is the *Summa* by Rainier Sacconi, an Italian who became not only a Dominican but also an Inquisitor and, most stunningly of all, did so having originally been no less than a Cathar perfect. It would be worthy of further research and investigation to determine what led a man such as this to be involved in the violence against those who had hitherto been not only his friends and colleagues but also the flock to whom he preached, for his *Summa* is perhaps one of the most objective texts on the relative theology of the two belief systems and in parts is almost wistfully sympathetic to the Cathar cause.

This learned battle led the Church to send numerous preachers and highly respected missionaries into the Languedoc in a bid to win back the hearts and minds of those who had crossed over to Catharism. When St Bernard visited the area he understandably could not reconcile himself with the fundamental differences in doctrine between the Cathars' faith and his own, but he was respectful enough of their way of life to state in one of his reports to the Pope that if one was to 'examine their mode of life, you will find nothing more irreproachable.'[5] This tacit respect for the Cathars was a defining feature in aspects of the ensuing horror.

The lack of any real success in reconverting 'heretics' and bringing them back to the fold of the Orthodoxy led to the next phase in the escalation of conflict. The Church decided to fight fire with fire and in 1205, sixty years after St Bernard's mission, a new body of travelling preachers was sent to the region to tackle the Cathars' own preachers head on. Among these roving Catholic shock troops was the Spanish monk and Catholic fanatic Dominic Guzmán, who would later found the Order of the Preaching Friars, or the Dominicans as they became known, and whose members were to be among the most fervent activists in the horrors of the Holy Inquisition.

However, even the persuasive techniques of Guzmán gained few converts to the Church. In 1207 Pope Innocent III took direct action against the Count of Toulouse, Raymond VI, excommunicating him for his tacit support of the heretics. When the Papal Legate, Pierre de Castelnau, who was charged with informing the Count of the Pope's decision, was murdered at St-Gilles, despite the fact that the crime seemed to have been committed by anti-Catholic rebels rather than pro-Cathar heretics, the Church of Rome wasted no time in laying the blame fully at the door of the Cathars and an enormous army was mustered to conduct a crusade, against not only the loathed heretics but also their supporters and sympathizers. Suspicion was enough evidence for condemnation and the threat of excommunication that had been directed at Raymond VI was used as implicit evidence of his supposed guilt.

A threat of excommunication generally resulted in the immediate capitulation of the king or nobleman involved. The excommunication of England's Henry II following the murder of Thomas à Becket in 1170 CE, and the subsequent public apology and act of humiliation that had been necessary for his pardon, were still remembered by many in France. Nor had they forgotten the upheaval that had been caused by the illegal divorce of King Philip II in 1200, which had resulted in the interdiction of the whole of France, which barred the entire population from participating in any of the Church's religious observances, especially the Mass. Once excommunicated, an individual was, legally speaking, dead and anyone, whether family, friend or vassal, was released from any obligations that they may have had towards that person. This resulted in the recipients of such threats going to extraordinary lengths to appease the Church and ward off the act that could unseat them from their power at a stroke. However, the Languedoc had already effectively severed itself from the control of Rome.

It was for this reason that the Pope, knowing that to place an interdiction on a land where the Church was already in decline would serve no purpose, decided to make the Count of Toulouse the personal target of his wrath. As early as 1204 he had written to Philip II: 'It is your responsibility to harry the Count of Toulouse out of those lands which at present he occupies; to remove this territory from the control of sectarian heretics; and to place it in the hands of the true Catholics who will be enabled, under your beneficent rule, to serve Our Lord in all faithfulness'.

It is interesting to note that at the time of this impending conflict those men who were to be the key players lived in an extremely cosmopolitan society. The English nobility all spoke French. Spanish and Italian poets were actually composing works in the 'langue d'Oc' of southern France and German Minnesingers were learning their art from the travelling troubadours from the same region. What is more, there were complex interconnections between noble families as a result of politically convenient marriages and feudal obligations. Raymond VI, Count of Toulouse, was himself not only a cousin of the King of France but also brother-in-law to both the King of England and the King of Aragon. He was also the Duke of Narbonne and Marquis of south-west Provence, which made him an extremely powerful feudal overlord whose authority extended over the regions of Agenais, Quercy, Rouergue, Albigeois, Comminges, and Carcassès.[6] Indeed so powerful was he that it is a source of amazement that the Papal 'Bull of Anathema' issued by Innocent III on 10 March 1208 was ever enacted.

The army raised against Raymond was gathered under the overall command of the Abbot of Cîteaux, with the military operation being conducted by Simon de Montfort. Originally a battle for the benefit of the hearts and souls of Catholics, the campaign quickly became far more political in nature. The cities of the south, with their high level of trade, had garnered huge resources, making the area a treasure house and many of the noble families extremely wealthy. This had incurred the envy of the poorer noblemen and landowners of the north, who avidly accepted the challenge of the fight on the side of the Catholics.

The Albigensian Crusade, as the conflict became known, had its opening battle in the town of Béziers in 1209 and continued until 1244. This horrific and extended period of brutality, to this day vividly etched on the collective memory of the region, saw no abatement when Simon de Montfort, proclaimed Count of Toulouse in 1213 on the death of Peter II, King of Aragon and Count of Barcelona, was then himself killed laying siege to Toulouse in 1218. Town after town was virtually razed to the ground in what can best be described as Europe's first scorched-earth warfare. Records of town and village officials were used to locate the heretics and those associated with them, and no mercy was shown in their dispatch, whether by fire or by the sword. Nor was the ferocity restricted to the Cathars. The large indigenous Jewish community of the Languedoc, which had hitherto been warmly accepted and supported by some of the noble families, and whose members were frequently holders of civic office, was also targeted.[7]

From 1216 until 1224 the Languedoc nobility fought bravely for the return of the land and property which the northern barons had taken from them, and this period saw the return of a level of localized normality, with Cathars returning to their homes and villages. But it was to be a short-lived respite, for King Louis VIII mounted a fresh crusade which once again sparked fighting in the Languedoc.[8] This led to the defeat of the Languedoc princes and in 1229 the Treaty of Paris ratified the region's conquest and annexation.

In 1233 the Holy Inquisition was born and took over the witch-hunt of heretics from the northern nobility. This continuation of the Albigensian Crusade saw yet more excesses of barbarism. The main towns and most Cathar strongholds had already fallen and those Cathars who remained alive had sought sanctuary in the remotest parts of the region, where isolation might afford them some protection. As a result the hunt for hidden Cathars was expanded to encompass the slaughter of any non-Catholic and was conducted with a rabid zeal designed to make the innocent inform on suspects in the hope of saving themselves.

The Albigensian Crusade culminated in the famous siege of Montségur, a medieval-European Masada. The defining moment of Cathar resistance, it virtually eradicated the Cathar legacy for ever. The château of Montségur, built in 1204, had served as a refuge for Cathars from the opening days of the struggle in 1209 and from 1232 it had become the seat of the forbidden Church. Home to some 250 Cathars and their leaders, it had even attracted the attention of Blanche of Castile, France's queen, who, realizing the importance it held to the loathed remaining Cathars, wrote that the Crusaders must 'cut off the head of the dragon'.[9]

But the Cathars had chosen their stronghold well. Surrounded by the beautiful if somewhat desolate Ariège hills, the chateau is situated on the *pog* of Montségur, a steep-sided, tall, rounded crag, resembling a smaller version of the Corcovado mountain with its enormous statue of Christ that dominates the skyline of Rio de Janeiro. Atop this easily defensible eyrie, the château itself is a squat, heavily fortified castle built from solid-stone blocks, the erection of which must at the time have been a civil-engineering wonder. The climb up to it is not to be undertaken lightly and one can only wonder at the effort that would have been required as those fleeing Cathars who were fortunate enough to have completed the perilous journey into the valley ascended the *pog*'s sheer slopes laden down with their few remaining possessions and the supplies they would require. Crusaders and Inquisitors, heavily weighted with armour, horses and the equipment of war, must have dreaded each attempt to climb up to its walls in order to mount an attack and it is little wonder that any hopes of a success from full-frontal offensives were quickly dispelled and the tactics changed to those of siege.

Although the attacking army numbered in excess of 10,000 men, the blockade lasted ten months, during which time those assaults that were mounted were met with the tenacious and desperate resistance that could be expected from those who knew only too well how barbaric and painful an end awaited them. Many of the besiegers were recruited from the local populace and would have had some sympathy with the Cathars, allowing them to pass through the lines in order to replenish supplies in the castle. The certainty that at some stage the siege would be over and the castle's occupants tortured and burned makes the actions of a number of the besiegers all the more extraordinary. For the records show that some of the attacking soldiers actually crossed over to the Cathar side during the course of the siege. Whether this was due to the respect that had been shown by some elements of the Crusade and Inquisition towards their foe is not recorded. However, it may also have been due to the way in which many of the Cathars approached their horrific demise with a grace and stoicism that many ascribed to their having some hidden knowledge which permitted them not to fear the flame or the blade. This may have been due in part to the Cathars' hatred of mortal flesh, leading some historians to conclude that for many of them the death of their physical body would have come as a welcome release, whatever the means, for this would allow their spirit to return to the divine spark. Alternatively, it may be that the attackers felt impelled to convert to a more convincing religion than their own.

Whatever the reasons, there is no doubt that some of the besieging army were impressed by the conviction of their foe. Perhaps this led to another of the extraordinary events of this history. On one night in January 1244, some three months before the siege came to an end, some of the perfects escaped from Montségur. According to reliable accounts taken at the time they were lowered by rope down the precipitous sides of the *pog* and took with them the bulk of the material wealth of the Cathars. The nature of this wealth has been the source of much speculation over the years, but whether it was physical treasure in the form of gold, silver, jewellery, or the more spiritual treasure of writings, knowledge or even the Holy Grail itself, as some have speculated, we shall probably never know. What is known is that the treasure disappeared without trace and has not been seen or heard of since that night.

On 1 March the Cathars capitulated. The terms of surrender that were negotiated are surprising, however. Of the 400 or so people remaining, there were some 160 perfects together with members of the nobility, knights and men, some of whom also had their families with them in the castle confines. The terms of surrender for the fighting men were different from those offered to the perfects. While the former would be allowed safe passage with all their possessions and full pardons for their supposed crimes, the perfects were promised fair penances and freedom if they refrained from their heretical beliefs and confessed their sins to the Inquisition. The Cathars requested, and actually received from the Inquisition, a fourteen-day truce in order to consider the terms and in return offered a number of hostages who would be executed if any escape attempts were made.

The Inquisition was not given to acts of bargaining, let alone gestures of generosity. If the Cathars knew that they were never going to renounce their beliefs, it is also strange that they would have wanted to prolong the agony for a further two weeks. Was there a reason for their request? The Cathars did conduct some sort of ceremony or festival on 14 March immediately before the truce ended. This date apparently held some significance for while it fell within the period of Easter – an orthodox festival to which the Cathars attached no significance – it was the date of the spring equinox that year and also the period during which the Manichaeans celebrated a sacred festival, the 'Bema', during which a book containing pictures illustrating the various aspects of duality was used.[10] While there has never been any evidence found for such a book or document ever being used by the Cathars, it is possible that something important was used during the course of the ceremony. Also, it has recently been discovered that the construction of the castle seems to have hinged around the summer solstice. Two arched 'windows' on one side of the building are arranged so that during the solstice light passes not only directly through them but also through the two corresponding arches on the other side of the building, the sun being visible as one looks through the building from one side to the other.[11]

At the end of the truce, on 15 March, the besieged gave their answer. To a man not one of them accepted the offer, and indeed many of those who had hitherto been 'believers' chose to take the *consolamentum*, thereby becoming perfects and ensuring that they would be treated even more harshly. Dawn the next morning saw some 200 of them escorted down the difficult, rocky slopes and placed in a wood-filled corral in the valley where, watched by their fellows in the castle who had been warned that any attempt to escape would result in death for them and the hostages, they were burned to death.

Those who remained in the castle had one last surprise in store. Despite the fact that hostages had been offered up as a guarantee against an escape, and having witnessed the horrific deaths of the 200, four of the perfects, on the night of 16 March after the ceremony had been completed, fled the confines of the castle by climbing down the sheer sides of the *pog* suspended from ropes. Local traditions maintain that these men also left with some other Cathar treasure. This has led to speculation that this dangerous flight was to remove something of great spiritual value from the clutches of the Inquisitors, something that had been used by the Cathars during the ceremony conducted on 14 March and which therefore could not be taken away during the January escape. Could there be a connection between this desperate act of evasion and the rumours of 'treasure' that were to surface with Abbé Bérenger Saunière's discovery nearly 600 years later? Local legends imply that what was removed was taken to the fortified caves at Ornolac, where more Cathars were killed some time later. However, only skeletons have ever been found there.[12]

Although Montségur became famous as the last stand of Cathar hope against the rising tide of the Inquisition, it did not signal the end of Catharism in the area. Pockets of activity remained, most notably in and around Rennes-le-Château in the caves and old mine workings that had been dug by the Romans in their search for the area's precious metals.

It is around this time that the various Grail legends arise. I have already mentioned some of the earlier works encompassing a string of legends, most notably those of Chrétien de Troyes and Wolfram von Eschenbach, and it is known that these, among others, are adaptations which draw upon a number of pagan stories and leitmotifs. Most notable among these is the continued focus on the grail itself. This is variously described as the cup from which Jesus and the disciples drank at the last supper, the chalice in which Joseph of Arimathea caught the blood of Jesus as he hung on the cross, or in some legends a large golden bowl or receptacle, not unlike the golden dish which was promised to Dagobert I for assisting Sisenant in the war against Sumtilla of Spain. What the legends and romances have in common, however, is the underlying association between them and the growing Knights Templar.

Volumes have been written on the history of the Knights Templar, both the accepted traditional history and the more esoteric background behind this order of warrior-monks. The consensus is that the Knights Templar, more properly named the Order of the Poor Knights of Christ and the Temple of Solomon, were formed in 1118 by Hugues de Payen, a nobleman from Champagne who answered to his overlord, the Count of Champagne.[13] De Payen one day presented himself and eight colleagues to the King of Jerusalem, Baudouin I, offering their services as knight escorts for the French pilgrims making the hazardous journey to the Holy Land. Their sole objective, as reported by Guillaume de Tyre who wrote the first historical record of the Knights' activities, was 'as far as their strength permitted, they should keep the roads and highways safe . . . with especial regards for the protection of pilgrims'.[14] Both King Baudouin and the Patriarch of Jerusalem seem to have accorded the Knights every privilege, allowing them to set up their quarters on the remains of the ancient Temple of Solomon, from which the full name of the order derives. However, there is today a complete dearth of material to shed light on the activities of the Order for the first nine years after its foundation. It would seem unlikely, if not downright impossible, that only nine knights could patrol the hazardous route to the Holy

Land, yet they were obviously doing something significant, for when they do resurface in the literature of the period, they are lauded as being model Christians. It is from ecclesiastical records that we learn of this reputation, and especially the writings of no less a personage than St Bernard of Clairvaux, whose attempts to quell the Cathars we have already seen. Indeed it was Bernard who, in writing his work *In Praise of the New Knighthood* hailed them as models of virtue and upholders of the highest Christian ideals. This effusive commendation led to the Knights returning to France, to a hero's welcome, and subsequently to the establishment of the Order as a military-religious group under official recognition at the Council of Troyes – the seat of the Count of Champagne – in 1128. The vows of chastity, poverty and obedience that, like all monks, members were required to swear seems to have had no restraint on the growth of the Order, for the next few years saw an extraordinary rise in the membership, with many men agreeing to the multitude of obligations imposed on them in order to be a member of this élite force. In many ways they were the 'Special Forces' of their age, both feared and admired by allies and enemies alike. Initiates were obliged to keep their hair short but not to cut their beards and wore a distinctive white garb – reminiscent of the white stoles worn by the Essenes – to which the famous splayed red cross was introduced in 1146.

The rules of battle under which each Knight fought were equally strict. If a Templar suffered the misfortune of capture he was not permitted to demand mercy nor was he allowed to ransom himself. Surrender was such anathema that it was forbidden unless the odds were three to one against the fighting force and even then the permission of the force commander had to be given. Their courage and skill in conflict became a byword and the Order's ranks were soon swelled further by the youngest sons of the nobility of both France and England, keen to align themselves with the reputation of bravery which membership of that body of men bestowed. This membership of the Order goes a long way to explaining the enormous wealth that it accumulated in a relatively short time. Following a European fund-raising journey undertaken by Hugues de Payen, the Order received huge donations, with money, land, jewellery and property all being added to the coffers. All new recruits were required to donate all their own wealth and property to the order – indeed de Payen himself did so – and within ten years of the Council of Troyes, the Knights Templar owned estates as far-flung as Portugal, Scotland, Hungary, Germany and the Holy Land, in addition to vast tracts of France, England and Spain. The financial astuteness of an order who welcomed all gifts and donations while disposing of nothing soon made them not only a fighting force of repute but also the first truly international bankers of Europe. Indeed so strong were they financially that they were in a position to lend money to kings, becoming at some time the backers of nearly every crowned head in Europe, and were relied upon by the merchant classes as the only safe way of transferring money from one place to another, both as physical currency and in the form of promissory notes. As the crusades against the Saracens continued unabated, the Knights Templar gained the respect of both the secular and spiritual power-mongers across Europe and for a hundred years they reigned as a supreme power with unrivalled international connections.

This extraordinary rise in fortunes could not last. Such enormous wealth and power soon led to jealousy and challenges to their authority and as early as 1252 Henry III of England threatened to confiscate some of their property, accusing them of 'excessive pride'. Although he was put down by the then Master of the Order this charge was not unfounded, for unchecked power had led to excesses and arrogance within the

Order. It was beginning to lose its reputation as the upholder of Christianity, instead becoming notorious for its corruption.

In 1291 the Holy Land came under relentless Muslim attack, and despite the bravery and tactics of the Crusaders the city of Acre, the last bastion of Christian territory in the Holy Land, fell into Saracen hands. The Order moved its centre of activities to Cyprus, but with its *raison d'être* now lost it was not long before it returned to mainland Europe to focus on managing the portfolios of wealth it had accumulated. Many of the Order's leaders returned to France, where they proceeded to revel in their wealth and position. But while exempt from taxation and answerable only to the Pope, they soon found that, far from returning as patriots and heroes, they were castigated as profligate wastrels. Indeed even their allegiance to the Pope had stretched relations with the Church of Rome to the limit and in 1307 the *coup de grâce* was set in motion. Philip IV of France, or Philip le Bon, wanted to rid his land of the Templar establishment and as early as 1303 he initiated a train of events that would see the threat that it posed to his monarchy eradicated. It is now widely held that he was responsible for the kidnapping and subsequent execution of Pope Boniface VIII and it is also thought that he may have been behind the murder of Pope Benedict XI. Certainly the next Pope, hitherto the Archbishop of Bordeaux, was a candidate put forward by Philip IV and his subsequent election to the pontiff's throne as Pope Clement V gave Philip a degree of control over the stance Rome took towards the Knights Templar. The position of the Order was decided when Philip took the decision to suppress it, and armed with information he had gained from spies who had infiltrated the Order, he had heavy charges laid against it.

At dawn on Friday 13 October 1307 Philip's troops struck and rounded up the Templars, placing them under arrest, sequestrating their assets and confiscating their properties. This shock attack was meant to have two prime objectives: to wipe out the Templars for ever and to make available to the King the vast wealth that they had accumulated. However, neither of these aims was achieved. Those Templars who were caught were 'put to the question' – tortured and subsequently burnt to death – most notably the Grand Master, Jacques de Molay, who suffered death by fire on the Île de la Cité in Paris in 1314, but many made good their escape. Nor was the much-vaunted treasure of the Templars ever found, its whereabouts remaining a mystery to this day. Those members of the Order who escaped found sanctuary in a number of places. Scotland, at war with England, had not ratified the Papal Bulls dissolving the Order and as a result became a host to many who fled, some of whom fought on the side of the Scots at the Battle of Bannockburn. Portugal had cleared the Order of any wrongdoing and those Knights who found their way there simply reformed under the name 'The Knights of Christ', continuing in much the same fashion as they had in France. Their famous red-cross insignia was the flag under which both Vasco da Gama and Christopher Columbus sailed on their voyages of discovery in recognition of the Knights' partial patronage.

Although 1118 is the year in which it is believed that the Templars were formed, there has been recent conjecture that the Order may have been in existence long before that date and that its founding was for a specific purpose more related to discovering the true origins of Christianity than the protection of itinerant pilgrims. This is alluded to in part by two aspects of the Templars' specific practice of their own creed. One of the objects which they revered was the image of a decapitated head and from at least one of the Templar preceptories such a head, fashioned from gilded silver, was removed. The connection that such an object may have with early Christianity is confirmed by the degree to which the Templars revered John the Baptist and, bizarrely for a group who had been lauded as the highest manifestation of the Christian ideal, shunned Jesus. Indeed there are records which show that some Knights thought of Jesus as a false prophet. Jean de Chaumes stated during his interrogation: 'You believe wrongly, because he is indeed a false prophet. Believe only in God in Heaven, and not in him',[15] while Deodatus Jefet is on record as saying: 'Do not believe that the man Jesus whom the Jews crucified in Outremer is God and that he can save you.'[16]

Perhaps most extraordinary are the words of Fulk de Troyes, who claimed that he was told not to believe in the false prophet Christ, but only in a higher God. Shown a crucifix, he said: 'Set not much faith in this, for it is too young.'[17]

As had been the case with the Cathars during the Albigensian Crusade, the sexual practices of the Templars were also brought into question, with charges of homosexuality, teaching women how to abort and obscene kissing becoming intermingled with accusations of denying Christ and spitting on the Cross. Indeed the connection with the Cathars is far more than that of shared spurious accusation by demented anti-heretics. For at about the same time that the Cathars were seeking sanctuary in the isolated villages of the Languedoc, the Knights Templar were fast becoming the biggest landowners of the same area. As much as the area around Rennes-le-Château was a Cathar stronghold, so also was it a bastion of Templar activities with, at one time, up to a third of the Templar landholdings being in the Languedoc. The remains of many Templar castles can still be found in the area and, as contemporaries, many Knights would have come from Cathar families and vice versa. In all records of the Albigensian Crusade the Knights Templar are notable by their absence; it is entirely possible that in the same manner that they had fought for the side of Christianity in the Holy Land they would have lent their support to the 'Good Christians' of south-west France.

Another factor in the pogrom against the Templars is of great interest. During the interrogation of those soldier-monks who were captured, one name recurs, Baphomet. This name, intoned by many before they were burned to death or as the result of the application of thumbscrews and yet more horrific torture, has long been a mystery. It has been thought to be variously the name of the revered severed-head image, the name of a devil – sometimes a cat – worshipped by the Knights on a corruption of the name Muhammad resulting from their contact with Arabic influences during the Crusades. One other explanation is that it is a bastardized form of the Arabic 'abufihimat', or 'Father of Wisdom'.[18] This last definition may be close to the truth, for recent work on the Dead Sea Scrolls has revealed the use of a code called the Atbash Cipher which, if applied to the word 'Baphomet', gives the translation 'Sophia'.[19] As we know from the *Pistis Sophia* in the *Codex Askewianus*, this is the Greek word for 'wisdom', although why, and perhaps more intriguingly, how, the Knights Templar were using a code that had been employed more than 1,000 years before their own founding remains a mystery. A possible answer to the question 'why' may be that offered by the authors Richard Andrews and Paul Schellenberger.[20] In their controversial and much-criticized work they postulate that, given the vehemence with which any Gnostic thought was being quelled, any reference to Sophia – a focus of Gnostic attention through association with Mary Magdalene, linked to the Kabbalah through Chokmah, an Old Testament feminine figure who was thought of as being not only the partner but also the adviser to God and also through the references to both the Egyptian Isis and the Greek Athena – would be sure to attract unwanted attention and therefore such allusions were hidden by the Templars using the Atbash Cipher. However, despite my best efforts, I am no further forward than any of my predecessors in answering the question of how this came to be the case.

That the Templars established so much of their property and activities in an area which was central to the pursuit of non-orthodox traditions, and that in many ways they seem to have displayed what can only be described as Gnostic sympathies while not actually aligning themselves fully with the 'heretics', fascinates me. It has been a matter of conjecture for many Templar historians that men who had hitherto laid down their lives for the protection of the Christian faith were subsequently hunted down and accused of the most un-Christian of practices. Why was this?

There is an undercurrent of a secret tradition associated with the Templars which would seem to indicate that they were the holders of some form of esoteric knowledge. It has long been thought that while they were stationed at the Temple of Solomon during the Crusades they undertook a series of excavations in the so-called 'Stables of Solomon', but what they found, if anything, has never been satisfactorily explained or proven. However, this may miss the point. For assuming that the initial party of nine Templars had a hidden agenda which did not involve giving protection to the travelling faithful – a reasonable enough assumption in view of the length of the journey and the modest number of Knights – could it have been that they went to Jerusalem in order to try to find something, and that the knowledge that such a thing even existed gave them power enough to build the organization which followed? Whatever this 'thing' may have been, the knowledge of it would have certainly required a level of protection, a coding of the information, that would allow its transmission among those who were privy to it without endangering them. It seems clear that the Templars were used to using codes – as we have seen with the possible use of the Atbash Cipher. However, we also have evidence that they employed methods of hiding information in the most unlikely places.

Some of the finest bequests made by the Templars to the areas in which they lived were the beautiful and extraordinary places of worship they constructed. From the cruciform churches dug into the ground in the horn of Africa to the cathedrals, such as Chartres, which were raised upon it, the Knights Templar left their mark on the landscape in the most dramatic fashion. But in these edifices, raised to the glory of God and built specifically for the practice of Christian worship, they displayed decidedly non-Christian imagery. Some of the greatest builders and architects of the Middle Ages, the Templars were obviously aware of the principles of sacred geometry, the same rules that had been used by the Egyptians in the construction of the pyramids, and used them in their own construction methods. Indeed it is the geometrical harmony and sense of proportion that imbue cathedrals like that of Chartres with the sense of majesty for which they have become renowned. Based on the precept of the Golden Mean, this understanding may have been a result of the time they had spent in Jerusalem, where the Temple of Solomon was deemed to be the zenith of human construction, its dimensions being in perfect proportions and tapping into a spiritual harmonic that could only be achieved through such perfection.

Nor was the broad architecture of their buildings the only point of reference the Templars employed in hinting at the knowledge gained by a long-gone civilization. Many of the decorative symbols and emblems that were carved both on the inside and the outside of these structures show that they were both aware of and had an understanding of what we today dismissively call esoterica. Astrological signs and pagan symbolism abound in Templar cathedrals and churches, as evidenced by the sign for Aries which can be seen over the doorway of many cathedrals, together with many symbols derived from the alchemical heritage of the Egyptians and the Kabbalah. Indeed there are distinct parallels between the Templars' secreting of knowledge in codified form in public places of worship and the strange decoration used by Bérenger Saunière when he was renovating the church at Rennes-le-Château.

One final point on this issue is another strangely coincidental set of circumstances. Hugues de Payen, the founder of the Order of the Poor Knights of Christ and the Temple of Solomon, was from the region around Troyes and, as was mentioned earlier, was a vassal of the Count of Champagne. Two of the other original nine Knights were also associated with the area and were bondsmen of the same Count, and evidence suggests that these three knew each other before the formation of the Order. There had also been at Troyes a Kabbalist school, founded by the Rabbi Rashi, which had existed in the town since the mid-eleventh century – the same town not only in which the Order was founded but also in which it was officially recognized at the Council of Troyes in 1128. And it was in the same town that Chrétien de Troyes not only wrote one of the earliest (and possibly the first) of the Grail stories, but from which he also took his name.

There is no doubt that the Grail legends, based as they are now acknowledged to be on older Celtic and pagan tales, are anything but highly symbolic versions of a Christian story. Much of the Christian surface detail may be largely due to the later 'Christianization' of Chrétien de Troyes' *Le Conte de Graal*. However, nothing can mask the fact that the basis of these stories is not only highly heretical in nature, but also richly peppered with Templar imagery. In *Perlesvaus*, those who attend the Grail are clothed in white robes bearing the distinctive red cross of the Templars, while one of the passages describes the hero finding 150 decapitated heads, some of which are encased in gold and silver, some in lead – a reference not only to Templar tradition but also to the alchemy of base and precious metals. The whole basis of the Grail legends may also be seen as fundamentally Gnostic, focusing as they do on an individual's personal quest. Yet this brand of Gnostic allegory is inextricably linked with both the upholding of the Knights' traditions and the dissemination of highly particular imagery, linking alchemy with Christianity and Templar traditions with the principles of Gnosticism. And it does so using images and symbols that would be fully understood only by those who had been initiated into their inner meaning.

Thus we have the Knights Templar privy to some secret information of religious importance, from a town with a Kabbalist tradition, using codes and secret symbolism to transmit ideas and information and with their activities preserved in the highly visual, ritualistic and equally symbolic Grail Romances. Further, when their mandate is rescinded, we find them moving to the homeland of European heresy.

A codification of information using esoteric symbolism that would either not be understood or would be disregarded by outsiders brings us back to the riddles of the paintings. I was now certain that there had to be a link between the codes in the paintings and the myths, legends and religious heritage of the Languedoc. The number of strands of my enquiry that had led to this region and its own mysteries, the connections there appeared to be between religion, history and the personalities involved, all seemed to be crystallized in this land of Magdalene myth, heresy and the enigmatic discovery made by Bérenger Saunière.

It appeared to me that all the clues in this Arcadian cipher were pointing not only to this specific region, but also to a particular place within it. What is more, I felt that there may well be 'treasure at the end of the rainbow' – a rainbow itself being a historical symbol of Arcadia – and that the treasure would be of spiritual importance rather than of material value.

My next step seemed obvious. If I was right I would have to apply the code that I had uncovered to the region which seemed to be the focus of so much related activity. It would be the acid test of all the work that I had done. Hitherto no one had found anything tangible – no treasure, no tomb, nothing – and there was no guarantee that I would be any different. Yet so many pieces of the puzzle that I had found had fitted together so well that I could not really believe I would not find anything. My first step was to turn to the maps of the region and to get a feel for the lie of the land.

CHAPTER NINE

THE KNIGHTS OF NAZISM,
THE CHARTS AND THE STARS

☆

Writers of the early twenty-first century are the heirs to a long tradition of attaching particular significance to the area around Rennes-le-Château. After all, Mary Magdalene herself is said to have been a regular visitor to Rennes-les-Bains – the original name for which was Les Bains de Rennes at the time when Rennes-le-Château was just called Rennes – just along the valley, where the warm springs have attracted visitors since before Roman times. Rhedae, the original name of the area surrounding Saunière's village, was regarded as a sacred site by the Celtic tribe of the Redones who lived there and who gave it this name. During the fifth and sixth centuries what is now a small village was a thriving town of some 30,000 inhabitants and seems to have been the northern capital of the empire ruled by the Visigoths and the county town of the diocese of Rhédénium. In the Middle Ages it was a bastion, not only of Templar landholdings but also of the Cathars, those carriers and upholders of the ancient Gnostic faith, considered by many to be the true meaning of the words of Jesus. The Templars themselves, the knight-mystics, warrior-monks with their mysterious excavations which can be seen even today in the Temple of Jerusalem, were and are inextricably linked with the area through their ownership of land and villages and undoubtedly knew that it lay on an important pilgrim route. Even Hitler is reputed to have dispatched a team of miners and archaeologists to the area during the Second World War in a bid to locate a supposed 'treasure'.

Interestingly, there is another curious link between Fascist Germany and the area. A sister organization to the Knights Templar was active in both northern Europe and in the Holy Land at the same time as both the Templars and the Hospitallers of St John. Called the Teutonic Knights of Saint Mary's Hospital at Jerusalem, they were, as were the Knights Templar, a religious order, formed by German Crusaders in 1190–1 in Acre, now in Israel, but at the time in Palestine. In the beginning they were associated with the Order of Hospitallers, founding their own German hospital, hostel and a church during the reign of Badouin I and drawing their membership solely from the German nobility. In 1199 they were recognized by Pope Innocent III, who in his Papal Bull confirmed the Teutonic Knights' right to wear the white mantle of the Templars and follow the Hospitallers' rule. By 1279 the Teutonic Knights had conquered the Slavs of Prussia and had embarked on a programme of building many towns and fortresses, expanding their area of influence until by 1329 they held the entire Baltic region from the Gulf of Finland in the north to Poland in the south as a papal fief. In the sixteenth century, however, the lands in the south were secularized as the Duchy of Prussia and the Order was abolished, losing its northern influence when its territory was divided between Poland, Russia and Sweden in 1558.

In Germany, however, the Order continued to survive, especially in the south, until Napoleon's dissolution of it in 1809. Twenty-five years later it underwent a revival and re-establishment in Austria but now restricted its efforts to charitable undertakings, a work it continues to this day through its many houses in Austria, Germany and Italy.

But it was with the rise of the Nazi Party that the by then romanticized tradition of knightly chivalry and the higher purpose of the Teutonic Knights was to see a renaissance. Heinrich Himmler, a member of the Party since its emergence after Germany's defeat in the First World War, was also a member of an organization called the Thule Society, proponents of a combination of ideologies which was to have a large bearing on the next twenty years of European politics. The Thule Society was a highly nationalistic group which took its name from one of the mythical homelands of the German people and subscribed to a quasi-mystical belief in the inherent greatness of the Germans. To its members the secrets of the 'Volk', the entire race rather than the 'people' alone, lay deep in the nation's past, when, in the forests of Teutoburg in 9 CE, the Teuton tribes led by Arminius defeated and destroyed the Roman army's legions. They were also inspired by the writings of the Roman, Tacitus, who held that the Teutons, while primitive, were uncorrupted, noble and masculine whereas the Romans, who had once been great, had now degenerated into nothing more than a collection of self-seeking and corrupt effeminates. (Tacitus probably had his own reasons for stating this in the context of contemporary Roman politics – tactful it certainly wasn't!) The Thule Society supported this ideology by invoking the operas of Richard Wagner, especially his *Parsifal* with its references to the Grail Romances, Arthurian legends and the writings of the late-nineteenth-century philosopher Houston Stewart Chamberlain, a leading exponent of the racial superiority of the northern-European Aryans, and from which the premise that the early Germans were the original Aryans was derived.[1]

Hitler was as aware as Himmler of the potential power of

this version of history for the purposes of propaganda, legitimizing Nazi aims with a veneer of historical gravitas. It even lent a degree of intellectual credibility to the view that National Socialism was 'more than a religion; it is the determination to create a new man',[2] and it had a further advantage: part of the creed of the Thule Society was devoted to confirming its determination to destroy the racial enemy of the Aryans – the Jews.

Hitler's rise to power as Chancellor of Germany in 1933 gave Himmler the opportunity to pursue and propagate his Thule Society interests with a vengeance. As commander of Hitler's bodyguards, the Schutzstaffel 'protection squadron', or SS, he oversaw an expansion of the organization from its original 300 members to as many as half a million by 1939, a figure that would continue to grow during the early years of the war. Most of its divisions are well known: the Waffen SS, who fought alongside the regular troops; the Allgemein or 'general' division, who staffed the concentration and death camps and were responsible for managing the deportation of the Jews of occupied Europe; and the Einsatzgruppen or 'special formations', who sought out the Jews in eastern Europe. But there was also another division, formed as a result of Himmler's personal quest for evidence to support the Thule Society's supremacist views: the Ahnenerbe or 'Ancestral Heritage Society'.

Drawn from Germany's scientific community, and including some of the country's finest archaeologists, ethnographers and anthropologists, members of the Ahnenerbe were inducted into the SS and held military status and titles, but their prime function initially was to provide conclusive proof of the German origins of the people of western Russia. However, expeditions soon ranged from the study of Indian medicines in South America to the analysis of the ethnicity of Tibetan tribespeople – and even resulted in another, more esoteric expedition: to locate the lost city of Atlantis, thought to be one of the original centres from which the Aryans developed.

In Himmler's eyes the SS was no less than a reincarnation of the glory of the Teutonic Knights, fused with the glamour and ideals of the Knights of Arthur and the Round Table. The oath taken by new recruits to the SS even echoed the Teutonic Knights' oath of allegiance. He also went so far as to try to recreate a Camelot for his SS, in 1934 renting Wewelsburg Castle in the district of Büren to transform it into a shrine and spiritual home for the entire SS organization. Some of the renovations that he oversaw there have led many to believe that it would one day house no less an object than the Holy Grail, which would have given the castle, the SS and Himmler himself the unquestionable, almost divine, affirmation that he sought.

It is thought to be the search for the Holy Grail that brought German miners and members of the Ahnenerbe to Rennes-le-Château. How the findings and story of Saunière had come to Himmler's attention is unclear. One possible explanation is the link with Richard Wagner and his work. John Millar, in an article for the Saunière Society newsletter entitled 'Richard Wagner, Rosslyn and the Mystery of Rennes-le-Château',[3] explains that when reading one of the early French works which focus on the village and its mystery he came across a reference to the burial of a 'love child' of Wagner's in the cemetery of the village's Church of the Mary Magdalene, the church that Abbé Bérenger Saunière had preached in and renovated. While attempting to authenticate this claim Millar received a letter from a correspondent explaining that a 'gentleman from Carcassonne' had called at Rennes-le-Château requesting to see the documents relating to the child and had taken them away for examination, since which time they had never been returned. Millar does not name this correspondent, nor does he state when these documents were removed, but his article does put forward evidence that Wagner did indeed visit the Languedoc, and he goes on to speculate that Wagner himself may have been aware of a secret in the area years before Saunière discovered his parchments.

Wagner's interest in these matters can be seen in particular in the opera *Parsifal*, his last great work and the one that he considered to be the culmination of his musical achievement. This opera is also known as *The Spear and the Sponge*, a direct reference to the lance that was used to make the wound in Christ as he was on the cross and the sponge which was passed to him, supposedly giving him vinegar to ease his pain. The spear covered in the blood of Jesus became very important later in the art of the Grail legends and in Templar iconography. The knight Parsifal, the opera's central character, is seen on a personal quest to find a state of spiritual enlightenment that will only be granted to him on his seeing the Grail. In order to achieve this he forgoes the earthly pleasures of drink, meat and knowledge of women as distractions from his one true aim. These personal sacrifices are almost identical to the privations undergone by the Cathar perfects *en route* to their returning to the divine light. Parsifal's quest would appear to be a direct analogy to the inner spiritual quest of the Cathars.

The Cathar heartland, the Languedoc, has a powerful, rugged beauty. Even the armchair traveller has only to glance at a map of the area to gain an idea of how rugged and varied the terrain is, with its soaring peaks and wide, fertile valleys. Water, locked within the porous white limestone of the area, is plentiful. The mountainous foothills of the Pyrenees, with their steep-sided valleys, rocky hills and scattered villages, are also the most ideal of hiding places – the ancient mineshafts and caves which abound in these parts have often been used as such. It is a veritable Arcadia, in the true meaning of the term

– a land of the rustic. The whole area is ripe with curious place names and architectural anomalies which seem to conspire together in some ancient mystery. For instance, a recurring motif in many of the churches in the area is the Star of David which features in stone windows or as an adornment to exterior stonework. The semi-derelict cathedral at Alet-les-Bains, six kilometres north of Rennes-le-Château, has two enormous round windows, in each of which is a large masonry Star of David, as does the cathedral at Limoux and the Cathedral of St Vincent at Carcassonne. Stranger still is the anomaly in what was only ever a Roman Catholic place of worship: the intricate carvings on a stone capital found within the grounds of the cathedral at Alet-les-Bains. Now stolen along with many other artefacts, the capital bore symbols and designs which have only ever been associated with Hinduism. It had at its centre a depiction of the god Ganesh and carved elephants. Indeed the whole village bears evidence of non-Christian symbolism, many of the houses having esoteric signs decorating them, and has a history which ranges from being the seat of the local bishopric until it became based at Carcassonne, to Templar connections through the lands that were granted to the Knights according to documents signed there. The church itself has even been shown to have been designed around the geometry of the Templar cross, although it was not actually constructed until the late fourteenth century, long after the Templars had been disbanded.[4] The town even features a Templar cross on its flag and civic armoury.

Alet-les-Bains was also once the home of the parents of Nostradamus, before they moved to the more famous St Rémy in Provence, and there has been much conjecture through the ages to suggest that he would have visited the town during the Middle Ages as it was known to be was an alchemical centre of some renown. The Stars of David which form the windows of the church, in addition to their obvious Judaic connection, may also be a reference to this history, this symbol being known to represent the alchemical unification of the male and female principles. Further, the most famous bishop to have been incumbent at the church, Nicolas Pavillon, whose bishopric lasted from 1637 until 1677, is associated with both St Vincent de Paul and Jean-Jacques Olier, the builder of the church of St Sulpice in Paris. These three men were the leading figures in the formation of an organization called the Compagnie de Saint-Sacrement, known among its members as the 'Cabal of the Devout' and who used the seminary of St Sulpice as its headquarters. Some see the organization as an ultra-orthodox Catholic body, while others are of the opinion that it was utterly heretical. The latter interpretation may be close to the truth, for St Vincent de Paul (1580–1660) who was canonized in 1737, claimed during his lifetime to have been an alchemical scholar.

The cathedral at Limoux, just north of Alet-les-Bains, has, as well as a number of windows built in the shape of the Star of David, a statue of St Vincent in its grounds, and the cathedral at Carcassonne is dedicated to none other than him. Limoux Cathedral also is the site of one of the Black Madonna shrines of France, and the eleventh-century statue of her that is still on public display is associated with many miracles.

The village of Arques is set on the northern side of a widening in the valley along which the River Rialsesse runs, and is about four kilometres east of Rennes-le-Château. Its name recalls both the Ark of the Covenant, the gold-covered box in which were carried the stone tablets bearing the Ten Commandments, and the vessel constructed by Noah, the same vessel that appears in the background of the Poussin painting *Winter* or *The Deluge*.

There has been a fortified site at Arques since as early as 1154 and in 1231 Pierre de Voisins, one of the companions of

Simon de Montfort, gained possession of the village. It was his descendants who built the first château, which was started in 1280 and completed in 1319, the renovated remains of which are a popular tourist attraction today. Its completion post-dates the Albigensian Crusade and the pogrom against the Cathar heretics, yet a local tradition maintains that the building was destroyed by Simon de Montfort.

What drew my attention to this part of the landscape, however, was the siting here of a 'tomb' which, until its destruction, was the focus of much attention by those on the Rennes-le-Château trail. Similar in shape and dimensions to the tomb in Poussin's *The Shepherds of Arcadia*, it was known locally as the 'Arques tomb' although it was situated some two kilometres west of the village near the hamlet of Les Pontils. Here the road follows the river and curves around a spur created by it. On this rocky outcrop, and easily visible by anybody travelling the road east from Rennes-le-Château, was placed a large rectangular stone monument which, according to some accounts, was built early in the twentieth century by one Jean Galibert before being sold to Mr Lawrence, an American, around 1921. Owing to constant disturbance and vandalism, the new owner destroyed the edifice, according to some accounts blowing it up with dynamite, so that all remains is the concrete base on which it once stood.

Lynn Picknett and Clive Prince[5] make two claims for this tomb based on an account by a friend of theirs who lives in the area. The first is that, according to those who live locally, there has always been a tomb on that site, a claim which has been used by many writers to suggest that Poussin saw the tomb and painted it into *The Shepherds of Arcadia* from life. This argument is often reinforced by claims that the hills in the background of the work are an exact match for those which form the south side of the valley, but it is in fact very hard to discern any

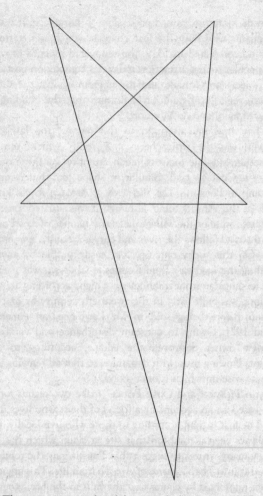

The pentagram isolated from Nicholas Poussin's 'The Shepherds of Arcadia' (see plate section)

direct similarities between the painting and the actual landscape. Their second contention is that, in accordance with local legend, the tomb was either the final resting place of Mary Magdalene or that it acted as a signpost to the site of her burial – they state that the original slab bore an arrow running its length. Yet another tradition claims that this same inscribed slab was removed from the Arques tomb and placed in the cemetery of the church at Rennes-le-Château, where it was subsequently defaced by Bérenger Saunière.

We already know that the area is rich in Magdalene traditions, but the relative modernity of the tomb may associate it more with these traditions than with any underlying historical fact. Its own late history and the fact that it would have been highly visible from the road lead me to believe that it may have been nothing more than a folly, placed there so that easily satisfied visitors to the area could go home happy that they had seen either the tomb from the Poussin painting or the tomb of Mary Magdalene and search no further. If it is a tomb, and a significant one at that, it occupies an unlikely, unprotected site. Even the idea that it once contained the body of the first owner's mother seems unlikely, especially in an area where most villages, no matter how small, have their own cemeteries.

Monuments aside, further inspection of the map reveals yet more strange place names. At the head of the valley east of Arques is a collection of topographical features which curiously bear the name 'Paradis'. There is the Col du Paradis, the Paradise Pass, through which the road from Rennes-le-Château runs east towards the villages of Albières and Mouthoumet and continues towards Narbonne. Associated with it is the 'Paradise Stream', which appears as a spring in the western approach to the col before flowing eastwards down the hill to join up as a tributary of the Rialsesse. Where it joins the river there is a small hamlet which bears the name Le Paradis (and which is just across the stream from a place called Bibet, possibly originating from the Latin word for 'to drink', the crystal-clear waters certainly having a refreshing purity and sweetness). While most of the local rock is white limestone, this end of the valley is made distinctive by the prevalence of a coarse-grained sandstone which, presumably as the result of a high iron-oxide content, is bright red. When the river is in full spate this gives it the appearance of running with blood. Indeed just west of the Col du Paradis is a small hill called the Roque Rouge, a geographical clue to the underlying geology, and many of the small local cemeteries have tombs and graves bearing the name Rouge – testimony that, minerals aside, at one time the 'Red' family were prevalent in the area and were rich enough to have built a number of sizeable mausoleums to the memory of their forebears.

My investigations had hitherto revealed the existence of a true pentagram behind the design of Poussin's *The Shepherds of Arcadia*, one that made sense of much of the composition of the painting and which, through the colours of the clothes worn by the characters portrayed, could be linked with *Winter* or the *Deluge*, which not only depicts the holy family coming ashore but gives clues to the Egyptian origins and meanings of the colours employed through the pyramids painted discreetly in the background. As I have revealed, the history of the people involved in these works, whether as friends of the artist or as the men that commissioned them, led me to what had hitherto been considered unrelated pictures and two more pentagrams. Having explored the region and its legacies, I believe that there is a causal relationship between some secret that these men wanted to conceal, their knowledge of the teachings of the ancients and the mysteries of these valleys.

Concentrating my interest at the head of the valley marked

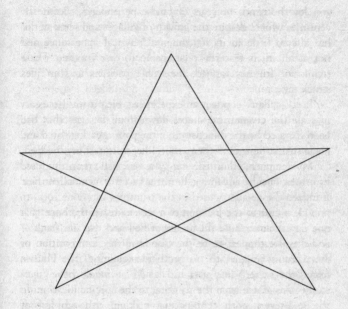

The pentagram isolated from Nicholas Poussin's 'A Dance to the Music of Time' (see plate section)

by the Col du Paradis, I noticed that there was an assortment of well-defined hills, forming a natural pattern that I had seen before. These features would have remained virtually unchanged for thousands of years, a landscape enduring down the centuries which, despite the growth of villages and settlements, has altered little in its fundamental physical appearance and not at all in its features' relationship to one another. These significant features formed discernible patterns and an idea struck me.

It was time to conduct an experiment. First it was necessary to scale the geometrical shapes down from the sizes that had been dictated by the dimensions of the paintings. I isolated and made smaller images of them, then I began to test my theory.

My approach, admittedly far more simplistic than that used by others, has the advantage that it is based on one salient fact. If indeed the geometry used in the paintings was done so as to provide a clue to the location of a secret site, in the hope that one day the secret would be discovered and the site found – and this does appear to be the case from the letter written by Abbé Louis Fouquet to his brother, explaining that Poussin feared the secret's loss after his death – it would have to be easily transferable from the painting to the specific location. In the mid-seventeenth century map-making, although already highly advanced, was not as accurate a science as it is today and therefore it would have to have been simple enough to be understood and at the same time easily employed by the user. And indeed this appears to be the case as the geometry of the paintings employs the symbol now well known to us.

Initially I took the pentagram that had been derived from Signorelli's *The Education of Pan* and laid it over the map. After some moments moving it around over the surface I found a most extraordinary fit. The point of one of the legs of the pentagram, that which had been formed at the bottom of the staff held by the elder in the painting, when aligned with the summit of the hill closest to the Col du Paradis, allowed the point of the other leg, formed at the feet of the Isis/Mary figure, to sit on top of another well-marked hill to the south. What is more, the head of the pentagram which had been at the top of the painting seemed to fit exactly with the most westerly part of the Roque Rouge, giving the shape an exact east-west alignment.

Cautiously, I then took the scaled down version of the pentagram that I had first discovered, that from Poussin's *The Shepherds of Arcadia*, and placed it over the same area. Bizarrely, it also made a fit, seeming to interlock with both the previous pentagram and with the map. The leg formed from the top of the white-robed figure's staff, when positioned on the top of the Col du Paradis hill, allowed its counterpart, formed from the top of the Horus/Jesus figure's staff, to sit on top of another hill, called Le Pech and exactly due south of the Col du Paradis hill. Like the previous pentagram, this one was also aligned east-west, with its head falling on the same spot at the tip of the Roque Rouge and pointing down the valley towards Rennes-le-Château.

So far there seemed to be a direct correlation between geographical features at the head of the Rennes-le-Château valley and two of the pentagrams that I had isolated. The acid test was whether or not the third would also result in a fit. This one had been taken from the second Poussin work, *A Dance to the Music of Time*, a female-dominated painting and one which I had associated strongly with both the Magdalene and the Virgin Mary figures. If the pentagrams in the other two paintings were based on an east-west alignment, the feminine principle behind this painting ought to imply a complementary north–south, polar arrangement, so I turned it through ninety degrees and placed it over the two pentagrams on the map. I

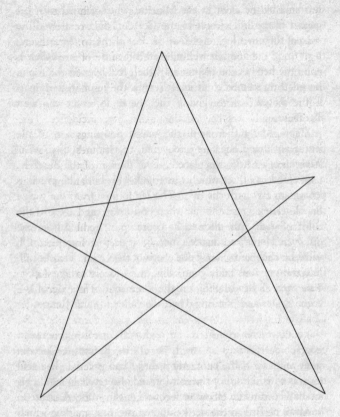

The pentagram isolated from Luca Signorellis's
'The Education of Pan' (see plate section)

was stunned by what I saw. Matching its north-easterly foot, gained from the cherubim blowing the bubble of creation on the painting, with the same hill as the other two, and its other leg, from the cherubim holding the sands of time in the painting, with a tumulus just to the north of the Roque Rouge, revealed that its head pointed south to correspond with a tall hill to the south of the col.

This surely was beyond the realms of coincidence. Three pentagrams, drawn from three separate paintings with similar histories, fitting on a map of geological features, that would have changed little since the time of Christ, of the head of a valley, the mouth of which is overlooked by an ancient village known to be the focus of great esoteric enquiry. Then, while double-checking that I had made no errors and that wishful thinking had not made me stretch the credibility of this discovery, I noticed another strange fact. The intersection of each of the pentagrams, which had fallen on Jesus in *The Education of Pan*, Mary Magdalene in *A Dance to the Music of Time* and the head of John the Baptist in *The Shepherds of Arcadia*, all seemed to point to one place on the map.

The hill on which this intersection falls forms the end of the valley. At its northernmost part is the small plateau across which the pass of the Col du Paradis runs. The pass extends southwards for half a kilometre before turning westwards to end in a spur, at the foot of which runs the River Rialsesse. In the crook of this rocky elbow is the Roque Rouge. But east of this outcrop, nestled in the apex of the curve, is a small collection of buildings, a settlement whose name has come to be the same as the hill itself. It is called Estagnol.

In Old French this translates as 'Lamb of the East'. Yet more fascinating is the derivation given by Brochart in *Huguet's Dictionary of France*, which bases its origins in the ancient French of the area, the language of Oc (the *langue d'oc*) or

Occitan, from which the region takes its name. Brochard states that *estagnol* can also be rendered as 'the essence of the sacrifice'. The very name of this place was imbued with religious significance! But was there any confirmation hidden in the paintings that would confirm Estagnol's meanings as being worthy of interest?

In *A Dance to the Music of Time* Orion in his golden chariot makes his bountiful sweep across the skies at the top of the painting. What is more, his head forms the head of the pentagram. Was Orion himself also relevant?

Like many of the ancient gods, Orion is immortalized in the heavens, an easily discernible constellation in the star map. His shoulders and head, his jewelled belt and the sword which hangs from it are easily visible, as is his raised arm shaking his club defiantly in the face of the bull Taurus. As he circles the sky it is not hard to imagine that this great hunter of antiquity is still in pursuit of his quarry. Having no rival for the wealth and brilliance of its composite stars, his constellation had an importance to the ancients that was unequalled, in many civilizations being associated with the sun – all the giants and heroes with which he has been linked being to a greater or lesser extent sun gods. He himself was a sun god to both the Egyptians and the Phoenicians; to the Greeks he was Phaethon, the reckless driver of the chariot of the sun who crashed from heaven into the River Eridanus, which in the world of the stars flows under the feet of Orion. He was also Uru-Anna, the 'Light of Heaven', an ancient Sumerian sun god, from whom it is thought that his later name may originate. He was also Tammuz, whose story of descent into hell and subsequent release by the goddess Ishtar served as a template for many of the sun-darkness, winter-summer and light-versus-dark myths that were to follow. Star worship, perhaps the earliest form of human religion, was also frequently coupled with the belief that man absorbed the qualities of the food that he ate – an ancient 'you are what you eat' theory. Early pyramid texts depict him as an omnipotent god who fed on both the bodies of other gods and, according to some, human sacrifices.

There is a description in the tomb of the fifth-dynasty Egyptian King Unas (c.4300 BCE) which describes the dead pharaoh as having 'become one' with the god Sahu, who is an interpretation of Orion. He roamed the limits of heaven preying upon gods and men, feeding on their slain bodies and absorbing the magic qualities that they possessed. It is thought that the identification of Unas with the exploits of Orion is probably a later development, a bid to ensure that the deceased monarch would also share in the magic of the star-gods.

With the advent of the Osiris- and Isis-based religions in dynastic Egypt, Orion was portrayed in carvings and inscriptions as a man running, looking back over his shoulder and holding either a star or the hieroglyph of life in his right hand. Sometimes he was depicted as sailing down the long river of the sky in a small boat that was formed by the constellation of Hare, which lies underneath him in the firmament. This association with water was continued by the Greeks and the Romans – for whom he was the son of Neptune, having the power to walk unharmed over the waters of the Earth. In Graeco-Roman mythology he fell in love with Merope, the daughter of the island king Oenopion, and sought her hand in marriage. However, her father was deeply opposed to the union and sent Orion on a range of difficult challenges, promising to consider Orion's request of marriage when he returned. It was not long before Orion realized that Oenopion's promises meant nothing and he derived a plan to carry Merope away but was discovered and held prisoner in the Palace. Oenopion condemned the giant to be blinded and cast out, helpless, on the shore of the island. Wandering alone and sightless, Orion wept for his fate, until he heard the sound of Cyclops' hammer ringing out in the far distance. He followed the noise to its source, finally reaching Lemnos and the forge of Vulcan, where the god, on hearing his story, took pity and gave him one of his blacksmiths as a guide to lead him to the land of the sun. Thanking Vulcan, Orion lifted his guide to his shoulders so that they could move faster and they strode out towards the east to find the land where the sun god rises, the source of all light. Arriving just as the sun was lifting from the horizon, Orion felt the warmth of the rays, opened his eyes and his vision cleared so that he was as far-seeing as he had ever been.

Also in the Graeco-Roman tradition is the significant association that Orion has with Diana. Diana the goddess of the moon and hunting, although sometimes driving her pale chariot across the night skies, often preferred to go hunting on Earth, leaving the night sky in darkness when she did so. (This story accounted for the fact that unlike the sun, the moon varied from day to day, frequently being completely absent from the sky.) One night Diana was hunting wild boar in the forest when she came across the mortal Orion and instantly fell in love with him. Forsaking her duties, she left the night sky in darkness as she followed Orion through the forests of the Earth.

Her brother, Apollo, the sun god, was furious on hearing that Diana had deserted her duties and made even more angry when he was told that she had fallen in love with a mortal. He tried to reason with her but she would not listen. On his daily race across the skies he thought about the problem and concocted a plan by which to resolve it. As he neared the horizon that evening he saw the figure of Orion bathing at sea, alone and some distance from the shore. Focusing all the powers of his golden rays on the figure of the giant, he made the water around him sparkle and leap until it was blinding to the eyes, making Orion nothing more than a shapeless blur among the waves. Leaning down from his chariot, he called out to his sister, wagering that even the goddess of hunting could not hit the faint dark object on the horizon. Seizing the challenge, she took up her bow and aimed so accurately that its dart pierced the head of Orion, who sank beneath the waves. When she stood on the shore waiting for her lover to arrive, the waves washed his body ashore, and she realized Apollo's treachery. Furious with anger and grief, she stepped into her own silver chariot, and carrying the body of Orion with her, set off across the sky.

When she reached the place where the sky was darkest, she set him down and the heavens lit up with stars, marking his head, his shoulders, his sword and his belt. Even the lion's skin which he carried over his arm was sprinkled with stars. Under his feet ran the River Eridanus in order that he might still walk its waters. Closely following him, Diana placed the two stars Sirius and Procyon to represent his favourite hunting dogs – which we now recognize as Canis Major and Canis Minor. When she stepped back to look at her work and saw how splendidly he shone there, she thought that even her brother the sun would be jealous of his beauty. Her heart was now cold and ever since then the moon, although sometimes bright, has always appeared lifeless.

Even in Norse mythology Orion plays a part as one of the big toes of Orvandil, the giant archer whose other toe was at one time frozen so hard that the god Thor was able to break it off and throw it up to the northern skies, where it can still be seen among the stars of Ursa Major. The three stars which form his belt are known in Scandinavia as the Spinning Wheel of Frigg, the Queen of Heaven, while in Mongolia they are the Three Dogs, and in New Zealand Maori tradition they are referred to as the elbow of the god Maui and also represent the stern of the canoe whose anchor is the Southern Cross. In

Hindu mythology Orion is regarded to be the giant 'Lord of the Creatures', an ascription which is virtually identical to the Middle Eastern recognition of him. Even in early Jewish traditions he was recognized as the giant Nimrod, fixed to the sky as a punishment for his rebellion against Jehovah, and he also forms a keystone in Zoroastrianism.

More recently Orion has been shown to have a renewed importance in our understanding of the ancients. Robert Bauval, an Egyptian-born engineer, is credited with being the first person in modern times to link the configuration of stars which form Orion's Belt with the strangely asymmetric positioning of the pyramids at Giza. His book *The Orion Mystery*[6] showed that, far from being important to the ancients merely as a source of legends, the configuration of stars in Orion was used as a template for the positioning of the pyramids. His discovery put the significance of Orion in a completely new light for modern readers and researchers, and although the debate continues, it is clear that there is a strong correlation between the star map of the constellation and Giza's world-famous landmarks.

Given the significance of Orion in terms of both mythology and the physical and intellectual composition of *A Dance to the Music of Time*, I decided to conduct a further experiment along the same principles as I had employed for the pentagrams. Orion is comprised of seven main stars of which the most widely known are Betelgeuse, which marks his right shoulder, and Rigel, his left knee. While his shoulders and knees are in a rough, slanted rectangle, the three stars which form his belt bisect this, angling down to the giant's left-hand side, his sword delineated by what is now known as the Great Orion Nebula hanging from the 'belt'. I first scaled the star map to that of the map of the region I was using and, as with the pentagrams, placed it over the area that the pentagrams seemed to indicate as being of interest. Again the fit was both immediate and extraordinary. Each of the main stars corresponded to a particular hill or tumulus and the stars which marked the belt fell on the ridge of Estagnol, in exactly the same places as the intersection of the pentagrams.

While aware that this may have been the result of mere coincidence, I was nonetheless stunned at the apparent connection. Here was seeming confirmation that the paintings were indeed a coded message leading to a site of great significance that actually existed, the importance of which derived from its connection with a holy family. And it was a secret that had been kept for nigh on 2,000 years.

All the evidence pointed to the ridge at Estagnol, but there was no real indication of what lay there. Surely if there had been anything of import left to find in this much-studied region, it would have been discovered by now. Yet amid all the published material I could find no mention of this place. Most researchers had concentrated their attentions on the village or immediate environs of Rennes-le-Château itself, or places to the west of Estagnol. And as yet, nothing tangible had been found.

Whether the paintings, the pentagrams, the coded clues and the Orion link amounted to anything worthwhile, or were just an extraordinary accumulation of coincidences, had to be tested. The only way to find out was to follow these esoteric signs and visit the place that they all pointed to: Estagnol, that small hill ridge at the head of the valley.

CHAPTER TEN

THE SITE AND THE

ARCADIAN TOMB

☆

At the foot of the hill on which Rennes-le-Château lies is the village of Couiza, from which a road, the D613, runs eastwards through the hamlets of Serres and Arques. Just before Serres there is a turning to the right which follows a small river called the Sals, of which the Rialsesse is a tributary, and which flows down from the village of Rennes-les-Bains. According to the local tradition Mary Magdalene would have passed through the entrance to this steep-sided valley, guarded to the east by the volcano-shaped hill of Pech Cardou, of which so much was made by Paul Schellenberger and Richard Andrews, and to the west by a peak that has at its summit the remains of the Château de Blanchefort, thought to have been the ancestral home of Bertrand de Blanchefort, the fourth Grand Master of the Knights Templar during the twelfth century.[1] As the road winds up the picturesque valley the hills to the right become almost sheer cliffs until, just before reaching Rennes-les-Bains, the valley widens a little and the river broadens out to reveal the site of the ancient spa, the waters that have percolated through the rock bubbling out into a small grotto before passing under the road to tumble into the river.

Rennes-les-Bains is a tidy, clipped village, nestling among

the hills. Popular with tourists, it attracts people from all over Europe to take the waters at its thermal spa and to sit in the square watching pétanque. The fittest brave the steep climb up the wooded hill which lies to the south of the village to see the 'Fauteuil du Diable', the Devil's Armchair, a rock carved into the shape of a seat (which bears a striking resemblance to the chair on which Pan is seated in Signorelli's *The Education of Pan*), and to admire the view down into the village and across the surrounding hills to the east.

If instead of turning right off the D613 one carries straight on, the road continues past Serres before coming to the hamlet of Les Pontils, curving left and then right in a lazy hairpin. On the right of this bend juts the rocky spur, carved out by the Rialsesse, on the top of which used to stand the 'Arcadian tomb'. The plinth on which it once stood until its recent destruction is easily visible from the road and still attracts sightseers.

It was along this road that I drove, my exhilaration at being so close to the site that all the evidence I had accumulated pointed towards tinged also with a sense of apprehension. I placed a cassette in the stereo and let the strains of Debussy's *La Mer* and *Prélude à l'Après-midi d'un Faun* ease away some of my fears. Could this be nothing more than a wild-goose chase? Could there really be a link between the supposed banishment of a living Jesus – sent into exile with Mary Magdalene as an act of political expediency – and a succession of learned, wealthy and powerful men who had become privy to such a secret and sought to protect and guard it through esoteric and Kabbalist coding in works of art? The notion did seem preposterous. As with any major discovery, the time between collating and analysing the evidence and actually testing for the proof of it was fraught with doubt. To be so close to knowing for certain whether there was anything there, or merely a bare and barren hillside that would prove nothing, gave a normally pleasant drive an air of heart-thumping anticipation.

From Les Pontils the road continues east, the valley first thinning to a small notch between two squat hills before broadening out to a wider basin containing a patchwork of pastures and small, wooded areas. On the left of the road is the château of Arques, its tall, square tower seemingly supported by the round turrets at each corner, set on a rising knoll and surrounded by the high wall which encloses its grassy grounds. Protected by a steep hill to its rear, it is well positioned to keep guard over the entrance to the basin, looking south over the Lac d'Arques towards the precipitous wooded hills of La Berco Grando and La Berco Petito and with a clear line of sight east and west along the axis of the valley. Driving past, it is hard to ignore the almost 800-year history of this building, the hewn and dressed stones of its solid walls giving silent testament to the bold tradition of the Templars and the atrocities carried out against the Cathars in the name of a broader Christian Church. The road continues past the château towards the village of Arques itself, a collection of quiet rural homes and farms which straddle what is no more than a metalled country lane which once would have a been a dry, dusty track along which rode knights resplendent in their Templar garb and farmers and families taking their produce to the village to trade or sell. Beyond the village the river runs alongside the road, joined by streams which flow down from the hills on the left. As the road winds up the slopes its turns and bends become tighter, negotiating the gullies through which the winter rains run as torrents. The map tells of ruins and carved standing stones on the hilltops and caves and ancient mine workings in the gullies and along the river's steep banks, giving this end of the valley an air of contemplative antiquity.

Leaving Arques behind, the valley starts to close in again,

the white stone of the hill's rocky outcrops and the eroded sides of the river's course giving way to the deep-red stone of the Clot da Rous and the Roque Rouge a kilometre to the south. Here all is quiet. It is a true Arcadia, both beautiful and desolate, welcoming and harsh. The underlying rock can be seen more frequently, poking up through the thin soil on the hillsides, while on the valley floor in small, meadowed fields bordered with wild flowers, cattle and sheep graze and fatten.

Ahead the valley floor starts to rise and the modest pastures of the smallholdings give way to a mixed forest of pines and oaks. The air cools in the shade of the trees and the warm, comforting smells of grassland and damp river banks are replaced by the crisp, clean fragrance of pine needles and fresh leaves. Here there are no villages, no houses to detract from the natural beauty of the countryside. Only the road, winding up the hillside, reminds the traveller of the people living in the valley.

About two kilometres from the start of the climb up the hill's western slope, the road crests the ridge and there on the verge, in a clearing in the woods which surround it, is a small road sign bearing the name of the hill over which the pass cuts, Estagnol. To the left is a picnic area for those who wish to stop and savour the still, cool beauty of the woods, but to the right is a small track, made by those who tend the forest, running down the spine of the ridge. From here it is necessary to continue on foot, the four-wheel-drive vehicles used by the forestry workers having made such deeps ruts in the track that no saloon car can negotiate them. Soon the track veers off to the right, going down the hill to a collection of two or three recently constructed buildings which are used to store the equipment necessary for the forest's upkeep and to fight the fires which occasionally break out during the summer months. Although the map shows that there is a footpath running the length of the ridge, there is no indication of it on the ground, no signs or clearly defined pathway, just a thick growth of long grass, brambles and thistle along the open space of the ridgetop, with the trees falling away down the slopes to the right and left. This is a place visited by few people, a rural idyll with beautiful views westwards along the valley through which the road traces its path towards Rennes-le-Château, eastwards towards the rising slopes of Le Pech, and beyond to the Forêt Domaniale de Fourtou.

Slowly the ridge begins to curve to the right and the view changes to follow the peaks of the crest that forms the valley's southern edge, a jagged-line that ends in the distant summit of Pech Cardou, easily visible in the clear, still air of a summer's afternoon. A track that is marked on the map as crossing the ridge of Estagnol has obviously fallen into disuse and has been reclaimed by the woodland, for there is no trace of it as the walker proceeds westwards. The ridge starts to rise ahead before culminating in its highest point, marked on the map as being 705 metres above sea level and giving a spectacular view of the entire area. Even to the seasoned walker or hill-climber this place seems to exude a special quality, a sense of peace and calm stillness that belies the effort of making progress through the thick vegetation.

And then as the ridge starts to descend from its modest summit, before dropping down to the valley floor in increasing levels of steepness, one's attention is drawn to a feature which seems to jar on the eye. On the right-hand side of the spur is a tall block of the rough limestone which dominates the immediate area. Standing alone like a solitary white tooth among the trees, it is invisible from the road, now nearly two kilometres away, so that although it is distinctive and at odds with the rest of the steep-sided, highly eroded ridge, it is not until one is close to it that it becomes visible – a lone sentry, well camouflaged from the eyes of the casual observer, but obvious to anyone who has made their way far enough through the woods to this striking spot.

It was to this point that I came, leaving the car parked on the roadside and walking the length of ridge, spade and map in hand, to the point that the pentagrams had indicated. I walked up to and inspected this imposing rock, some five metres tall and four wide. While I was excited at finding something at the exact site suggested by the years of research with the paintings and their pentagrams, my sense of discovery was nonetheless curbed by the fact that this in no way could be described as a tomb. Certainly it was an impressive piece of local geology that had somehow remained standing while the bedrock around it and of which it was obviously comprised had been eroded away. At its foot lay a small collection of boulders which appeared to be more in keeping with the processes which had formed them and served to highlight the monolithic appearance of this naturally formed edifice. Its potential as a tomb, as a place of burial, was non-existent. But the area itself did seem to be in keeping with the landscape in which Poussin had placed his tomb in *The Shepherds of Arcadia*, the jagged ridges in the background of the painting echoing the appearance of the ridge which runs westwards towards Rennes-le-Château. Even the trees to the sides of and behind the lone rock appeared to be the same species as those in the painting, and at the foot of the standing stone was a small, flat-topped rock which looked identical to the stone on which the Jesus figure was resting his white-sandled foot, the same foot that had formed one of the points of the pentagram.

As I neared this standing stone to inspect it more closely, I could see that its position gave it a commanding westerly view along the whole length of the valley. But as I picked my way through the few boulders which were scattered around the little plateau I became aware of something else. Behind the stone, where the ridge falls away sharply, there was nothing.

The stone was on the edge of an escarpment. It was an immense finger of rock which marked the edge of the ridge, beyond which there was a ten-metre cliff dropping vertically away, and at the bottom more dense vegetation, the forest carpeting the steep slope down to the valley floor. But there was something else. From my position by the side of the standing rock, as I looked down over the edge I could make out a large slab of rock which had obviously fallen away from the crest where I stood and had landed so that its uppermost edge rested against the cliff face.

At this point my mind began to race with the implications of this. The visual clues in *The Shepherds of Arcadia* seemed to point to this being the site, confirming what the pentagrams in the paintings and even the strange coincidence of the Orion star map had already shown. But the tomb in the painting is the work of human masons, carrying the enigmatic inscription 'Et in Arcadia Ego'. But what actually is Arcadia? Dictionaries define it as a land of shepherds and shepherdesses, a rustic place. Perhaps then this is the real clue: the tomb is not actually a man-made structure, like the one that had been placed by the roadside at Les Pontils, but a naturally occurring place made by nature, by Pan, the rustic god of the earth – who stands to the left of the tomb in Poussin's rendering of the scene.

If this were the case, then the vertical rock would fit with the position of the tomb in the painting, acting like a headstone and just visible enough as a marker to those in the valley who knew where to look. Even the little flat-topped stone was in the right place to suggest that this could be the site and seemed to imply that Poussin must have actually been here in order to have noticed such details. But, in the absence of any other features, the site of what?

In order to find out I lowered myself down one side of the cliff using tree limbs to support myself until I reached the bottom, finding myself standing on the massive stone slab leaning against the cliff face. I had noticed from the top of the bluff that there seemed to be a hole to one side of the slab, a gap in the accumulated vegetation and moss that was acting like a cork. Working my way across the steep incline, I approached it and tried to peer in, but the opening was too small to see if there was anything inside. I started to tug at the plugs of moss, finding that large handfuls came away easily until I had opened up a hole about a metre square. Now that I was able to see inside, there appeared to be a large cavity between the fallen slab and the cliff face, with a level earth floor some two metres beneath me. I eased myself through the hole that I had created and dropped down to the floor, finding myself in a triangular cave some five metres long and a metre and a half high. On hands and knees I crawled along the packed-earth floor of the cavity, noticing a small triangular opening at the other end through which I was able to crawl out. Exiting the cave, I stood with my back to the cliff face looking down the steeply inclined, heavily wooded slope. To my left was another fallen slab, one that had been invisible from the top of the escarpment but which also leaned against the cliff and formed another triangular cave.

Amazed by this, I looked up at the solitary stone, now some six metres above my head, and contemplated my discovery. The single finger of white rock looked increasingly as if it could have been designated as the headstone of a tomb, the actual burial site positioned at the bottom of the cliff where it would be both less noticeable and less likely to be disturbed. As I had crawled through the first cave I had certainly noticed a number of things that now struck me as odd. The earth floor had underneath it, where I had scraped away the soil to make an exit, a bed of stones which on closer inspection appeared to have been deliberately placed there. Each of them had been turned so that the rougher sides, where the faces were jagged and irregular, were placed face down in the earth and the largest, smooth side, face upwards. They were closely embedded in the underlying soil to form a stable, horizontal floor upon which the blown earth and dust of the wood that had entered the cave over the years had formed a top stratum which covered this stony level.

Back in the cave, I set about clearing some of this accumulated level of earth to reveal more of the underlying stones and as I did so I noticed something else that seemed strange. For such an ideal hiding place and despite the fact that there had been a small opening at ground level – which I had had to widen in order to make an exit – there were no signs of any animal having ever used the place. It would be reasonable to expect that such a well-secreted natural lair would be used by any of the abundant wildlife in the area and yet here there were no signs of fur or feathers that might have been left by resident fauna, no bones or evidence of the place having been used by a predator as a safe place to hole up and eat captured prey. Nor was there any spoor or faeces. The interior of the cave was utterly devoid of any sign of ever having been used by an animal.

As I worked with the spade to clear away the earth I had disturbed at the exit of the first cave, I noticed something else. Despite the fact that it was a hot summer's day and the walk along the top of the ridge to the site had been made harder by the absence of any breeze, here at base of the cliff the cooling shade of the trees was aided by a gentle current of air, a breeze which came up from the valley floor and which not only cooled the area at the foot of the cliff but also kept the interior of the cave much cooler than the ambient air temperature. It also seemed to have the secondary effect of keeping the cavern dry, for whereas the earth outside, covered by leaf litter and vegetation, was moist, that inside was dust-dry and showed no signs of ever having been sodden by winter rainfall. As I took this in, it began to look increasingly as though this site, marked by the large monolith at the top of the cliff and with the two cave-like structures formed by the fallen slabs below, could have been, if not formed by human design, then certainly adapted by human hands for some purpose. But created how and for what purpose?

Answers to either of these questions can only be speculative. Given the nature of the rock, it is entirely possible that each of the leaning slabs at one time stood either side of the remaining upright at the top of the cliff, but as a result of weathering became weak enough at the base to topple over on to the escarpment below. Indeed, given the intensity of the summer sun in this region and the cold weather which comes down from the Pyrenees in winter, it is conceivable that such weathering may have had a thermal component which would have hastened the process. But it is equally plausible that, the slabs perhaps already having been weakened by the natural and meteorological conditions that prevailed, their descent from the top of the cliff was hastened by manpower to create their present rough structure. We can only assume that such 'builders' had to rely on the chance that the slabs would fall to rest against the cliff, leaving a triangular aperture beneath each. Then again, given the prevalence of new theories relating to the construction of Stonehenge and the Pyramids, perhaps there was little luck involved. There may have been engineering techniques known to the ancients but subsequently forgotten.

In either case, the structures exist. They have also at some stage in their history been worked to provide a solid, flat floor – although the headroom, even in the larger cave which I found first, does not lend itself to human habitation by anyone other than short children or pygmies; both are so narrow that each can take only one adult.

I thought back to the clues that had brought me to this place, specifically the three paintings – of which *The Shepherds of Arcadia* was central and the same painting in which Abbé Bérenger Saunière supposedly showed so much interest during his trip to Paris. I thought of the image of the tomb and confirmed to myself that the position in which it was depicted in the painting was too uncanny a match with where I now stood for it to be the product of coincidence. The pentagram that had been concealed in it had been one of three that had directed me to this specific – and hitherto unknown – site. The painting being an allegorical image of the holy family, which portrays the duality of the flesh and the spirit through the figures of Jesus and Pan, and contains a reference to the physical connection between Jesus and the Magdalene, it seemed ever more possible that the actual lives of these very real people had been thoroughly researched, and embedded in a work which seemed only to make sense when viewed as the pictorial result of a secret told to the artist, the secret of a heresy which could not be publicly proclaimed. Abbé Louis Fouquet had alluded to such a secret in the letter he had sent to his brother after meeting Poussin in Rome. The men who were behind this picture and the other two were men whose quest for the lost knowledge of the ancients, whose erudition and understanding of the languages and esoteric beliefs that they held, could so easily have led them to uncover a veiled truth that the Catholic Church would fight to suppress: namely, the real facts surrounding not only the death but also the whereabouts of the mortal remains of the man who had founded that Church and in whose name its works continued. All these elements played on my mind as I surveyed the site and thought of the mixture of fact and conjecture, hard evidence and supposition that had led me here.

A little further down the slope from the bottom of the cliff and the slab-roofed caves was an overgrown patch of rocks and boulders that looked as though it had spread out as the result of a rockfall. From my vantage point between the two cave entrances and with my back to the small cliff face, the scree looked as if it had originated from where I stood. Indeed, judging from where it had come to rest, the rocky debris could only have come from where my feet now were, between the two cave entrances. Instantly I grasped another piece of the puzzle, which linked this discovery with my translation of the coded message on one of the parchments discovered by Bérenger Saunière.

We know that Dagobert I was something of an early commercial archaeologist, raiding abandoned Roman hoards of jewellery, coinage and precious stones to fill his coffers and fund his armies. What is more, he was connected with the area and is known to have been an active tomb-robber. But there is one tomb of particular interest. A tomb where he found not only inscribed artefacts but also two bodies which he left on the hillside while taking the treasure to Paris. The inscriptions had led his wife to insist that he return the artefacts to where he had discovered them, but he went instead to the Abbey of St Denis, which subsequently rushed a party of monks to the tomb to recover the bodies and transport them to Paris and then on to Rome.

The warning inscription on one of the pieces of treasure stated that 'anyone removing them from the tomb would be cursed and their line would be cursed also'. Here was an echo of the coded phrase in the Saunière parchment, for which the new translation reads 'To Dagoberti I King and to Sion is this treasure and he/it is there dead' or alternatively 'To Dagoberti I King and to Sion is this treasure and it is death'.

We have seen already the likelihood that Dagobert, while in the area, would have been aware of the local legends of treasure hidden by the Visigoths and the Romans alike, and would no doubt have been familiar with the tradition that Mary Magdalene once lived and travelled throughout the district. We have also seen that *Le Serpent Rouge*, that curious collection of zodiacal prose poems, while of uncertain authorship and even less certain origins, does state: 'But how many have pillaged the house leaving only the embalmed corpses and a number of metal things they could not carry'. Could it be that this was in fact the tomb that was raided by Dagobert, and the rocky debris is the remains of a pile of stones and small boulders that had been placed between the mouths of each of the cave tombs to seal them? The stones would have been pulled away and thrown down the slope as Dagobert and his party tried to gain access to the interiors. It is certainly within the realms of possibility that these curious structures are in fact rustic tombs. The possibility of living in them is severely restricted by the lack of space that they offer, but their long, narrow chambers are similar in design to the spaces in which coffins are laid in the crypts beneath churches.

Returning to the interior of the larger of the tombs, I could discern from about halfway down the length of the interior, towards the far end where the triangular opening had been sealed with large boulders, a vertical line of flat slabs of rock. Positioned so that they abutted on to the angled roof of the cave-tomb, they gave the appearance that they may at one time have been placed in such a way as to contain a body, a form of stone sarcophagus within the larger space of the tomb itself.

The smaller, western, second cave also had a chamber formed by a huge fallen slab leaning against the face of the cliff. This had the same flat floor of packed earth in which small stones and pebbles had been set so that their flattest side formed a stable, horizontal deck and an interior lining of flat slabs aligned with the sloping roof mass. Both chambers could easily have formed rectangular stone coffins.

I returned to my rucksack at the top of the cliff to check the paintings for any other details which might be specific to the location. The ground behind the tomb in *The Shepherds of Arcadia* certainly fell away sharply. In the picture this can be seen best at the right-hand rear corner of the tomb itself, where the earth angles down, revealing another step on the tomb's plinth. If my interpretation that the tomb in the painting was meant to denote the solitary natural headstone of the location was right, then it was painted with remarkable accuracy.

I was also reminded of an engraving I had seen by Athanasius Kircher, the classical scholar and esotericist from whom Poussin had taken lessons in perspective. Purporting to be a drawing made from descriptions brought back by a Father Martini of an effigy near the town of Tunchuen in the Fukien province of China, it depicted a rocky spur set in a barren, hilly landscape. The spur took up the fore and mid-ground of the work and on both its left- and right-hand flanks there was vegetation in the form of sprouting bushes and small trees. The key elements of this work were a male human bust on top of the spur with his arms folded in the sign of a cross over his chest and mounted on two boulders. Not only could that be seen as a representation of the ridge of Estagnol but the bust was positioned, near the right-hand flank, in exactly the same position as the headstone at which I was looking. The face of the bust also showed European, not Oriental features. Nor was this all. Below this ridgetop statue, further down the right-hand side of the hill, were two fallen slabs of rock, their bases resting on a narrow escarpment and their top edges leaning against the small cliff at the base of the statue. I also recalled a severed head at the base of one of the fallen slabs which, with its pointed nose, highly defined cheekbones and brow ridge, let alone its pompadour hairstyle, was indisputably not that of an Oriental. What was Kircher trying to suggest? Had he veiled an artistic description of the site with a false Chinese setting? Poussin need not have visited the site himself – some scholars have doubted his presence in the Languedoc – but may have executed a painting under the eyewitness Kircher's instructions. The result was a painting which Poussin's patron and Athanasius's employer, the man who would become Pope Clement IX, could hang in his private apartments for his personal viewing, an informed masterwork by one of the most fashionable artists of the day. Poussin and Kircher may both, of course, have visited the site, and maybe even together, in order to gain a sense of the place that would be conveyed by the finished work. Later checks showed that the notes accompanying the Kircher engraving did imply a special significance to the scene, and as a representation of life. Father Martini, when discussing the supposedly Chinese monument: 'could not say whether it was artificial or natural. It seems to be an exteriorisation of that magnetic or etheric quality of a landscape which we call "spirit of place".'[10] The term 'spirit of place' could even be construed to be a covert reference to 'the place of the spirit'.

I was also minded of the recurring image in Leonardo da Vinci's two versions of the The Virgin of the Rocks. The triangular formation depicted in both of these paintings was, to my mind, nothing less than a reference to the tombs which I had just discovered. The fact that the X-ray of the Louvre version of Poussin's The Shepherds of Arcadia bore exactly the same image served only to confirm to me that the connection that I had made earlier was correct.

The late-afternoon sun was now far over to the west, floating languidly over the village of Rennes-le-Château and picking out the relief of the hills on either side of the valley in long shadows. I sat on the edge of the cliff, my legs hanging down towards the two tombs. The sequence of discoveries that had led me to this isolated spot in the Languedoc countryside was far-ranging but incontrovertible in the associations that it established between them. The reinterpretation of the Rennes-le-Château parchment which had brought the history of Dagobert I to the fore for the first time. His extraordinary deal-making with the Church, which had founded the strength of a united France, the origins of that deal in the discovery of a tomb with its treasure and bodies, and the dire warning that had so disturbed his wife. The local legends of Mary Magdalene, so closely woven into the traditions of the area. The mystery surrounding the crucifixion and the subsequent disappearance of the body of Jesus, which had led to the Church's claims of resurrection but which could so easily have been a well stage-managed event, designed to protect the political careers of two powerful men and at the same time appeal to the fragile sensibilities of the Jewish Council of elders.

The fact that both Pontius Pilate and Herod had been exiled to this place, Herod to the same area even, gave enormous credibility to the theoretical banishment of Jesus to this land, with its international and multicultural population that would have been conducive to his continuing his ministry. All this led to the possibility that he had been here, in a countryside which, although more temperate than his home-land, was so similar in topography, vegetation and atmosphere that it could have been a home from home.

And then there were the paintings, which drew together so many strands. Those images of a holy family coming ashore, rich in esoteric symbolism and references, of the spiritual education of the young Jesus at the feet of Pan, the mortal brother of the man who held the spirit, the two halves which make the whole, and finally of the allegorical resting place of the senior members of that family, the return of their bodies to the god of the Earth from whence they had come. My investigation of the painters, patrons and personalities behind these works led in each case to the implication that there was a secret that had to be both protected and continued, a shrouded truth that, if exposed, would be refuted, denied and subsequently lost.

I set about packing my papers and equipment, pausing first to take some photographs of the site and the tombs while the light was still strong enough to pick out details. As I did so I thought too of the area's rich heritage of so-called heresy. Could it have originated from the words of a travelling preacher from the other side of the Mediterranean, a man whose sermons contained a subtext that was so Gnostic in meaning, so close to the basis of the beliefs of the Cathars who had once made this same valley their home? His words of wisdom had emphasized a quest for enlightenment, a path of self-determination which also formed the bedrock of the actions which both the local people and the Knights Templar who had eventually settled in the area had undertaken. The same knightly endeavours which had become surrounded in mystery and mystique and which had led to the Grail Romances, those stories of chivalrous asceticism and of a quest for either the most holy of objects or the most personal of truths – so akin to the principles of Gnosticism.

All these factors had led me here, not knowing what to expect or even if there would be anything to find. And yet I had made a discovery. A very real and tangible unearthing of two tombs, marked by a headstone and which conformed to every aspect of the intellectual and paper trail which had guided me to this site. Checking that I had left nothing behind, I secured my bag and with a last look around, I turned my back to my discovery and walked back up the ridge that only a few hours before I had walked down so expectantly yet with such trepidation. But now I knew I had physical proof that I had indeed managed to crack the code of the Arcadian Cipher.

EPILOGUE

☆

I had known when I embarked on investigating this mystery that its conclusion would probably not involve the discovery of incontrovertible proof. The likelihood was that there would be no hidden treasure in the form that Hitler and others both before and after him had sought. Indeed there had been clues along the way which suggested that if anything were to be found it would more than likely be spiritual rather than material in nature. What I had discovered however was a place which was not meant to exist. A place that the centuries were meant to have covered up. A place which I had come to as a result of interpreting an interconnected string of facts. Those facts had existed for all to discern although the specific interpretation had been my own. It had led to this ridge, a place called Estagnol, 'the lamb of the east', and to two tombs that could so easily be the rustic sarcophagi in which were laid the bodies of the man who gave birth to a religion and the woman who gave birth to his child.

Unknown to me as I left the site there was to be one final revelation, an extraordinary phenomenon which I had not seen and could not have imagined during the time I had spent there. On my return to London I developed the films that I had exposed on the afternoon I spent on the ridge. As I flicked through the photographs of the surrounding landscape, the headstone and the two tombs, there was one particular image that caught my eye. It had been taken from the space between the two entrances, the area that had at one time been covered with the mound of boulders and rocks which had blocked access to the tombs and protected their contents. It was of the entrance to the first tomb, the larger of the two and that which I had first climbed into. At first glance it appeared to show nothing more than a white rock slab on the left hand side, the rock that had fallen from the top of the cliff, and the darkened interior of the tomb itself, lit only by the flash of the camera. But then I noticed something else. On the right of the frame was the vertical side of the tomb, formed by the wall of the cliff and covered by ivy and moss. Whilst this did not look odd and was exactly as I remembered it, it was what lay just inside the entrance that held my attention. Up against the wall, indeed actually part of it, was the image of a man, either naturally formed from the lie of the strata or carved by some unknown hand. A man with long hair and a beard whose face reminded me of an image I had seen before, in paintings, drawings and on the Shroud of Turin. The face of the man called Jesus.

There can be no absolute proof that these tombs once contained the bodies of Jesus and the Magdalene – but the connection, and the tomb's existence there, is uncanny. To my mind it stretched credulity to say there is no meaning to this place, given the signs that point towards it, and that there was indeed such a remarkable place to be found at the end of the trail I had discerned. Why did Grimo's monks, on recovering the bodies, take them on to Rome? They must have held some significance to the Church. And could not my discovery be the resolution to the Rennes-le-Château mystery, the explanation for the sudden rise to wealth of its priest and the secret that was cryptically alluded to by his housekeeper Marie Denarnaud?

Proof of the significance of what I have discovered may only lie within the neutral confines of the Vatican State in the form of two bodily remains, one of which, according to the Church which has its worldwide base there, should not even exist in the form of mortal biological material. Does it lie within the power of that Church to either prove or disprove my theory? Perhaps the time is now right, two thousand years after the birth of the man in whose name the Church was founded, for it to relax its insistence on a physical resurrection and present the world with the mortal remains of Christ.

Late News

Another strange episode occurred more recently. In the spring of this year (2000) I returned to the site in order to take photographs which could be used as illustrations for this book. On arrival at the ridge, as I walked along the crest, I neared the jagged tooth of the 'headstone' and saw that something was draped over it. As I drew near it became obvious that someone had covered this curious standing stone with a piece of fabric.

Dark vermilion in colour, it had obviously been there for some time as the part of it which had been exposed to the sunlight had become more faded than that in the shade. Taking it off the rock, I laid it on the ground to see it better and immediately realized that what I was looking at was a piece of thick woven cloth that had the dimensions of a prayer mat. My curiosity piqued, I surveyed the site for further evidence that someone had been there, but found nothing.

My attention returned to the prayer mat and on inspecting it more closely I was astonished to find that there was a design woven into two of its borders that I had seen before. At the front and rear edges of the mat was a single row of interlocking Templar crosses, the *croix pattées* that the Knights Templar had worn on their white over-mantles and which had been carried on the sails of the ships under Christopher Columbus' command when he discovered America. What is more, at the centre of each cross, intricately woven into the design, was a small letter 'T', seeming to confirm that this was in some way related to the Knights Templar.

What it was placed there for and who may have brought it to the site can only be guessed at.

Having taken my pictures I replaced the mat where I had found it and walked away as I had done many times before, leaving nothing but footprints and taking nothing but memories.

NOTES

☆

CHAPTER ONE: THE PAINTINGS AND
THEIR PATRONS

1. Pastor Freiherr von Ludwig, *The History of Popes*, Routledge & Kegan Paul, London, 1952.
2. Ademollo, *Teatri*, Rome, 1888.
3. Ludwig.
4. In 1623, when he had been transferred from Koblenz to Heiligenstadt, he undertook the dangerous journey dressed in his Jesuit robes, having stated, 'I would rather die in the robes of my order than travel undisturbed in worldly dress.' But for the intervention of a young soldier who took pity on the novice monk, this would have been what happened.
5. *New Encyclopaedia Britannica*, 1988 edn.
6. *Oedipus Aegyptiacus*, p. 419. Cited in J. Godwin, *Athanasius Kircher: A Renaissance Man and the Quest for Lost Knowledge*, Thames and Hudson, London, 1979.
7. Godwin.
8. Godwin.
9. This is thought by some authors to be the Château Mornay et Saintonge where the gallery burned down in 1947 but which is known to have been decorated with mythological scenes and to have been inscribed 'Nicolas Poussin pinxit anno 1614'. The one piece that was salvaged from the ruins, *Diana and*

Actaeon, is generally considered to be the artist's earliest surviving work.

10. Quoted in Richard Verdi's *Nicolas Poussin*, Royal Academy of Arts, London, 1995. Poussin himself wrote that he 'suffered extreme hardship and exhaustion' on the journey.

11. This young man was Gaspard Dughet, who was to become one of the greatest landscape painters of the seventeenth century.

12. Alain Merot, *Poussin*, Hazan, Paris, 1990.

13. The letter from which this cryptic extract is taken was kept in the archives of the Cosse-Brissac family, who have been prominent in French Freemasonry since the eighteenth century. Lèpinois, *Lettres de Louis Fouquet*. Cited in Michael Baigent, Richard Leigh and Henry Lincoln, *The Holy Blood and the Holy Grail*. It may be of interest to learn that Abbé Louis Fouquet subsequently had to flee France, having been involved in a failed plot to murder the Marquis de Louvois, a senior minister of Louis XIV.

14. It is important to note that only comparatively recently has the term 'occult' become imbued with overtones of devil-worship. Its more specific and exact meaning is of the religions, creeds and knowledge that fall outside the teachings of the Church of Rome, that huge body of learning that with the rise of Roman Catholicism was decried as heretical and became largely forgotten.

15. Cited in Eliphas Lévi, *Transcendental Magic*, Rider and Company, London, 1984 (first published 1896).

16. He also wrote such works as *History of the Jews* in 1650, *Codex Cabbala* in 1651 and *Reformation and Science* in 1663.

17. Giovanni Pietro Bellori, *Le Vite de' pittori, scultori et architette moderni . . .*, Rome, 1672.

18. K. Dorothea Ewart, *Cosimo de' Medici*, Macmillan, London, 1899.

19. Marcel Brion, *The Medici*, Elek Books, London.

20. We know this from Ficino's letters to Lorenzo de' Medici and the inscription on his translation of the commentaries of Plotinus: 'mihi Mercurium primo Termaximum, mox Platonem mandavit interpretandum' – cited in Frances A. Yates, *Giordano Bruno and the Hermetic Tradition*, Routledge & Kegan Paul, London, 1964.

21. Charles L. Mee, *Lorenzo de' Medici and the Renaissance*, Cassell, London, 1971.

22. Serge Bramley, *Leonardo – the Artist and the Man*, HarperCollins, London, 1992.

CHAPTER TWO: THE ESOTERIC ARCHAEOLOGY OF FINE ART

1. Anthony Blunt, *Nicolas Poussin*, the A. W. Mellar Lecture in the Fine Arts, London and Washington, 1967.
2. Both religions were centred around bull worship, from which is thought to have derived the Old Testament worship of the Golden Calf idol or the God Sin, who was the focus of idolatry for the Semites of Babylon. Cited in Georges Roux, *Ancient Iraq*, Allen and Unwin, London, 1964.
3. It is for the same reason that John the Baptist is frequently depicted as a bearded rustic, signifying his closeness to nature, the normal world, through his natural conception and birth.
4. Henry Lincoln, *The Holy Place*, Jonathan Cape, London, 1991.

CHAPTER THREE: BABYLON, EGYPT AND THE KABBALAH

1. *The Oxford Classical Dictionary*, ed. by Simon Hornblower and Anthony Spawforth, Oxford University Press, Oxford, 1996.
2. Adrian Room, *Dictionary of Astronomical Names*, Routledge, London, 1988.
3. Room.
4. Sadly, George Smith is largely one of the forgotten heroes of archaeology, many of the dictionaries and encyclopaedias on the subject ignoring him completely, The information here is largely drawn from *Gods, Graves & Scholars – the story of archaeology*, C. W. Ceram, Sidgwick & Jackson, London, 1952 (first published as *Götter, Gräber und Gelehrte*, Rowohlt-Verlag, Hamburg, 1949), which although now dated handles the subject movingly. Further research into Smith has shown that he died in Aleppo, Syria, in 1877 and his position as Director of the British Museum's expeditions was

taken on by none other than Hormuzd Rassam, the man who
discovered the tablets.

5. Ceram, pp. 274–5.

6. *The Atlas of Mysterious Places*, ed. by Jennifer Westwood, Weidenfeld
& Nicolson, London, 1987.

7. *The Macmillan Dictionary of Archaeology*, ed. by Ruth D. Whitehouse,
Macmillan, London, 1983.

8. Gerald Massey, *Ancient Egypt and the Light of the World*, Black Classic
Press, Baltimore, 1992 (originally published 1907).

9. Morton Smith, *Jesus the Magician*, Victor Gollancz, London, 1978.

10. Smith.

11. Lynn Picknett and Clive Prince, *The Templar Revelation*, Bantam
Press, London, 1997.

12. Picknett and Prince.

13. This is derived from the Hebrew version of Mark xvi: 15–34, *Eloi,
Eloi, lama sabach thani*, more usually thought to mean 'My God, my
God why hast thou forsaken me?' or 'Father, Father, why hast thou
forsaken me?'

14. There are many ways of spelling this, including Kabbala, Qabalah
and Cabala.

15. From the point of view of those passing on the knowledge it is
would be *masorah*, which is the exact equivalent of the English
'tradition'.

16. Ezekiel i.

17. S. Mathers, *The Cabala*, Kegan Paul, Trench, 1909.

18. Joy Hancox, *The Byrom Collection*, Jonathan Cape, London, 1992.
Cited in Picknett and Prince.

CHAPTER FOUR: GNOSTICISM

1. According to some sources he may have lived even earlier, *c.*1400
BCE.

2. Paul Johnson, *A History of Christianity*, Weidenfeld and Nicolson,
London, 1976.

3. James Robinson (gen. ed.), *The Nag Hammadi Library in English*, E.
J. Brill, Copenhagen, 1988.

4. Giovanni Filorama (trans. Anthony Alcock), *A History of Gnosticism*, Basil Blackwell Ltd, Oxford, 1990.

5. The correct, but little used, spelling is in fact Naj' Hammadi.

6. Koran 4:157.

7. As we have seen, the writings of Valentinus and to a lesser extent Basilides have survived through the copies of the hostile accounts and refutations by such writers as Irenaeus and Clement. It was Tatian, a Syrian Gnostic convert, who in the second century was the first to combine the four Gospels into a single work, the *Diatessaron*, and Heracleon who wrote the earliest commentary on the Gospel of St John, extracts of which were preserved through the writings of Origen. Likewise it is through the work of that arch antiheretic Epiphanius that writings such as the 'Letter to Flora' by the Valentinian Gnostic Ptolemaeus, which gives the rules for interpreting the Mosaic law of the *Torah* in a Christian sense, were preserved; as was the work of Theodotus, a disciple of Valentinus, whose comments on the system of thought employed by his master come down to us through the excerpts used by Clement of Alexandria.

8. Theosophy is religious study with a view to finding the hidden essence of all religions, a theme which is not dissimilar to Esoteric Buddhism.

9. Filorama.

10. Tobias Churton, *The Gnostics*, Weidenfeld & Nicolson, London, 1987.

11. Michael Baigent, Richard Leigh and Henry Lincoln, *The Holy Blood and the Holy Grail*, Jonathan Cape, London, 1982.

12. Baigent, Leigh and Lincoln, citing James Robinson (gen. ed.), *The Nag Hammadi Library in English*, E. J. Brill, Copenhagen, 1988.

13. The Arabic originals of this work are thought themselves to be a translation of earlier Egyptian texts. This leads us to believe that this work may be closely related to the original books of Solomon (971–631 BCE).

14. W. Förster (ed.), *Die Gnosis II*, Zurich, 1971 (Eng. trans. by R. McL. Wilson, *Gnosis*, Oxford, 1972); R. Macuch, *Zur Sprache und literatur der Mandäer*, Berlin, 1976; K. Rudolph, *Die Mandäer, I Prologomena: Das Mandäerproblem*, Göttingen, 1961; K Tröger (ed.), *Gnosis und Neues Testament*, Berlin-Gütersloh, 1973. All cited in Filorama.

15. Hugh Schonfeld, *The Passover Plot*, Hutchinson, London, 1965.

16. E. S. Drower, *The Mandaeans of Iraq and Iran: Their cults, customs, magic, legends and folklore*, Clarendon Press, Oxford, 1937.

17. Lynn Picknett and Clive Prince, *The Templar Revelation*, Bantam, London, 1997.

18. In the *Book of the Zadokites*, the Zadokites being a group of religious teachers who had instructed John, it states that 'they were in favour of releasing the word from the strict ways of the ruling of the sects of the Pharisees and the Sadducees'.

19. Quoted in Kurt Rudolph, *Mandaeism*, E. J. Brill, Leiden, 1978.

20. Drower.

21. Quoted in Rudolph.

22. Aside from those sources which we have cited for specific references, much of the information on the Mandaeans has been drawn from the *Encyclopædia Britannica*, The Gnostic Society Library (http://gnosis.org/mandaean), http://home.sn.no/~noetic/libe.htm, and Lynn Picknett and Clive Prince, *The Templar Revelation*, Bantam, London, 1997; and on the Marsh Arabs through the Iraqi National Congress website at www.inc.org.uk, which is one of the few sources giving relatively objective and up-to-date information on the plight of the marsh tribes.

23. Norman Golb, *Who Wrote the Dead Sea Scrolls?*, Michael O'Mara, London, 1995.

CHAPTER FIVE: THE CRUCIFIXION MYTH

1. Michael Baigent, Richard Leigh and Henry Lincoln, *The Holy Blood and the Holy Grail*, Jonathan Cape, London, 1982.

2. Baigent, Leight and Lincoln.

3. *A History of the Jewish People*, ed. by H. H. Ben-Sasson, Weidenfeld & Nicolson, London.

4. Martin Goodman with Jane Sherwood, *The Roman World 44* BC–AD *180*, Routledge, London and New York.

5. Goodman with Sherwood.

6. Lynn Thorndike, *A History of Magic and Experimental Science*, Columbia University Press, New York, 1958.

7. F. W. Farrar, *The Herods*, Service & Paton, London, 1898.
8. Farrar.
9. Harold W. Hoehner, *Herod Antipas*, Cambridge University Press, 1972.
10. Farrar.
11. R. Runcie, 'Blood on His Hands', *The Times*, London, 21 March 1999.
12. *Acta Pilati*, ed. by G. Sluter, 1879.
13. Eusebius, *The Ecclesiastical History and the Martyrs of Palestine*, trans. Hugh Jackson Lawlor and John Ernest Oulton, Macmillan, London.
14. Eusebius.
15. William Barclay, *The Gospels and Acts*, SCM Press Ltd.
16. There is an interesting passage in the Gospel of Luke (x:i) which states that Jesus appointed seventy-two disciples and sent them 'into every city and place'. This appears to illustrate that Jesus had a knowledge of the Kabbalah and of the zodiac as there are seventy-two quinaries in the zodiac and this fact is also confirmed by Tatininus in the *Detesteron*: 'he sent out seventy-two disciples'.
17. This is thought to refer back to the passage in the Talmud of Babylon, *Gemarara*, p. 83, Book II, which states that 'the bone must not be broken of the sacrifice'.
18. *Idolomania*, Investigator Abhorrens, London, 1859.
19. *Idolomania*.
20. There are many works which focus on differing theories about the crucifixion, including the role of the eclipse, the use of drugs and potions, the replacing of Christ, the identities of the robbers and other hypotheses too numerous to mention.
21. This echoes an earlier Bible story which tells of Moses being ordered to speak God's word. Moses incurred God's anger by explaining that His words would 'crowd on his lips', meaning that he was not a speaker, and he suggested that his brother Aaron would be a better man to carry out God's wish (Exodus iv: 10–16).

CHAPTER SIX: THE FRENCH CONNECTION

1. Harold Hohner, *The Life of Herod*, Cambridge University Press, 1972, pp. 262, and F. W. Farrar, *The Herods*, Service & Paton, London, 1898.

2. Eusebius, *The Ecclesiastical History and the Martyrs of Palestine*, trans. Hugh Jackson Lawlor and John Ernest Oulton, ii7, Macmillan, London.
3. Luke, viii:2.
4. Laurence Gardner, *Bloodline of the Holy Grail*, Element Books, Shaftesbury, 1996.
5. Margaret Starbird, *The Woman With the Alabaster Jar*, Ch. 3, p. 98. Cited in Laurence Gardner.
6. Jacobus de Voraigne, *Legenda Aurea*, London, 1483 (cf. Gardner).
7. Lynn Picknett and Clive Prince, *The Templar Revelation*, Bantam Press, London, 1997.
8. Ean Begg, *The Cult of the Black Virgin*, Arkana, London, 1985.
9. Begg.
10. Karbra Nagast's book *Magda* (1908) states that the first Magdalene was of Ethiopian origin, was black, wise and full of magic. It also suggests that she was married to Solomon and bore a son who was named David.
11. Cited in Picknett and Prince.
12. Bokenham, p. 158, lines 5780–6.
13. Helen Meredith Garth, 'Saint Mary Magdalene in Mediaeval Literature', *The Johns Hopkins University Studies in Historical and Political Science*, Series LXVII, Number 3, 1950.
14. W. M. Metcalfe, *Legends of the Saints* in the Scottish dialect of the fourteenth century, XVI, 'Magdalene', p. 263, lines 263–6.
15. De Voraigne, p. 77.
16. Most Ahmadi information here cited is drawn from the excellent work by Paul C. Pappas, *Jesus' Tomb in India*, Asian Humanities Press, California, which explores the Ahmadi claims in great depth.
17. Michael Baigent, Richard and Henry Lincoln, *The Holy Blood and the Holy Grail*, Jonathan Cape, London, 1982.
18. Picknett and Prince.
19. Picknett and Prince.
20. A. N. Wilson, *Jesus*, Sinclair-Stevenson, London, 1992.
21. Picknett and Prince.
22. Karl W. Luckert, *Egyptian Light and Hebrew Fire*, State University of New York Press, New York, 1991. Cited in Picknett and Prince.

23. Picknett and Prince, taken from Owen St Victor, *Epiphany*, Sancta Sophia, Leuven, 1991.

24. Picknett and Prince, citing G. R. S. Mead, *Simon Magus: An Essay*, Theosophical Publishing Society, London, 1892.

25. Picknett and Prince.

26. Picknett and Prince.

27. Picknett and Prince, citing Susan Haskins, *Mary Magdalene*, HarperCollins, London, 1993.

28. Baigent, Lincoln and Leigh.

CHAPTER SEVEN: A VILLAGE, A MYSTERY AND A MEROVINGIAN KING

1. Henry Lincoln, *The Holy Place*, Jonathan Cape, London, 1991.

2. Lincoln.

3. Michael Baigent, Richard Leigh and Henry Lincoln, *The Holy Blood and The Holy Grail*, Jonathan Cape, London, 1982.

4. Lincoln.

5. Ian Wood, *The Merovingian Kingdoms 450–751*, Longman.

6. St Gregory of Tours.

7. It is perhaps interesting to note that his name is a precursor of the name Louis. Indeed the Emperor Louis the Debonair is recorded as saying that Clovis 'bears the same name' as him. If one removes the first letter of his name this becomes more obvious.

8. Arianism was the doctrine of Arius of Alexandria (fourth century CE), who denied the divinity of Christ.

9. St Gregory of Tours.

10. Usually known as St Remi, he lived from 437 CE to 533 CE and is thought by some historians to have been the brother of Principius, Bishop of Soissons.

11. Wood.

12. Eddius Stephanus, *Vita Wilfridi*.

13. Digot, *Histoire de Royaume d'Austrasie*, Nancy, 1863, and Folz, *Tradition Hagiographique et culte de St Dagobert, roi de Francs, Le Moyen Age*, Brussels, 1963.

14. Lanigan, *An Ecclesiastical History*, Vol. 3.

15. Eddius Stephanus.
16. Baigent, Leigh and Lincoln.
17. Michael Baigent, Richard Leigh and Henry Lincoln, *The Messianic Legacy*, Jonathan Cape, London, 1986.
18. Baigent, Leigh and Lincoln, 1986.
19. According to Eddius Stephanus, *Vita Wilfridi*, he did not actually return until 676.
20. J. M. Wallace-Hadrill, *The Frankish Church*, Clarendon Press, Oxford, 1983, discusses in full this confusion which stems from one charter of Grimoald's in which he donated the villa at Germigny to the monasteries of Stavelot-Malmédy. It appears to suggest that Dagobert II's first reign was from the death of his father, Sigisbert III, in 656, until his usurpation in 660–1 by Grimoald. He would therefore have been no more than a child king, allowing Grimoald to hold the reins of power.
21. J. M. Wallace-Hadrill, *The Long-Haired Kings and other studies in Frankish History*, Methuen, London, 1962.
22. Eddius Stephanus.
23. Henri Lobineau, *Dossiers Secrets d'Henri Lobineau*, 1967.
24. Edward James, *The Origins of France 'From Clovis to the Capetians'*, Methuen, London.
25. James, p. 141.
26. Gregory of Tours, *Decem Libri Historiarum* V 44; Chilperic, *Ymnus in sollemnitate s. Medardi*.
27. D. Ganz, *Bureaucratic shorthand and Merovingian learning*. Cf. Ian Wood, *The Merovingian Kingdoms 450–751*, Longman.
28. Fredegar, IV 47.
29. According to some research it is possible that Haldetrude was Dagobert's mother and that Berthetrude was the mother of Charibert. See Ewig, *Die Namengebung bei den ältesten Frankekönigen und im merowingeschen Königshaus*, p. 64.
30. *Gesta Dagoberti I*, 5.
31. Fredegar, IV 67; Wood, *The Merovingian Kingdoms 450–751*, Longman.
32. *Vita Faronis*, 78.
33. Paul Fouracre and Richard A. Gerberding, *Late Merovingian France 640–720*, Manchester University Press. Also Wallace-Hadrill 1960, ch.78.

34. In Wallace-Hadrill 1960, following Fredegar, this Visigoth king's name is Suintila.
35. J. M. Wallace-Hadrill 1962.
36. Lionel and Patricia Fanthorpe, *Rennes-le-Château, its mysteries and secrets*, Bellevue.
37. *Vita S. Pauli, Episcopi Virdunensis*, 899, 900, 901, 902, 903. Grant of land and libraries.
38. Formigé, *L'Abbaye Royale de Saint-Denis*.
39. Bruno Krusch and Wilhelm Levison, *Passio sanctorum martyrum Dionisii, Rusticii et Eleutherii*, Ed. MGH Auct Antiq IV.
40. Edward B. Foley, *The First Ordinary of the Royal Abbey of St.-Denis in France*, The University Press, Fribourg, Switzerland, 1990.

CHAPTER EIGHT: THE HOME OF THE HERESY

1. Michael Baigent, Richard Leigh and Henry Lincoln, *The Holy Blood and the Holy Grail*, Jonathan Cape, London, 1982.
2. Baigent, Leigh and Lincoln, citing D. de Rougement, *Love in the Western World*, New York, 1940.
3. David Christie-Murray, *A History of Heresy*, New English Library, London, 1976.
4. The Cathars called themselves 'Christians' and 'Good Christians' and were also termed 'friends of God'. The few surviving Cathar documents and texts comprise two dogmatic treatises, one of which is in Florence, and two rituals. The bulk of our knowledge of the Cathars today comes from the judiciary sources of the Crusade and the Holy Inquisition in the form of interrogation statements, of which there exist more than 7,000. The statement of one poor soul opens with the 'Pater' the renowned 'Lord's Prayer' of the Cathars, the opening lines of which are: '*Payre sant Dieu dreyturier de bons speritz . . .*' ('Holy Father, Legitimate God of good spirits').
5. Walter Birks and R. A. Gilbert, *The Treasure of Montségur*, Crucible, London, 1987.
6. Zoé Oldenbourg, *Massacre at Montségur*, Weidenfeld and Nicolson, London, 1961.
7. There are local records which show that Jews were appointed to the offices of consul or magistrate in many towns of the region.

8. Michel Roquebert, *Cathar Religion*, Editions Loubatières, 1994.

9. Cited in Lynn Picknett and Clive Prince, *The Templar Revelation*, Bantam, London, 1997, although their source is not quoted.

10. Picknett and Prince, citing F. Niel, *Les Cathares de Montségur*, Paris, 1973.

11. *Montségur et le Catharisme*, http://207.253.12.33/montsegur-intro.html.

12. Michael Baigent, Richard Leigh and Henry Lincoln, *The Holy Blood and the Holy Grail*, Jonathan Cape, London, 1982.

13. In a book called *The Templars' Chart*, by Jeremy Cross, Newhaven, USA, 1821, there is a reference stating that King Cyrus of Persia commissioned a new order of knights to be called the Knights of Est and who were charged with escorting the treasures of the Temple of Solomon on their return to Jerusalem from Babylon and the rebuilding of the Temple in 530 BCE. This order is considered by some scholars to have been a precursor to the French Knights of the Eagle, the Knights of the Sword in Palestine and subsequently the Knights of the Red Cross.

14. Willliam of Tyre, *A History of Deeds Done Beyond the Sea*, trans. Emily Atwater Babcock and A. C. Krey, New York, 1943.

15. Baigent, Leigh and Lincoln, citing M. Michelet, *Procès des Templiers*, Paris, 1851.

16. Baigent, Leigh and Lincoln, citing *Der Untergang des Templer-Ordens*, Berlin, 1887.

17. Baigent, Leigh and Lincoln, citing Michelet.

18. Baigent, Leigh and Lincoln.

19. Hugh J. Schonfield, *The Essene Odyssey*, Element, Shaftesbury, 1984, cited in Picknett and Prince.

20. R. Andrews and P. Schellenberger, *The Tomb of God*, Little Brown, London, 1996.

CHAPTER NINE: THE KNIGHTS OF NAZISM, THE CHARTS AND THE STARS

1. Houston Stewart Chamberlain was born in Portsmouth in 1855 and went to study in Switzerland, where, then in his twenties, he first heard the music of Richard Wagner. He is perhaps best known for

his work *Die Grundlagen des neunzehten Jahrhunderts* (*The Foundations of the Nineteenth Century*) in which he expounded his theories which linked ancient anti-Semitism with the then modern racist ideas. He was of the view that the Jews had poisoned the 'Aryan doctrine' and regarded Hitler as the one man who could implement his ideas and eradicate forever the Jewish race. The book was first published in 1910 and is thought by many to have had a seminal influence on Hitler's thinking. Chamberlain died on 9 January 1927 in Bayreuth, Germany.

2. Chamberlain.

3. *Newsletter of the Saunière Society*, Vol. Two, Number 5/II, 1 January 1999.

4. Cited in Lynn Picknett and Clive Prince, *The Templar Revelation*, Bantam, London, 1997, who quote from work done by Franck Marie in his book *Alet les Bains*.

5. Lynn Picknett and Clive Prince, *The Templar Revelation*, Bantam, London, 1997.

6. Robert Bauval and Adrian Gilbert, *The Orion Mystery*, William Heinemann, London, 1994.

CHAPTER TEN: THE SITE AND THE ARCADIAN TOMB

1. This is mentioned in Michael Baigent, Richard Leigh and Henry Lincoln, *The Holy Blood and the Holy Grail*, Jonathan Cape, London, 1982. However, Richard Andrews and Paul Schellenberger in *The Tomb of God* (Little Brown, London, 1996) state that Bertrand de Blanchefort was actually the sixth Grand Master of the order, having been elected in 1156 and that the château had not been owned by him but by a Bernard de Blanchefort, who appears to have had no links with the Order of the Knights Templar.

2. Joscelyn Godwin, *Athanasius Kircher: A Renaissance Man and the Quest for Lost Knowledge*, Thames and Hudson, London, 1979.

TIMELINE

☆

	4300	Birth of Egyptian Fifth Dynasty King Unas (approx.)
	4000	Dating of the 'Island of the Dead', Bahrain
	3000	Approximate dating of the *Epic of Gilgamesh*
	2650	Beginning of the First Dynasty of Uruk
	2550	End of the First Dynasty of Uruk
	2000	Judaic culture commences migration through Mesopotamia to Egypt
	1792	Beginning of Hammurabi's rule over Babylon
	1750	End of Hammurabi's rule over Babylon
	1595	Founding of Babylonia as a territorial State with Babylon its capital
	1298	Rameses II installed as Pharaoh
	1232	Death of Rameses II
7TH	660	Birth of Zoroaster/Zarathustra
	604	Birth of Nebuchadnezzar
	587	Nebuchadnezzar sacks Jerusalem
	583	Death of Zoroaster/Zarathustra
	562	Death of Nebuchadnezzar

BEFORE COMMON ERA BCE

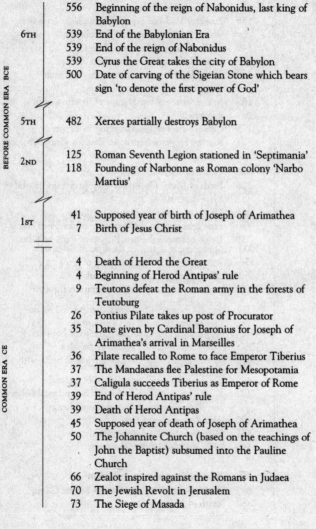

	556	Beginning of the reign of Nabonidus, last king of Babylon
6TH	539	End of the Babylonian Era
	539	End of the reign of Nabonidus
	539	Cyrus the Great takes the city of Babylon
	500	Date of carving of the Sigeian Stone which bears sign 'to denote the first power of God'
5TH	482	Xerxes partially destroys Babylon
2ND	125	Roman Seventh Legion stationed in 'Septimania'
	118	Founding of Narbonne as Roman colony 'Narbo Martius'
1ST	41	Supposed year of birth of Joseph of Arimathea
	7	Birth of Jesus Christ
	4	Death of Herod the Great
	4	Beginning of Herod Antipas' rule
	9	Teutons defeat the Roman army in the forests of Teutoburg
	26	Pontius Pilate takes up post of Procurator
	35	Date given by Cardinal Baronius for Joseph of Arimathea's arrival in Marseilles
	36	Pilate recalled to Rome to face Emperor Tiberius
	37	The Mandaeans flee Palestine for Mesopotamia
	37	Caligula succeeds Tiberius as Emperor of Rome
	39	End of Herod Antipas' rule
	39	Death of Herod Antipas
	45	Supposed year of death of Joseph of Arimathea
	50	The Johannite Church (based on the teachings of John the Baptist) subsumed into the Pauline Church
	66	Zealot inspired against the Romans in Judaea
	70	The Jewish Revolt in Jerusalem
	73	The Siege of Masada

BEFORE COMMON ERA BCE

COMMON ERA CE

132	Second Jewish Revolt
135	Emperor Hadrian expels all Jews from Jerusalem, which is renamed Aelia Capitolina
140	Birth of Iraneus, Bishop of Lyon
150	Birth of the anti-Gnostic Tertullian
160	Justin Martyr writes of Jesus the 'Galilean Magician'
165	Justin, writer of the first anti-Gnostic works, martyred
175	Celsus writes of Jesus working in Egypt
193	Roman Emperor Septimius Severus visits Babylon
200	Death of Iraneus, Bishop of Lyon
216	Birth of Mani, Gnostic teacher and founder of the Manichaeans
225	Death of the anti-Gnostic Tertullian
250	First reference to the existence of the *Pistis Sophia*
251	Denis becomes the first Bishop of Paris and dies during the persecution of Decius
276	Death of Mani, Gnostic teacher and founder of the Manichaeans
337	Small Church of St Denis, constructed by St Genevieve enlarged by Constantine
350	*Nag Hammadi Scrolls* written
410	Visigoth King Alaric sacks Rome
431	Palladius becomes first Bishop of Ireland
447	King Merovee ascends the throne and establishes the Merovingians or 'Long-Haired Kings'
450	The Romans leave Gaul
451	Battle of the Catalaunian Fields
496	Gaul invaded by the Alemanni
605	Birth of Dagobert I
613	The Edict of Paris, the French *Magna Carta*, written

622	Dagobert I takes up the rule of reduced Austrasia
628	Dagobert I's father, Chlothar, dies
628	Dagobert succeeds to the throne of the Franks and becomes overall king
651	Dagobert II born
656	Dagobert II's father, King Sigisbert III, dies
664	Council of Whitby. Celtic Church dissolved and subsumed into the Roman Church
674	Dagobert II returns from England and Ireland to France to take up the throne
679	Dagobert II dies
872	Dagobert II canonized
995	The apocryphal gospels *Abd al Jabbar* written to establish Muhammed as a true prophet
1012	First Cathar heretics arrive in Limousin
1059	Church at Rennes-le-Château consecrated to Mary Magdalene
1118	The Order of the Poor Knights of Christ and the Temple of Solomon founded
1128	Templar order officially recognized at the Council of Troyes
1143	Peter the Venerable of Cluny condemns the Jews of Narbonne
1145	St Bernard de Clairvaux arrives in the Languedoc
1146	Introduction of the *croix pattée* to Templar garb
1149	Establishment of the first Cathar Bishopric
1170	Murder of Thomas à Becket and excommunication of England's King Henry II
1190	Formation of the Teutonic Knights of St Mary's Hospital at Jerusalem
1205	Commencement of the Cathar pogroms by Dominic Guzman

1208	Papal 'Bull of Anathema' issued by Pope Innocent III
1209	Start of the Albigensian Crusade, Béziers, France
1213	Simon de Montford proclaimed Count of Toulouse on the death of Peter II
1218	Siege of Toulouse
1229	Treaty of Paris
1233	Commencement of the Holy Inquisition
1244	End of the Albigensian Crusade
1244	Siege of Montségur ends
1252	Henry III of England accuses the Templars of 'excessive pride'
1279	Teutonic Knights conquer the Slavs of Prussia
1291	Acre falls to the Saracens
1307	King Philip IV of France dissolves the Templar order, Friday, 13 October
1314	Templar Grand Master, Jacques de Molay, burned to death, Île de la Cité, Paris
1389	Birth of Cosimo de' Medici (Cosimo the Elder)
1424	Florence Baptistry doors created by Lorenzo Ghiberti and Andrea Pisano
1434	The Medicis' rule over Florence and Tuscany commences
1441	Birth of Luca Signorelli
1463	Leonardo del Pistoja returns from Macedonia with *Corpus Hermeticum*
1464	Death of Cosimo de' Medici (Cosimo the Elder), 4 August.
1469	Death of Piero the Gouty
1478	Assassination of Giuliano de' Medici in the Pazzi Conspiracy
1483	Leonardo da Vinci paints the first version of *The Virgin of the Rocks*
1492	Luca Signorelli commissioned to paint *The Education of Pan* by Lorenzo de' Medici

1492	Jews expelled from Spain
1492	Death of Lorenzo de' Medici (Lorenzo the Magnificent), 9 April
1508	Leonardo da Vinci paints the second version of *The Virgin of the Rocks*
1523	Death of Luca Signorelli
1532	Shroud of Turin discovered in Chambery, France.
1562	Start of the Wars of Religion
1585	Birth of Armand-Jean du Plessis de Richelieu (Cardinal Richelieu), Poitou, France
1594	Birth of Nicolas Poussin, Les Andelys, Normandy, France
1598	End of the Wars of Religion
1602	Athanasius Kircher born, Fulda, Germany
1607	Armand-Jean de Richelieu ordained as a priest and consecrated to the Holy See of Lucon
1610	Assassination of King Henry IV
1618	Start of the Thirty Years War
1623	Cardinal Maffeo Barberini elected to Papal throne as Urban VIII
1624	Richelieu appointed First Minister of France
1631	Death of Johannes Kepler
1650	Poussin commissioned to paint *The Shepherds of Arcadia* by Cardinal Rospigliosi
1661	Disappearance of Gaffarel
1664	Duc de Richelieu commissions Poussin to paint *The Four Seasons* series
1692	Birth of John Byrom
1723	The Medicis' rule over Florence and Tuscany ends
1763	Death of John Byrom
1778	First appearance of the *Codex Askewianus*
1809	Napoleon dissolves the Teutonic Knights
1840	George Smith born Chelsea, London, England

1852	Birth of Bérenger Saunière, 11 April, Montazels, France
1868	Birth of Marie Denarnaud
1872	George Smith discovers the *Epic of Gilgamesh*
1879	Bérenger Saunière ordained
1885	Bérenger Saunière becomes parish priest of Rennes-le-Château
1886	Bérenger Saunière embarks on the restoration of the church at Rennes-le-Château
1891	Abbé Bérenger Saunière discovers the parchments
1917	Bérenger Saunière dies, 22 January, Rennes-le-Château
1932	Ethel Stevens (Lady Drower) publishes her work on the Mandaeans
1933	Hitler becomes Chancellor of Germany
1934	Himmler rents Wewelsburg Castle as spiritual home of the Schutzstaffel
1945	Discovery of the *Nag Hammadi Scrolls* in Egypt
1967	Publication of Gerard de Sede's book *L'Or de Rennes*
1953	Marie Denarnaud, housekeeper to Saunière, dies, 29 January, Rennes-le-Château
1982	Publication of *The Holy Blood and the Holy Grail*
1984	Joy Hancox finds the *Byrom Collection*
1990	Bishop of Durham suggests that it is not necessary to believe in a literal resurrection to be a good Christian
2000	Publication of *The Arcadian Cipher*

BIBLIOGRAPHY

☆

Abhorrens, Investigator, *Idolomania*, Effingham Wilson, London, 1859

Andrews, R. & Schellenberger, P., *The Tomb of God*, Little, Brown, London, 1996

Baigent, M., Leigh, R. and Lincoln, H., *The Messianic Legacy*, Jonathan Cape, London, 1986

—— *The Holy Blood and the Holy Grail*, Jonathan Cape, London, 1982

Barclay, W., *The Gospels and Acts*, SCM Press, London, 1976

Bauval, R. and Gilbert, A., *The Orion Mystery*, William Heinemann, London, 1994

Begg, E., *The Cult of the Black Virgin*, Arkana, London, 1985

Bellori, G. P., *Le Vite de' pittori, scultori et architetti moderni . . .*, Rome, 1672

Ben-Sasson, H. H., ed., *A History of the Jewish People*, Weidenfeld & Nicolson, London, 1976

Birks, W. and Gilbert, R. A, *The Treasure of Montsegur*, Crucible, London, 1987

Blunt, A., *Nicolas Poussin*, Phaidon and Bollingen Foundation, London and New York, 1967

Bramley, S., *Leonardo – the Artist and the Man*, HarperCollins, London, 1992

Brion, M., *The Medici*, Elek Books, London, 1969

Ceram, C. W., *Gods, Graves & Scholars – the story of archaeology*, Sidgwick & Jackson, London, 1952 (first published as *Götter, Gräber und Geleherte*, Rowohlt-Verlag, Hamburg, 1949)

Christie-Murray, D., *A History of Heresy*, New English Library, London, 1976

Churton, T., *The Gnostics*, Weidenfeld & Nicolson, London, 1987

Cross, J., *The Templar's Chart*, published by the author, Newhaven, Conneticut, 1821

Digot, Auguste, *Histoire de Royaume d'Austrasie*, Nancy, France, 1863

Drower, E. S., *The Mandaeans of Iraq and Iran: Their cults, customs, magic, legends and folklore*, Clarendon Press, Oxford, 1937

Eddius Stephanus, 'Vita Wilfridi', in Webb, J. F., ed., *Lives of the saints*, Penguin Books, Harmondsworth, 1965

Eusebius, *The Ecclesiastical History and the Martyrs of Palestine*, trans. Hugh Jackson Lawlor & John Ernest Oulton, Macmillan, London, 1927–8

Ewart, K. D., *Cosimo de' Medici*, Macmillan, London, 1899

Fanthorpe, L. & P., *Rennes-le-Chateau, its mysteries and secrets*, Bellevue Books, Ashford, 1991

Farrar, F. W., *The Herods*, Service & Paton, London, 1898

Filorama, G., *A History of Gnosticism*, Basil Blackwell, Oxford, 1990

Foley, E. B., *The First Ordinary of the Royal Abbey of St.-Denis in France*, The University Press, Fribourg, Switzerland, 1990

Folz, *Tradition Hagiographique et culte de St Dagobert, roi de Francs*, Le Moyen Age, Brussels, 1963

Formigé, Jules, *L'Abbaye Royale de Saint-Denis*, Presses universitaires de France, Paris, 1960

Förster, W., ed., *Die Gnosis*, vol. II, Artemis Verlag, Zurich, 1971 (English translation by R. McL. Wilson, *Gnosis*, Clarendon Press, Oxford, 1972)

Fouracre, P., and Gerberding, R. A., *Late Merovingian France: history and hagiography, 640–720*, Manchester University Press, Manchester, 1996

Gardner, L. *Bloodline of the Holy Grail*, Element Books, Shaftesbury, 1996

Godwin, J., *Athanasius Kircher: A Renaissance Man and the Quest for Lost Knowledge*, Thames & Hudson, London, 1979

Golb, N., *Who Wrote the Dead Sea Scrolls?*, Michael O'Mara, London, 1995

Goodman, M. with Sherwood, J., *The Roman World 44 BC–AD 180*, Routledge, London and New York, 1997

Hancox, J., *The Byrom Collection*, Jonathan Cape, London, 1992

Haskins, S., *Mary Magdalene*, HarperCollins, London, 1993

Hoehner, H. W., *Herod Antipas*, Cambridge University Press, Cambridge, 1972

——, *The Life of Herod*, Cambridge University Press, Cambridge, 1972

Hornblower, S. & Spawforth, A., eds, *The Oxford Classical Dictionary*, Oxford University Press, Oxford, 1996

Jacobus de Voraigne, *Legenda Aurea*, London, 1483. (Cf. Gardner)

James, E., *The Origins of France: From Clovis to the Capetians, 500–1000*, Macmillan, London, 1982

Johnson, P., *A History of Christianity*, Weidenfeld & Nicolson, London, 1976

Lévi, E., *Transcendental Magic*, Rider and Company, London, 1984 (first published as *Dogme et rituel de la haute magie*, 1896)

Lanigan, *An Ecclesiastical History of Ireland*, vol. 3, Hodges and M'Arthur, Dublin, 1822

Lincoln, H., *The Holy Place*, Jonathan Cape, London, 1991

Luckert, K. W., *Egyptian Light and Hebrew Fire*, State University of New York Press, New York, 1991

Macuch, R., *Zur Sprache und literatur der Mandäer*, Berlin, 1976

Massey, G., *Ancient Egypt and the Light of the World*, Black Classic Press, Baltimore, 1992 (originally published 1907)

Mathers, S., *The Cabala*, Kegan Paul, Trench, Trübner, London, 1909

Mead, G. R. S., *Simon Magus: An Essay*, Theosophical Publishing Society, London, 1892

Mee, C. L., *Lorenzo de' Medici and the Renaissance*, Cassell, London, 1971

Meredith, Garth H., *Saint Mary Magdalene in Mediaeval Literature*, The John Hopkins University Studies in Historical and Political Science, Series LXVII, Number 3, 1950

Merot, A., *Poussin*, Hazan, Paris, 1990

Metcalfe, W. M., ed., *Legends of the Saints: in the Scottish Dialect of the Fourteenth Century*, Scottish Text Society, Edinburgh and London, 1896

Michelet, M., *Procès des Templiers*, Imprimerie Royale, Paris, 1841–51

Morton Smith, *Jesus the Magician*, Victor Gollancz, London, 1978

Niel, F., *Les Cathares de Montségur*, Seghers, Paris, 1973

Oldenbourg, Z., *Massacre at Montségur*, Weidenfeld & Nicolson, London, 1961

Pappas, P. C., *Jesus' Tomb in India*, Asian Humanities Press, Berkeley, California, 1991

Picknett, L. & Prince, C., *The Templar Revelation*, Bantam Press, London, 1997

Robinson, J. (gen. ed.), *The Nag Hammadi Library in English*, 3rd edn., E. J. Brill, Leiden, 1988

Room, A., *Dictionary of Astronomical Names*, Routledge, London, 1988

Rougement, D. de, *Love in the Western World*, Harcourt, Brace and Co., New York, 1940

Roux, G., *Ancient Iraq*, Allen and Unwin, London, 1964

Rudolph, K., *Die Mandäer*, vol. I, *Prolegomena: Das Mandäerproblem*, Vandenhoeck & Ruprecht, Göttingen, 1960

——, *Mandaeism*, E. J. Brill, Leiden, 1978

Runcie, R., 'Blood on his Hands', *The Times*, London, 21 March 1999

St Victor, O., *Epiphany*, Sancta Sophia, Leuvens, 1991

Saunière Society Newsletter, vol. 2, no. 5/II, 1 January 1999

Schonfield, H. J., *The Essene Odyssey*, Element, Shaftesbury, 1984

——, *The Passover Plot*, Hutchinson, London, 1965

Schottmüller, K., *Der Untergang des Templer-Ordens*, Berlin, 1887

Sluter, G., ed., *Acta Pilati*, M. B. Robins, Shelbyville, Indiana, 1879

Thorndike, L., *A History of Magic and Experimental Science*, Colombia University Press, 1958

Tröger, K.-W., ed., *Gnosis und Neues Testament*, Gütersloher Verlagshaus Mohn, Gütersloh, 1973

Verdi, R., *Nicolas Poussin*, Royal Academy of Arts, London, 1995

Wallace-Hadrill, J. M., *The Frankish Church*, Clarendon Press, Oxford, 1983

——, *The Fourth Book of the Chronicle of Fredegar* (trans.), Nelson & Sons, London and New York, 1960

——, *The Long-Haired Kings: and other studies in Frankish History*, Methuen, London, 1962

Westwood, J., ed., *The Atlas of Mysterious Places*, Weidenfeld & Nicolson, London, 1987

Whitehouse, R. D., ed., *The Macmillan Dictionary of Archaeology*, Macmillan, London, 1983

William of Tyre, *A History of Deeds Done Beyond the Sea*, trans. Emily Atwater Babcock & A. C. Krey, New York, 1943

Wilson, A. N., *Jesus*, Sinclair-Stevenson, London, 1992

Wood, I., *The Merovingian Kingdoms 450–751*, Longman, London, 1994

Yates, F. A., *Giordano Bruno and the Heremetic Tradition*, Routledge & Kegan Paul, London, 1964

INDEX

☆